THE FLETCHER JONES FOUNDATION
HUMANITIES IMPRINT

The Fletcher Jones Foundation has endowed this imprint to foster innovative and enduring scholarship in the humanities.

D1496271

The publisher and the University of California Press Foundation gratefully acknowledge the generous support of the Fletcher Jones Foundation Imprint in Humanities.

Academic Apartheid

RACE AND THE CRIMINALIZATION
OF FAILURE IN AN AMERICAN SUBURB

Sean J. Drake

UNIVERSITY OF CALIFORNIA PRESS

University of California Press
Oakland, California

Cover art by Brian Stauffer.
Interior photographs are by the author.

Library of Congress Cataloging-in-Publication Data

Names: Drake, Sean J., author.
Title: Academic apartheid : race and the criminalization of failure in an
    American suburb / Sean J. Drake.
Description: Oakland, California : University of California Press,
    [2022] | Includes bibliographical references and index.
Identifiers: LCCN 2021046115 (print) | LCCN 2021046116 (ebook) |
    ISBN 9780520381353 (cloth) | ISBN 9780520381377 (paperback) |
    ISBN 9780520381384 (epub)
Subjects: LCSH: Segregation in education—California, Southern. |
    Educational equalization—California, Southern. | Racism in schools—
    California, Southern. | Minorities—Education—California, Southern.
Classification: LCC LC212.522.C2 D73 2022 (print) | LCC LC212.522.C2
    (ebook) | DDC 379.2/63097949—dc23/eng/20211022
LC record available at https://lccn.loc.gov/2021046115
LC ebook record available at https://lccn.loc.gov/2021046116

31 30 29 28 27 26 25 24 23 22
10 9 8 7 6 5 4 3 2 1

Contents

Acknowledgments   vii

Introduction   1
Segregated Schools and Disadvantaged
Students in an Affluent Neighborhood

1. "If You're Not in AP Classes, Then Who Are You?"   24
2. The Symbolic Criminalization of Failure   65
3. The Segregation of Teaching and Learning   108
4. The Institutionalization of Ethnic Capital   144
5. "We've Failed These Kids"   180
    Missed Opportunities and Signs of Hope

    Conclusion   198

Methodological Postscript   209
Notes   217
Bibliography   225
Index   243

Acknowledgments

First and foremost, thank you to the students, parents, teachers, faculty, and staff who welcomed me onto their campuses and into their lives. They were gracious hosts, and this book would not have been possible without their understanding, curiosity, and cooperation. I am especially thankful for the teachers who let me observe in their classrooms, and for the students who accepted me and urged me to tell their stories.

This project began as my doctoral dissertation in the Department of Sociology at the University of California, Irvine. The faculty and my fellow graduate students at UCI provided a wonderful network of intellectual and social support that sustained me throughout my graduate studies. Gilberto Conchas took me under his wing as soon as I arrived on campus, helping me navigate the hopes and fears that are endemic to the early stages of graduate school, and getting me involved in research projects right away. His first book, *The Color of Success*, changed the way I thought about the unequal distribution of resources and opportunities in schools. Gil provided critical feedback on an intermediate draft of the manuscript, and I am so appreciative of his guidance and friendship.

A special thank you to Jennifer Lee, who served as my primary advisor and chaired my dissertation committee at UCI. Jennifer's strategic and pragmatic approach pushed me to become a more effective writer, and to formulate research questions that cut to the heart of the issues that I examine in this book. Our regular meetings throughout the data collection and analytical phases of the project were always fruitful and inspiring. She helped me make sense of all that I was seeing, hearing, and experiencing in the field. I am grateful for her support over the years in all aspects of my career.

Thank you to David Snow and Jacob Avery, who co-taught an ethnographic research methods seminar that served as the springboard for the research that appears in this book. I gained access to my field sites while I was a student in that course, and their insightful feedback on the early stages of the project helped me tremendously. Dave's detailed comments on my first sets of field notes set the tone for the rest of the project, and Jacob always knew just what to say to keep me focused when the data seemed overwhelming.

During my time at UC Irvine, numerous faculty members served as informal advisors or sounding boards at various stages of this project. Among this constellation of supporters, I am particularly grateful to Lilith Mahmud, Ann Hironaka, Belinda Robnett, Cynthia Feliciano, Nina Bandelj, Geoff Ward, Frances Leslie, Evan Schofer, Doug Haynes, Thomas Parham, and Kaaryn Gustafson for their interest in my development as a sociologist and the trajectory of this project. I also received constant support from the Graduate Division at UCI, including a series of fellowships and grants that carried me through the bulk of my fieldwork.

I benefited from a collegial and supportive group of graduate students at UC Irvine across the social sciences and humanities, including Ali Meghdadi, Dana Moss, Raul Perez, Pablo Torres, Sharmaine Jackson, Burrell Vann, Miles Davison, Martin Jacinto, Alma Garza, Hector Martinez, Sheefteh Khalili, Matt Rafalow, Brendon Butler, Briana

Hinga, Nayssan Safavian, Alex Lin, E.J. Johnson, Kreshnik Begolli, Cathery Yeh, and Phil Walsh. These were the fellow doctoral students with whom I checked in, workshopped ideas, sharpened arguments, and hung out with casually from time to time. I am indebted to them all.

Thank you to the Ford Foundation for supporting the later stages of data collection and analysis through a Dissertation Fellowship, and for the opportunity to present and receive feedback on an early, skeletal version of this work at the 2016 Annual Conference of Ford Fellows in Washington, D.C. Various sections and chapters of the book were also significantly strengthened by participants' questions and comments at the 2014 Yale Urban Ethnography Project Conference, the American Sociological Association's Annual Meeting, the Race Research Workshop in the Department of Sociology at UC Irvine, the colloquium series in the Department of Sociology at UC Berkeley, the colloquium series in the Department of Social Science and Humanities at NYU Steinhardt, and the Ethnography Workshop in the Department of Sociology at NYU. Thank you to all who attended those sessions and gave me feedback.

A special thank you to Elijah Anderson, whose books got me excited about ethnographic methods, and whose generous mentorship has been instrumental to my progression as a sociologist. Eli invited me to present at his Urban Ethnography Project Conference at Yale University in 2014 despite the fact that I was only in my second year as a sociology doctoral student and I had only about six weeks of observational data to work with. (Thank you, Jacob, for helping me prepare!) That gathering introduced me to a broad network of ethnographers and kindred spirits, and it was a turning point in the development of my research agenda. I received encouraging comments and critiques from Colin Jerolmack, Waverly Duck, Forrest Stuart, Jooyoung Lee, Jeffrey Lane, Leslie Paik, Alice Goffman, Fred Wherry, and Jeff Guhin. Their interest in my work boosted my confidence, and I left New Haven that weekend with a renewed sense of purpose and direction.

After completing my dissertation, I spent four years at New York University, first as a Provost's Postdoctoral Fellow and then as a

Visiting Assistant Professor. NYU was an ideal place for me to transition from a doctoral candidate to a professor, and those interstitial years gave me the time and space to reacquaint myself with my data and write this book from beginning to end. I am grateful for the unwavering support and guidance of many terrific colleagues at NYU, but I would particularly like to thank Kwame Coleman, Matthew Morrison, Cybele Raver, Farooq Niazi, Jim Fraser, Colin Jerolmack, Iddo Tavory, Pat Sharkey, Lisa Stulberg, Ravi Shroff, Stella Flores, Ann Morning, Linsey Evans, Mike Funk, Gary Anderson, Pamela Morris, Noel Anderson, Eric Klinenberg, Lynne Haney, David Kirkland, Mike Amezcua, Mireya Loza, Sebastian Cherng, Charlton McIlwain, Liang Zhang, Ann Marcus, Kayla Desportes, Colleen Larson, and Letizia La Rosa. Thank you as well to the NYU undergraduate and graduate students for commenting so thoughtfully on the portions of this book that I presented in class.

I would also like to thank Tomás Jimenez for believing in my work and offering such helpful advice along the way. Thank you to Nicole Hirsch, a good friend since long before we reconnected as sociologists, for many clarifying and enjoyable conversations. Tristan Ivory and Kwame Coleman strategized with me in December of 2019 when a setback forced me back to the drawing board for a few weeks, and I am grateful for their wisdom and friendship then and now. Brandon Finlay has been and continues to be a wonderful friend and steady source of support.

There are a few other scholars who I would like to thank because their work inspired me during all phases of this project: Claude Steele, Pedro Noguera, Carla Shedd, Tony Jack, Victor Rios, and Shamus Khan. They have all led me by example in terms of their research and writing. Tony and Victor also gave me helpful advice on the process of securing a book contract. I look forward to thanking them all in person someday soon.

Thank you to Jennifer Eberhardt and David Nussbaum, who steered me through my first research project when I was an undergraduate at Stanford University, and helped instill in me a love of social science that has only grown since then.

Thank you to Min Zhou and Dana Moss, who each read multiple drafts of various chapters. Their critiques, questions, and suggestions were invaluable during the final months of writing and rewriting. They challenged me to address theoretical and analytical blind spots, and to be clear about the most pertinent implications of my findings.

My experience working with Naomi Schneider and University of California Press has been fantastic. From the first minutes of our first meeting to discuss this project, Naomi believed wholeheartedly in my data and plans for the book. She has been incredibly supportive at every stage, and her constant encouragement has helped me immensely. Thank you to Summer Farah at UC Press, for guiding me through the final stages of the process, and to Dominique Moore and Julie Van Pelt, for reading and editing the manuscript so carefully. Thank you to Brian Stauffer, whose artwork appears on the cover, and to the design team at UC Press for making the cover look better than I imagined.

Thank you to the wonderful faculty, staff, students, and deans in the Maxwell School of Citizenship & Public Affairs at Syracuse University for welcoming me with open arms. A special thank you to chair Janet Wilmoth and all of the faculty, students, and staff in the Department of Sociology, and to director Len Lopoo and the rest of the faculty and staff in the Center for Policy Research. I have felt tremendous support from the SU community since well before I arrived on campus. I am thankful to be part of such a talented and visionary community of scholars, and at a university where so many faculty members and students are committed to inclusive excellence and community engagement.

I would be remiss if I did not thank Jim Tracy, Mike Reilly, and Vin Lananna, three exemplary track coaches from my youth, who taught me how to train hard but smart, pace myself, and finish strong. I called upon those lessons many times throughout this project, but especially during heavy periods of writing and revision.

I am incredibly lucky to have a loving and supportive family in my corner. One day during my first year of graduate school, I called my big brother Chris to vent to him about something I was struggling with. I'll never forget what he told me: "It's supposed to be hard," he said. "If the things you're doing were easy, they wouldn't be worth it." He was right, and I recall that message whenever the going gets tough.

Thank you to my parents, Brenda and Michael Drake, for their steadfast support. My mom has always been my fiercest advocate, and my dad is my role model and the best teacher I have ever had. Thank you to my aunts, uncles, and cousins who asked helpful questions about the book and rooted for me to finish it, and to my grandparents, who endured decades of Jim Crow laws and overcame so much to expand opportunities for future generations of our family. This project would have been impossible without their courage and perseverance.

Writing a book of research findings is a journey of sorts, and my wife and best friend, Panya, has been with me through all of it. She celebrated with me at various milestones and lifted my spirits during those stressful times when the path forward was entirely unclear. She came to my rescue late one night when my technological incompetence led me to mistakenly delete an important section of the manuscript. She made many sacrifices so that I could complete this book, and her unconditional love and support has been more than anyone could ever ask for. I appreciate her and love her very much.

Finally, I thank our amazing daughters, Alya and Renée, for the curiosity and joy that they exude each day. They were incredibly patient with me on days when the organizing and categorizing and writing seemed endless. For instance, during periods of intense writing, they taped an envelope to the wall outside the door of my home office and routinely stuffed it full of motivational notes and artwork for me to discover when I emerged. They inspired me and pushed me across the finish line. I am so proud of who they are, and so excited for what the future has in store for them.

Introduction

SEGREGATED SCHOOLS AND DISADVANTAGED
STUDENTS IN AN AFFLUENT NEIGHBORHOOD

I grew up in San Francisco, a progressive metropolis famous for its hilly terrain, majestic views, and cold summers. In the 1990s, when I was in elementary and middle school, SF was an eclectic and cosmopolitan city, a bastion of liberal urbanism. I used to ride the municipal bus home on the days when I didn't have sports practice after school, which provided me with a front-row seat to the tremendous ethnic and racial diversity of the city. I would sit at the back of the bus because it was customary for youth to sit there, and because it gave me the best vantage point to observe my surroundings. Folks of all backgrounds and identities clambered on and off at different stops, and I took it all in.

I was proud to live and learn in a city as diverse and intriguing as San Francisco, but my pride would soon be tested. It did not take long for my bus rides to introduce me to residential segregation and socioeconomic inequality. I began to notice that the race of those who got on and off the bus roughly corresponded to the property values around those stops; the Black and Latinx riders—the riders

1

who looked most like me—boarded and exited the bus in lower-income neighborhoods. Over time, I saw that societal opportunities were not distributed equitably and that many people and communities were disadvantaged through no fault of their own. I remember being struck by the rigidity and consistency of it all. The school segregation that I saw and experienced was even more jarring. I was fortunate to attend schools at which resources were plentiful and opportunities to prepare for high school and college seemed endless. My elementary/middle school, which I attended from kindergarten through eighth grade, had a state-of-the-art gym and theater, a technology lab filled with new computers, richly appointed science classrooms, a two-story library, and multiple courtyards and other green spaces. In high school, my college counselor was on a first-name basis with admissions officers at the most elite colleges and universities in the country. I was, however, always one of only a small handful of students of color in my classes and grade level, a Black boy in what sociologist and seminal urban ethnographer Elijah Anderson refers to as "white space."[1] Moreover, I can count on one hand the number of teachers of color I had during my grade-school years, and I did not have a Black teacher until college. White teachers taught me about Christopher Columbus's "discovery" of North America, Native American genocide, the enslavement of Africans in America, the Civil War and Reconstruction, blackface minstrelsy, the Harlem Renaissance, Jim Crow segregation, and the civil rights movement of the 1950s and 1960s. They taught the work of Langston Hughes, Zora Neale Hurston, and Ralph Ellison, among others. We also read *Adventures of Huckleberry Finn*, in which author Mark Twain marshals the n-word no less than 219 times. They were good teachers and good people, but I wished for a deeper understanding, a kinship and perspective that they could not adequately provide.

When I was an adolescent, the dearth of students or faculty of color at school often engendered feelings of isolation and the need the prove myself—to prove that the color of my skin did not mean that I was less capable than my peers of lighter complexion. And I saw that many of my Black friends and family members outside of school attended schools that did not provide them with the same opportunities that I had. My peers who were Black or Brown, the ones whom I hung out with after school at track practice or on weekends, attended schools on the other side of town, schools that looked like dilapidated juvenile detention centers: massive blocks of concrete with peeling paint and cracked windows, surrounded by tall fences, thick bars, and foreboding gates. Inside, those school buildings were often dimly lit and in a state of general disrepair.

When I was twelve, my track teammates taught me how to fight since fights were routine at their schools, though I never ended up needing those skills at mine. We dressed the same and listened to the same music. We spoke the same slang. We were all Black and on the same team living in the same city, but our school experiences were worlds apart. They had aspirations and big dreams just like I did, but they lacked the opportunities that I had to see them through. We went our separate ways after track practice each day, and it all seemed so unfair. I wanted to go with them, to be with them at school. I wanted them at *my* school, because I knew, even at that young age, that the segregated school system around us was stunting their potential. Also, selfishly, I wanted them at my school so I wouldn't have to be the only one; so I wouldn't have to feel alone because I looked different; so I wouldn't have to be "the Black kid" in class anymore.

· · · · ·

I carried those childhood experiences with me through college and, eventually, on to graduate school as a doctoral student in sociology. I read dozens of scholarly journal articles and books about racial inequality and segregation, but those studies rarely, if ever, mentioned students like who I was as a youth. My experiences, and the experiences of others like me in similar educational and social contexts, were largely missing from the literature. Thus, I began this book project intending to examine my own experiences—the experiences of Black and Latinx students navigating affluent, elite, and academically stringent school culture, particularly in schools where they were one of very few Black or Latinx students enrolled.

I decided to conduct the study in Valley View, California,[2] a Los Angeles suburb where the majority of residents were middle class or affluent. As I began the project, the median household income in Valley View was nearly $100,000 and roughly 68% of adult residents over age twenty-five were college graduates.[3] The ethnoracial composition of the city reflected broader contemporary immigration flows in middle-class, coastal California communities: 45% White, 39% Asian, 9% Latinx, 2% Black, and 5% "other or mixed-race."

I chose Pinnacle High School—the flagship high school in the Valley View Unified School District—as my initial field site. Pinnacle's campus was spread over a sixty-acre plateau, and it featured a plethora of scholastic and athletic facilities. It was known as an academically elite school; the graduation rate was 95%, and the percentage of those graduates who went on to college was even higher. Approximately 89% of Pinnacle's 2,000+ students came from middle-class or affluent households.[4] Just over 50% were Asian[5] and roughly 40% were White, while Black and Latinx youth comprised approximately 2% and 7% of the student body, respectively.

I was drawn to Pinnacle in part due to its racial composition, which would allow me to study the experiences of Black and Latinx youth in a setting where they were vastly outnumbered by their White and Asian peers. Moreover, the racial diversity at Pinnacle would enable me to deviate from the Black-White racial binary that was, and remains, so commonplace in sociological studies of segregation and racialized schooling.[6] In 1960, approximately 84% of American high school students were White, and the overwhelming majority of the remaining 16% were Black.[7] As I began fieldwork for this project, the racial makeup of American children reflected America's new and increasing diversity: Whites, Blacks, Latinx, and Asians comprised 51.7%, 15.8%, 23.7%, and 5.1% of high school-age

children, respectively,[8] and Asian Americans were the fastest growing racial group in the United States.[9] As such, Pinnacle High School
presented an important, contemporary context of racial and ethnic
diversity—an educational terrain in which Asian and Latinx students were indispensable to the story.[10]

. . . . .

I began my fieldwork at Pinnacle by sitting in on a US history class
for sophomores. The class was taught by Ms. Miller, who was White,
in her early forties, and a Pinnacle alumna. Of the thirty-eight students in class that day, nineteen were Asian, twelve were White, four
were Black, and three were Latinx. Each student had an assigned
seat among several rows of desks.

Jamal, one of the Black students, stood 6'1" and was a legitimate
star on the varsity football and basketball teams. His assigned seat
was in the back row and in the far corner of the room, farthest from
the whiteboard and projector screen at the front. On my second day of
observation, during a PowerPoint lecture on the Civil War, Ms. Miller
projected a copy of the Gettysburg Address onto the screen. The letters and words were small enough that she asked the class whether
anyone was having trouble seeing and reading the text. One hand
shot up; it was Jamal's. "I am," he said. Several students around him
cracked smiles and chuckled. "How come you're having trouble seeing?" asked Ms. Miller. "I'm blind," replied Jamal. Half the class burst
into laughter, which quickly spread throughout the room. Ms. Miller
was not amused. She dismissed Jamal's statement as a joke, ignored
the laughter, and resumed the lecture.

I started paying more attention to Jamal during subsequent visits
to Ms. Miller's classroom because I saw my childhood self in him—a
Black student-athlete at an elite prep school where only 2% of his fellow students were also Black. Unlike my teenage self, however, Jamal
often appeared listless and disinterested during class. For instance,
after watching a PBS Civil War documentary, students were to write

a short essay in their notebooks on whether the United States could exist as two separate nations—North and South. Instead of responding to the prompt, Jamal chose to draw pictures while listening to music through one of his earbud headphones.

Ms. Miller then showed the class a painting of a scene and asked students to comment on it aloud, but Jamal kept doodling. He glanced briefly at the painting after several students had offered their interpretations, and then went back to drawing, his head bobbing ever so slightly to the beat of the song that he was listening to. Ms. Miller posed questions about the significance of various colors and symbolism in the artwork, but Jamal never looked up again after his initial glance. A few more minutes passed, at which point he leaned his elbow on his desk, rested his head in the palm of his hand, and closed his eyes. "Jamal, wake up," Ms. Miller said to him after a while, but her voice was flat and lacked urgency, and he continued to rest until the period was over.

Jamal was not always disengaged in class. His attention would wane whenever subject matter was presented visually—such as via PowerPoint—but his level of focus increased markedly whenever doing worksheets in class, and he often assumed a leadership role during breakout sessions, peer review assignments, and small group projects. There was a clear pattern to the discrepancy in his engagement, and I wondered why.

Exactly three weeks into my fieldwork, everything changed. As I stepped into the classroom, I noticed that Jamal was not in his seat. Ms. Miller used a seating chart to take attendance and, on any given day, she would circle the names of any students who were absent before handing me the chart so that I could see who was present. I noticed immediately that she had marked Jamal as absent by crossing his name off the chart.

After class I asked Ms. Miller about Jamal and why she had eliminated him from the class roster. She said that he had been "transferred to Crossroads for credit recovery." I asked her what Crossroads was and what "credit recovery" was, as I had never heard of that school or that term. She said Crossroads was a "continuation high school" located about a mile away in Valley View and that it was a public school within the Valley View Unified School District. She added that students were sent to Crossroads from each of Valley View's four comprehensive high schools, including Pinnacle, when they had fallen behind on their cumulative coursework such that they were no longer on pace to graduate on time with their class.

How and why did students like Jamal end up at Crossroads? How did they feel about changing schools in this fashion, in the middle of the semester? What was the transfer process like? Under what conditions, if any, could students return to Pinnacle? How did the academic culture at Pinnacle compare to the academic culture at Crossroads? These were some of the questions that I jotted in my notebook right away as I stood in the hallway outside Ms. Miller's classroom door that afternoon.

CALIFORNIA'S CONTINUATION HIGH SCHOOLS AND ALTERNATIVE SCHOOLS ACROSS THE NATION

Continuation high schools have existed since 1919 in California as an "alternative education" option for students enrolled in the state's comprehensive public high schools. In 1965 there were only thirteen continuation high schools in the state, but changes to state law that year mandated that most public school districts operate a continuation high school for sophomores, juniors, and seniors deemed "vulnerable to academic or behavioral failure." Consequently, the number of continuation high schools in California increased dramatically in the ensuing decades.[11] Then, during the George W. Bush administration, a central focus on improving public school test scores incentivized high schools to push lower-achieving students into continuation schools.[12] In 2018, there were 435 continuation high schools statewide, serving a total of 85,343 students, or roughly 5% of the public high school student population that year.[13]

The purpose of continuation schools is to provide an accelerated credit recovery program that gives students who are behind on their course credits a chance to catch up and graduate on time from high school.[14] As a "dropout prevention" strategy, continuation high schools are intended to be temporary off-ramps for students who eventually return to graduate from their comprehensive high school once they have gotten back on track. However, continuation high school students are far more likely to drop out than their peers at comprehensive high schools,[15] and most continuation school students who end up graduating remain there to do so, never returning to the high school from which they were transferred.[16]

A recent analysis of national data revealed that roughly 500,000 high school students across all fifty states were enrolled in an alternative education program at some point during the school year, and that those students were disproportionately Black, Latinx, and from lower-income backgrounds. Nearly two-thirds of state education departments implement policies in which students can be involuntarily transferred to an alternative school for disciplinary reasons. Nationwide, alternative high schools are generally housed in trailers, dilapidated buildings, or tucked into strip malls. There is often little instruction from teachers, and extracurricular offerings are sparse at best.[17]

A separate analysis found that in some states, such as Florida and Michigan, alternative high schools can operate as private charters, which means that students who drop out of them are not counted toward the official dropout count of the broader district. In Pennsylvania, once students are transferred to an alternative high school for credit recovery, their test scores are absorbed into the district average instead of recorded as belonging to any specific high school. Such arrangements have been criticized as ways for comprehensive public high schools and districts to skirt state accountability measures by concealing struggling students and dropouts.[18] In short, the mechanisms of segregation and inequality that I highlight throughout this book are far from unique to Southern California.

. . . . .

After I learned of Jamal's transfer, I left Pinnacle for the day seeking more information about Crossroads. I clicked through the Valley View Unified School District's website, and what I found in that simple search convinced me that what had up to that point been a study of race and academic culture at Pinnacle would surely need to expand to include Crossroads. These two public high schools, in the same school district, in the same upper-income suburb, were demographically divergent. According to district data, the student body at Crossroads was approximately 39% White, 36% Latinx, 11% Black, and 7% Asian. This meant that, at Crossroads, Black and Latinx students were conspicuously overrepresented, while Asian students were clearly underrepresented.[19]

I also came across evidence of socioeconomic and academic inequality. Whereas 11% of students at Pinnacle had been designated by the district as "socioeconomically disadvantaged," 51% of Crossroads students shared that label. I then read that over 90% of Pinnacle students who took the California High School Exit Exam (CAHSEE) as sophomores passed on their first try, but only 30% of Crossroads sophomores who took the test could claim that achievement. Taken together, these glaring racial, socioeconomic, and academic disparities were curious. The demographic features of Valley View, Pinnacle High School, and Crossroads High School—and the relationship between the two schools—were intriguing and warranted a thorough examination of the processes and practices that contributed to these inequalities.[20] This book is the result of that study.

Drawing on two years of ethnographic fieldwork at Pinnacle and Crossroads, as well as 122 in-depth interviews with students, parents, and faculty at each high school, I unveil hidden, institutional mechanisms of school segregation and inequality that disproportionately placed Black, Latinx, and lower-income students at risk. At Pinnacle High School, where exceptional achievement was commonplace, students who fell behind were framed as misfits who did

Table 1   Racial compositions of Pinnacle High School, Crossroads
           High School, and Valley View, CA, in 2015

Race	Pinnacle High School	Crossroads High School	Valley View, CA
Asian	52.2%	7.5%	39.1%
White	35.5%	39.6%	44.8%
Latinx	7.2%	36.5%	9.2%
Black	2.1%	11.4%	1.9%
Other	3.0%	5.0%	5.1%

not belong there. The presence of a continuation school in the district gave comprehensive high schools like Pinnacle the option of pushing out lower-achieving students and intensifying the focus of their considerable educational resources on high-achievers. A few days into my visits to Crossroads, Mr. Gregory, a thirty-year-old, second-year math and science teacher, described Crossroads and its relationship with Pinnacle in stark terms: "Here at Crossroads, we're essentially a dumping ground for the students that the comprehensive high schools don't want to teach and support," he told me one day after school. "It's really a form of school segregation, plain and simple."

A SUCCINCT SUMMATION OF SEGREGATED SCHOOLING IN AMERICA SINCE 1954

On May 17, 1954, the US Supreme Court ruled in *Brown v. Board of Education* that a system of "separate but equal" schools for Blacks and Whites was "inherently unequal." The ruling established that de jure racial segregation in American schools was unconstitutional. *Brown* was a pivotal legal victory of the civil rights movement, a resounding declaration that racial segregation had no place in the field of public education. But countervailing forces of segregation and integration after *Brown* resulted in periods of progress, stagnation, and backsliding, such that de facto racial segregation has remained an entrenched and defining feature of American schooling.[21]

Brown did not reduce school segregation at first because it lacked enforcement provisions. Furthermore, "freedom of choice" desegregation plans that were enacted by Southern school districts helped preserve school segregation in those districts in the 1950s and 1960s by placing the responsibility of integration on Black families.[22] Black parents had the "choice" to enroll their children in all-White schools, but White families, faculty, and staff at those schools were often overwhelmingly and openly hostile toward any racial integration whatsoever. For instance, in 1957, the Little Rock Nine—nine Black teenagers in Little Rock, Arkansas—were the first Black students to attend Little Rock Central High School. They faced a torrent of racist slurs and death threats, and President Eisenhower ordered the National Guard to escort them into the school building to ensure their safety. This sort of racist backlash had a chilling effect on school desegregation in the late 1950s.[23]

The situation improved somewhat with the passage of the Civil Rights Act of 1964, which ended the legal segregation of public spaces and criminalized employment discrimination on the basis of race, gender, religion, or national origin. The Civil Rights Act greatly increased the power of the executive and judicial branches of government to enforce school desegregation. The law granted the US Department of Justice the power to file lawsuits to force school districts to desegregate, and it cleared the way for the Department of Education to cut funding to districts that continued to segregate their schools.

Despite these momentous legal victories in the fight against a racially segregated school system, few lawsuits were filed to compel desegregation in the immediate aftermath of the Civil Rights Act, and school districts remained highly segregated across the country

in the late 1960s; in 1968, well over a decade after *Brown*, 50% of
Black students nationwide attended a school in which at least 90%
of all students were also Black.[24] Widespread desegregation did not
begin in public schools until the late 1960s and early 1970s, when
court orders began to require school districts to adopt more effective
integration plans.[25]

One such plan was busing. In 1971, in the Supreme Court case
Swann v. Charlotte-Mecklenburg Board of Education, the Court
ruled that busing was a constitutionally protected remedy for
racially segregated schools, particularly in districts where residential segregation made school integration even more challenging. By
the mid-1970s, hundreds of school districts across the nation were
subject to similar court-ordered desegregation plans,[26] and the plans
were effective because they had the weight of a federal judge's ruling
behind them.[27] At the end of the 1970s, school segregation was still
widespread in all regions of the country, but significant progress had
been made; in 1980, 33% of Black students nationwide attended a
school in which at least 90% of all students were also Black, a 17%
decrease since 1968.[28]

The 1980s and 1990s were decades of stalled progress on school
integration, and the period from the year 2000 to today has been
a combination of continued stagnation and the gradual resegregation of public school districts across the country.[29] A complex set of
social and structural forces undergird these dynamics. Residential
segregation between Blacks and Whites declined slightly between
1990 and 2010, but that decline did not correspond to a meaningful
decrease in school segregation between Black and White students.

One of the most important reasons for this incongruous finding
involved "White flight," in which White parents responded to the
racial integration of previously all-White neighborhoods and schools
by moving to Whiter suburbs,[30] or pulling their children out of public school and enrolling them in private options.[31] White flight began
in earnest in the late 1960s when school desegregation plans were
increasingly enforced through the courts,[32] and it gained traction in

subsequent decades as a response to further integration efforts. One of the primary consequences of White flight in metropolitan areas has been an increase in residential and school segregation *between* neighboring districts. In other words, as desegregation efforts led to modest reductions in segregation between schools within districts, school segregation increased between contiguous districts due to White enrollment losses in the integrating districts.[33] This between-district school segregation increased throughout the 1990s and up through 2010.[34]

Integration efforts were also hampered near the turn of the century by changes within the legal system. From the 1990s through 2010, hundreds of public school districts across the country that had been under court-ordered desegregation arrangements were released from court control and oversight.[35] This broad relaxation of desegregation enforcement allowed school segregation in a majority of these districts to climb back to levels unseen since the late 1960s and early 1970s.[36] Thus, a review of history makes clear that, after *Brown*, school segregation either remained unabated, or it went through periods of decline, stagnation, and resurgence that were, in effect, offsetting.

Ramifications of a Racially and Economically Segregated School System

Inequality in the US educational system reproduces inequality in society by affording fewer educational opportunities and resources to poor and working-class students compared to their middle-class peers.[37] Schools replicate societal "patterns of dominance and subordination, the distribution of ownership of productive resources, and the degree of social distance and solidarity among various fragments of the working population."[38] Stratified schooling conditions students for employment within a stratified economy; schools in middle-class neighborhoods are structured to prepare students for college and lucrative careers while schools in working-class and poor neighborhoods are typically not as well equipped to do so.[39]

Black and Latinx persons living in the United States are drastically overrepresented among the nation's poorest individuals and those residing in the lowest-income neighborhoods.[40] As such, school segregation patterns disproportionately concentrate Black and Latinx students in high-poverty schools.[41] High-poverty schools regularly lack the requisite layers of academic and social support that students need in order to flourish (e.g., consistent mentoring relationships, and opportunities to connect schooling to an attainable career goal), and this is particularly true for students who carry the burden of challenging life circumstances to school each day.[42] Consequently, Black and Latinx youth often receive an inferior education through no fault of their own, and their academic performance suffers dramatically as a result.[43] Segregated schooling depresses the academic performance of Black and Latinx students in terms of grades, test scores, graduation rates, and college enrollment figures.[44]

Black students are, on average, the most adversely affected group; they remain the most racially segregated youth, pay the highest achievement penalty for racially segregated school districts,[45] and experience the greatest academic and labor market gains from successful desegregation efforts.[46] Economist Rucker Johnson has found that these gains are due to greater access to educational resources in schools with higher percentages of White students, smaller class sizes in those schools, and higher per-pupil spending in Whiter districts.[47] The societal benefits of desegregation are overwhelming, but as a nation we have too often lacked the moral clarity and political will to sustain and build on the progress made after *Brown* and the *Civil Rights Act of 1964.*

Segregated Classrooms in Integrated Schools

The primary reason for the continued racial segregation of schools is the pervasive persistence of residential segregation, since the vast majority of students attend their neighborhood public school.[48] A large body of scholarship details the substantial challenges faced by

Black and Latinx students in racially segregated, low-income neighborhood schools,[49] but researchers have paid far less attention to the structural mechanisms of educational inequality in middle-class neighborhoods and those that are not highly segregated. School segregation takes many forms and is not solely the product of residential segregation and other neighborhood factors.

Even when integration efforts have been successful at the school level and able to overcome residential segregation, such efforts have generally fallen short of resulting in racially diverse classrooms. Starting in the late 1960s and early 1970s, fruitful attempts at integration were met with curricular tracking policies that proliferated in public school districts. Tracking resulted in the disproportionate placement of Black and Brown students in lower-level, remedial courses—a system of segregated classrooms within integrated schools.[50] Racialized tracking remains a routine and extensive practice, particularly in racially diverse public schools and in middle-class communities.[51]

HIDDEN MECHANISMS OF SCHOOL SEGREGATION AND INEQUALITY IN VALLEY VIEW

Apart from the extant literature on tracking, researchers have paid scant attention to the ways in which high schools in middle-class and affluent districts perpetuate racial and social class disparities. Moreover, research to date has overwhelming come from schools and districts in which racial diversity has largely existed in terms of Black and White.[52] My Southern California field sites—Pinnacle High School and Crossroads High School—reflect a particular racial and ethnic diversity that has not received much attention in qualitative studies of school segregation. Furthermore, though many studies of educational inequality take a comparative approach by analyzing the disparate school conditions and opportunities between students living in low-income, racially segregated urban neighborhoods and the

Whiter, wealthier suburbs nearby,[53] between-school segregation also exists within racially diverse, integrated suburban communities like Valley View.[54] The relationship between Pinnacle and Crossroads is a case in point.

Additionally, the mechanisms of educational inequality in highly affluent and privileged contexts have not been sufficiently addressed by social scientists, although there are two notable exceptions worth mentioning here. In *Privilege*, sociologist Shamus Khan examines elite high school culture at a remarkably wealthy, predominantly White, private boarding school in the Northeast[55]—a far cry demographically and geographically from Pinnacle High School in Southern California. In *The Privileged Poor*, sociologist Anthony Jack exposes multiple ways in which a highly prestigious, private college in a New England city exacerbates socioeconomic inequality among students of color on campus despite stated institutional commitments and initiatives to promote diversity, equity, and inclusion.[56]

Khan and Jack both focus on the embodiment of privilege at private institutions, and how that culture of privilege begets inequality. Their work reminds us that inequity and disadvantage can exist within some of the most privileged educational institutions, and their findings indicate a need for continued scholarship to further understand the mechanisms and processes that reproduce racial and socioeconomic advantage and disadvantage at a variety of schools, including those that are considered elite. This book is my attempt to push the sociology of education forward in that direction.

This book is also an extension of recent research on the criminalization of Black and Latinx youth. In *Unequal City*, an ethnographic study of Chicago public schools, sociologist Carla Shedd highlights surveillance practices by school staff and Chicago police that lend a prison-like, carceral feel to Black students' school experiences.[57] Shedd's research, and other similar work, has shown the frequently punitive nature of public schooling to be problematic; in the public schools on Chicago's South Side—and in other racially segregated, low-income districts across the country—the presence of surveillance cameras and law enforcement officers tend to distract educators from an understanding of students' most basic developmental needs.[58] Officials in these schools too often perceive Black and Latinx students as physically threatening and troublesome, and frequently label these youth as "difficult," "dangerous," or even "gang member[s]."[59] These alienating labels, and the harsh conditions that often come with them, can have a long-term negative impact on students' levels of academic engagement,[60] eventually pushing these youth out of traditional, comprehensive high schools.[61] In affluent, suburban Valley View, I found that Black and Brown students were similarly criminalized and labeled, but for reasons that had little to do with a threat of deviant behavior or illicit activity. Instead, these students of color were criminalized and discredited for struggling academically.

AN EXTREME FORM OF TRACKING

Sociologist Robert Zussman reminds us that successful ethnographic case studies "look at extremes, unusual circumstances, and analytically clear examples, all of which are important not because they are representative, but because they show a process or a problem in particularly clear relief."[62] Whereas conventional curriculum tracking is a process of segregation that occurs *within* schools, I encountered an extreme form of tracking that happened *between* schools. Students who struggled at Pinnacle High School were pushed out and tracked into neighboring Crossroads High School, a phenomenon that I refer to as *academic apartheid*.

Academic apartheid is between-school segregation based on one's academic standing rather than one's home address. Just as residential segregation purposefully creates and maintains racially homogenous, hyper-policed neighborhoods where an array of social problems are concentrated and amplified,[63] academic apartheid creates and maintains schools with a concentration of academically underperforming students and a criminalizing environment in which students frequently feel discarded, discredited, and punished.[64] Crossroads's presence in the district helped boost Pinnacle's reputation because Pinnacle used Crossroads as a "dumping ground"—a scholastic scrapyard for students who were behind on credits. Shepherding struggling students to a separate high school, and holding the vast majority of them there through graduation, helped Pinnacle manage and maintain its status as an academically elite high school.

In Valley View, this segregation was heavily racialized, as Black and Latinx students were starkly overrepresented at Crossroads. It was also tied to socioeconomic status, with lower-income students constituting nearly five times the percentage of the student body at Crossroads as they did at Pinnacle. In this book I show *how* this form of school segregation operated by elucidating the ways in which specific continuation school policies and practices in the district disproportionately affected Black, Latinx, and lower-income students.

AN OVERVIEW OF MY METHODS

My methods of data collection for this project included extensive observation and face-to-face, in-depth interviews with a variety of institutional actors at both schools. Over the course of seventeen months during which both schools were in session, I spent hundreds of hours making observations at Pinnacle High School and Crossroads High School. I observed in various spaces and at numerous events, such as classrooms, assemblies, conferences, faculty meetings, back-to-school nights, trophy presentations, and graduations. Observing in a wide variety of school spaces allowed me to minimize the extent to which important aspects of the settings and situations under study would be inadvertently excluded from the analysis.[65] I was often able to take copious field notes, by hand in a notebook, within these various school spaces. I supplemented these notes with memos to provide a "running record" of my early analytic hunches and "proto-conceptions."[66] I engaged in dozens of informal conversations on campus with teachers, administrators, students, and parents in accordance with the "interviewing by comment" technique of ethnographic data gathering—making comments to informants to spark conversations in the field in lieu of asking direct questions.[67]

My first six months of fieldwork were strictly observational with no formal interviews, a period during which I gradually built rapport with various institutional actors at both schools. As such, by the time I started conducting interviews, I had established a level of familiarity and trust that allowed me to have candid conversations with various members of each school community. To obtain student interview subjects, I introduced myself to each class in which I was observing and passed around a signup sheet for students to indicate their interest in being interviewed by me sometime during the school year. I distributed several signup sheets throughout the year, just in case one or more students in a given classroom changed their mind about their willingness to sit for a formal interview. I secured additional interviews with students, teachers, staff, and parents via snowball sampling—a process of referral from one informant to another.[68]

I conducted all student interviews on either the Pinnacle or Crossroads campus during regular business hours. I interviewed students during the lunch period, during class periods (with teacher approval), or on campus after school. I conducted all interviews with teachers during free periods or after school, typically in their classroom. I obtained consent from each informant to audio-record each interview, and all recordings were transcribed verbatim, either by me or by an undergraduate research assistant whom I trained.

At Pinnacle, I interviewed twenty-eight students (fifteen girls and thirteen boys), seven teachers, four administrators, and six parents.[69] At Crossroads, I interviewed fifty-nine students (thirty girls and twenty-nine boys), nine teachers, three administrators, and six parents—and I participated in a focus group discussion with twelve additional Crossroads parents. I asked all students to identify their

	Pinnacle	Crossroads	
Race	High School	High School	Total
Asian	8	3	11
White	7	20	27
Latinx	6	22	28
Black	7	14	21

Table 2   Self-identified race of student interviewees

race as part of the interview, and the results of that inquiry are presented in Table 2. The number of each racial group in my Crossroads student sample roughly corresponded to the percentage of each racial group in the entire student body at Crossroads. I oversampled Black and Latinx students at Pinnacle because Black and Latinx students were overrepresented among those transferred to Crossroads.

A PREVIEW OF THE UPCOMING CHAPTERS

Chapter 1 examines how institutional definitions of success and failure affect school policies and practices in ways that contribute to school segregation and inequality in Valley View. Pinnacle High School's academic culture was characterized by what I refer to as an exacting *institutional success frame*—a collective interpretation of academic achievement cultivated by institutional actors such as school administrators, teachers, parents, and students. At Pinnacle, the institutional success frame was competitive and unforgiving. Exceptional academic achievements were routine and expected. I show how and why a lofty institutional success frame was such a fundamental part of the academic culture at Pinnacle, as well as the ways in which it promoted division within the school community and marginalized students who struggled academically.

Chapter 2 details the transfer process between Pinnacle and Crossroads, and the ways in which the process places undue strain on Black, Latinx, and lower-income students. Transfer to Crossroads was voluntary, but students often faced unrelenting pressure from school counselors and administrators to transfer. Those from more privileged backgrounds were better positioned to resist and avoid a move to Crossroads. Once transferred, students experienced a criminalizing environment of social control: restrictive metal fences and gates; constant surveillance by faculty, staff, and an armed police officer; limited bathroom privileges; no off-campus privileges during the school day. Crossroads students were prohibited from visiting the campus of any comprehensive high school in the district, including the one from which they had been transferred. The curriculum at Crossroads was so sparse that it disqualified graduates from matriculating at a four-year college. Shepherding struggling students to Crossroads stigmatized these students as "failures" and fostered a student climate of academic apathy that was counterproductive to Crossroads's stated purpose as an academic rehabilitation center. And the arrangement benefitted Pinnacle; with low-performing students out of sight and out of mind, Pinnacle could focus its considerable resources on high-achieving students who would enhance the school's reputation by scoring top marks on standardized tests and gaining admission to the most selective colleges and universities in the country.

Chapter 3 highlights the day-to-day classroom experiences of specific teachers at Pinnacle and Crossroads to show the ways in which *academic apartheid* creates separate and unequal teaching and learning environments. Though located in the same school district in the same upper-middle-class suburb, Pinnacle and Crossroads diverged sharply in terms of the social and academic culture of a typical class in session. At Pinnacle, teachers rarely needed to spend any time quieting the classroom before beginning a lesson, or in maintaining students' attention while class was in session. These luxuries allowed Pinnacle teachers to spend nearly all of their time and energy on teaching, and Pinnacle students often assisted their teachers by helping classmates with challenging course material both during class and office hours. In contrast, at Crossroads, where some level of disorder among students during class time was common, the role of the teacher was often to be a classroom manager of sorts, striving to be effective and "get by" despite the challenges. When struggling students are concentrated in one school, the result is a set of classroom conditions that do little to motivate apathetic students, are challenging and distracting for students who *are* motivated, and undermine teachers' pedagogical efficacy and morale.

Chapter 4 shifts the focus to Pinnacle's Korean families, who had an important influence on the institutional culture, policies, and practices at Pinnacle and throughout the district. Ethnic capital—which refers to the social and material benefits that co-ethnic support systems provide—is crucial for immigrants' educational attainment. Rather than merely drawing on co-ethnic resources that were external to the school, such as those found in community organizations or religious congregations, Korean parents at Pinnacle embedded their ethnic capital within Pinnacle High School by forming their own ethnically segregated parent group—the Korean Parent Teacher Association (Korean PTA). I detail the ways in which the Korean PTA supported Korean parents and students at Pinnacle, raised money to support the school, and provided cultural education programs for teachers throughout the district. An examination of this ethnically exclusive parent organization sheds new light on how highly resourced immigrant groups mobilize those resources to succeed in a new society, and the ways in which immigrant incorporation involves a relational back-and-forth adjustment between newcomers and well-established individuals and institutions.

Chapter 5 probes for solutions to some of the problems detailed throughout the book. I illuminate portions of interviews and informal conversations I had with students, parents, teachers, and administrators that focused on ways to improve the high school experience for students who end up at Crossroads. Sometimes we discussed whether Crossroads should exist as a school at all, and what some alternatives to Crossroads might be. I also present my observations at Crossroads's annual career fair for students. The career fair was a memorable event because it was, by far, the most engaging and exciting gathering for Crossroads students all year. I discuss the implications of this heightened level of engagement for how schools like Crossroads can prepare students for productive, meaningful educational experiences and careers after high school.

In the conclusion, I address the implications of the study for our understanding of how schools and school districts reproduce racial segregation and socioeconomic inequality. Leaning heavily on my ethnographic observations and interviews throughout my time spent at Crossroads and Pinnacle, I suggest changes to policy and practice aimed at establishing a fairer and more equitable high school experience for disadvantaged students. I propose concrete, actionable steps toward easing the burden placed on struggling students to find success in school environments that, as currently structured, set them up for stigmatization, alienation, and failure.

1 "If You're Not in AP Classes, Then Who Are You?"

Pinnacle High School sat on a sprawling, fifty-five-acre suburban campus, with meticulously manicured lawns and stately school structures that rose above dozens of neatly pruned trees. Pinnacle boasted a theater/auditorium, gymnasium, all-weather track, football field, soccer field, baseball field, Olympic-sized swimming pool, several tennis courts, and separate buildings to house its math, science, humanities, arts, and athletic departments. There were two large parking lots on school grounds—one for faculty and staff that wrapped around the front of the school, and one for students located along a side of campus that bordered an attractive row of houses. Dozens of parking spaces in both lots were covered by broad solar panels, which provided ample shade from the Southern California sun and powered electricity throughout the buildings and classrooms on campus.

Pinnacle was an "open campus," meaning that there were multiple paths and walkways on the grounds that served as points of entry and exit and that there were no fences or gates around the campus perimeter. During the lunch period, I frequently witnessed a stream of dozens of students walking in small groups down one of the main streets near campus toward a gas station that sold a wide variety of snacks and beverages. Just across the street from that gas station was an upscale strip mall with a bank, a Starbucks, several popular neighborhood eateries, and a large grocery store. Students were free to leave and return during any free period throughout the day, and these businesses were popular destinations for those who ventured off campus.

Pinnacle was the leading public high school in Valley View, consistently ranking as one of the top public high schools in California and the nation. Their top ranking was reflected in their high school exit exam pass rates, graduation rates, and the percentage of graduates who went on to four-year universities immediately following graduation. Over 96% of Pinnacle's graduates enrolled in postsecondary institutions, and nearly 70% attended four-year colleges and universities. The curriculum offered twenty-nine honors and advanced placement (AP) courses, a variety of clubs and student government opportunities, and a robust peer tutoring program. Pinnacle enrolled over two thousand students each year from surrounding Valley View neighborhoods,[1] and school officials were quite proud of the school's academic profile given the size of the student body.

As is the case at many high schools, popular students at Pinnacle were those who wore designer clothing and exclusive sneakers, drove desirable cars, were standout athletes, or were cheerleaders. But students with high grade point averages (GPAs) and test scores were popular, too. At assemblies, the physics and debate teams drew cheers that were just as loud as those for the football and basketball teams. Moreover, the highest academic achievers were frequently the same students who donned the latest fashion, drove a "sick" or "dope" car, played one or more sports, or were on the cheer squad. In other words, the "nerds" and the "jocks" were regularly the same kids.

The student body was racially and ethnically diverse, though there were few Latinx students and even fewer Black students. During my

Table 3   Racial compositions of Pinnacle High School
          and Valley View, CA

Race	Pinnacle High School	Valley View, CA
Asian	52.2%	39.1%
White	35.5%	44.8%
Latinx	7.2%	9.2%
Black	2.1%	1.9%
Other	3.0%	5.1%

fieldwork, the racial composition of the student body was 52.2% Asian, 35.5% White, 7.2% Latinx, 2.1% Black, and 3.0% "other."

Pinnacle's academic culture was competitive and exacting. This achievement culture split the student body into two general types of students—those who were high academic achievers, and those who were not; those who had their sights set on gaining admission to the most prestigious colleges and universities in the country, and those who did not. Students who excelled were casually celebrated, while those who struggled or focused less on academics were often overlooked, devalued, and marginalized.

When I showed up in the main office for my first day of fieldwork, I knew that Pinnacle had a reputation for academic excellence, but I wanted to know more about how and why this was so. I was curious about what campus life was like for students and teachers. I entered the office and was immediately greeted by the receptionist, Deborah—a vivacious, middle-aged Black woman with a friendly smile. I introduced myself and told Deborah that I had an appointment to observe Ms. Quinn's third-, fourth-, and fifth-period AP classes. Deborah quickly produced a sign-in sheet and nametag for me to fill out. She also gave me a map of the school for visitors and drew a path to my destination, which was on the other side of campus in the humanities department. I thanked her and set off on my

Figure 1. Pinnacle High School administration building and auditorium

Figure 2. Pinnacle High School baseball field and training equipment

way, walking quickly just in case I got lost amid the buildings and corridors.

As I headed toward the classroom, I saw no more than a dozen students ambling about at first. Then I heard the school bell and, almost at once, students began to pour out of doorways, hallways, and from around every corner, flooding the open space between buildings. As I weaved my way between clusters of students, I thought about Pinnacle's reputation for high achievement and how that reputation might affect students in different ways. I paused outside the humanities building to jot two questions in my notebook that would guide my early days of fieldwork: 1) What are the most salient lines of stratification in this community? 2) How might acclaimed, high-performing public schools like Pinnacle contribute to the reproduction of inequality?

. . . . .

I arrived at Ms. Quinn's door just in time for the start of the first of her two AP psychology classes. Ms. Quinn's classroom, located on the second floor of the humanities building, was large enough to comfortably accommodate thirty desks. The desks were arranged in neat rows, and they appeared clean and unblemished. The wall farthest from the door was covered by a poster picturing a bubbling brook running through a temperate rainforest. Just to the right of the poster was a window overlooking a handful of parking spaces and a grassy knoll just beyond the asphalt. The rest of the room was sparsely decorated with various souvenirs and artifacts from Ms. Quinn's summertime excursions across Europe and Asia. There were also other, smaller posters depicting aspects of European or Asian history and culture, such as the one Ms. Quinn hung on the wall just behind her desk that listed all the British kings and queens, and another beside it that enumerated the tenets of Buddhism.

The racial composition of the students was overwhelmingly Asian and White, just like the student body overall; of the twenty students in class that morning, twelve were Asian, six were White, and two were Latinx. Ms. Quinn, who was White and in her mid-forties, stood at the front of the room dressed in a light blue t-shirt, red corduroy pants, and white canvas sneakers. She suggested that I sit behind her desk, which was located in a corner of the classroom, near the door.

Ms. Quinn was an engaging, energetic, and humorous teacher. She began class by reviewing answers to homework questions and previewing an upcoming assignment. She then lectured on the psychology of vision, presenting the material via PowerPoint slides projected onto a pull-down screen at the front of the classroom. Students feverishly copied all the information on each slide into their binders and notebooks, their brows furrowing with focus and determination. During the lecture, Ms. Quinn emphasized new and important information by indicating that it was likely to appear on "the test." "The test" was the AP psychology examination that students were scheduled to take in May, a little more than six months away. The entire course was geared toward preparing students to pass that test.

The school bell rang at the end of the class period to alert students that it was time to head to their next class. Ms. Quinn gave a few final instructions for homework as students began to pack their backpacks. Some students left immediately while others lingered briefly at or near their desks. A student approached Ms. Quinn to ask a question about optical illusions.

Once the entire class had left the room, I had an opportunity to speak with Ms. Quinn about the competitive academic environment that Pinnacle was known for. As a teacher who had been teaching various honors- and AP-level courses at Pinnacle for eight years, she was familiar with the school's culture of academic achievement. I began our conversation by commenting on what I had just observed in class:

SEAN: Those students seemed to be really focused and motivated.

MS. QUINN: Yeah, they really are good kids and good students. One thing you should know about our school is that there is a lot of interest from students and their parents in the honors and AP classes we offer. I only teach honors and AP level, and all of my classes are electives, and all of my classes are always filled to capacity. These kids want to take the rigorous stuff, and they want to challenge themselves. In fact, many parents choose Pinnacle because we offer so many honors and AP classes, and almost all of our students pass their AP exams. My students have a 97% pass rate on the AP exam since I've been here. We put out that data publicly and it really helps us attract and recruit new students and families who want to prepare for a top college and get a competitive edge.

SEAN: When you say that your honors and AP classes are "electives," that means that they are optional? [*I already knew that the answer was yes, but I was interested in how she would frame her response.*]

MS. QUINN: That's right; honors and AP are optional. We don't force any student into advanced classes or anything like that, but there is an expectation here that most students will at least take a handful of higher-level classes. We might suggest it or recommend it in some cases, but we usually don't have to.

SEAN: Students are already interested.

MS. QUINN: Exactly; they are already interested, and lots of them are here at Pinnacle specifically because of our variety of advanced courses. We actually often have to tell parents to back off and relax when it comes to the higher-level classes. Our academic counselors are always trying to calm parents down and lower the temperature a little bit. Sometimes we'll get a student whose parents are university professors with, like, three PhDs, and they'll be trying to push their kid into an AP class or several AP classes at once, and maybe that student isn't ready yet.

SEAN: And I've heard that there's a lot of competition here among students. Is that something that you see?

MS. QUINN: Oh yes! Students compete with themselves and each other constantly. They'll calculate their grades as soon as they receive a test back. I've never taught a math class, but I see lots of calculators in my classes because students are plugging in scores and figuring out their grades. And they do this while talking about it with their classmates and openly comparing scores. Sometimes students say things like, "If I don't bring home an A, my dad will kill me." I think the competitive environment motivates them because no one wants to be the one doing poorly when everyone else is doing well.

Ms. Quinn checked her watch. "Well, I have another batch of kiddos coming in now and they have a pop quiz," she said. I settled back into her desk chair and opened my notebook to a blank page.

In the days and weeks that followed, I began to focus my observations at Pinnacle on the school's culture of academic achievement. I was most interested in the institutional mechanisms that sustained this culture, and how it affected students of varying backgrounds and achievement levels. What I found was that the exacting achievement culture was promoted by a wide variety of institutional actors such that it was pervasive. Not all students, however, fit neatly within this academic climate.

PINNACLE'S INSTITUTIONAL DEFINITION OF SUCCESS

In *Frame Analysis*, sociologist Erving Goffman develops the concept of a sociological "frame"—a "schemata of interpretation" that allows people to "locate, perceive, identify and label" various episodes and circumstances in their lives and the world around them.[2] Frames are imbued with meaning; they help individuals make sense of their experiences, and, in turn, frames inspire both individual and collective action.[3] More recently, sociologists Jennifer Lee and Min Zhou have studied "cultural success frames," focusing on how Chinese and Vietnamese immigrant parents and their children define academic success in the United States. For many immigrant families, those definitions affect the educational and career aspirations, expectations, and decisions in a household.[4]

I submit that cultural frames of achievement are also applicable at the institutional level. In the context of education, an *institutional success frame* is a collective, institutional interpretation of academic achievement that is cultivated by institutional actors, such as administrators, teachers, parents, and students. According to the institutional success frame at Pinnacle High School, students were routinely expected to enroll in a challenging series of honors and AP classes, strive to attain a 4.0 grade point average, achieve top marks on AP exams and the SAT exam, and gain admission to one or more prestigious universities.

Pinnacle's rigid success frame affected many aspects of life on campus. Signs and symbols of academic excellence were visible throughout the school, but most notably on a brick arch that framed the front entrance to the administration building. "PINNACLE HIGH SCHOOL" appeared across the top of the arch in bold, metal letters fastened to the tawny bricks. Two phrases were affixed to the arch at eyelevel, one on either side. The phrase on the left side read, "California Distinguished School," and letters on the right spelled out, "National Exemplary School." Pinnacle had conspicuously tattooed these distinctions to its building as essential components of its institutional culture and identity.

Symbols of the institutional success frame were also visible within classrooms, often through decorations and other displays that reinforced prodigious expectations. For instance, Mr. Ventura, a biology teacher, lined the tops of the walls in his classroom with dozens of college pennants. These pennants represented a selection of the colleges and universities that Mr. Ventura's former students chose to attend. A scan of the pennants along the back wall read like a published list of top-ranked postsecondary schools: Stanford, Harvard, Princeton, Yale, Columbia, M.I.T., Duke, Brown, Dartmouth, NYU, Vanderbilt, Michigan, University of Chicago, Northwestern, Cal Tech, UCLA, UC Berkeley, UC Irvine, UC San Diego, UC Santa Barbara. For Mr. Ventura, and many of his colleagues, the enviable college enrollment of former students was a great source of personal pride, and these pennants served as badges of pedagogical honor. The display was also symbolic of the institutional success frame and

Figures 3a and 3b. Signs of the Institutional Success Frame at Pinnacle High School

a tacit reminder to current students of the level of achievement that was expected of them. "That's what success looks like at our school," he told me after class one day. "I want students to be reminded of what they can achieve here, of the opportunities that are available to them if they do well."

BACK-TO-SCHOOL NIGHT

Back-to-school nights can yield important insights into the culture of a school. These events allow parents to learn more about the curriculum, goals for the school year, and teachers' expectations for students. Parents also have the opportunity to meet teachers, ask questions, gather information about extracurricular activities, and socialize with other parents.

Back-to-school night at Pinnacle High School was the busiest and most crowded gathering of the year on campus. As I approached the major intersection in front of the school on my way to the event, cars were lined up in the turn lane to enter the parking lot. The main lot, which was expansive enough to accommodate hundreds of cars, was rapidly filling to capacity. Luxury cars were plentiful;

Mercedes-Benzes, BMWs, and Audis were commonplace, as were models from Tesla, Porsche, Lexus, Maserati, and Range Rover. These cars were status symbols and a clear indication of community affluence. I even saw—and heard—a red Ferrari, its engine growling as it eased into a space at the edge of the lot.

I parked in the student lot and walked onto campus toward the courtyard area in front of the gymnasium and theater complex. The mood was light and celebratory. Most parents were dressed in business-casual attire on what was a warm, September evening. Most men were wearing collared shirts with dark jeans or khakis and leather sneakers, and most women were wearing dresses with either heels or flats. When I reached the courtyard, it was teeming with activity as parents, administrators, and a handful of students mingled and made casual conversation. The space had been arranged like a small fair, with several student and parent organizations each occupying a different table. The organizations were there to greet parents, explain their purpose on campus, and pass out recruitment materials. For instance, the Parent Teacher Association (PTA) distributed an information sheet. One of the bullet points on their flyer read "Pinnacle PTA coordinates a number of programs featuring knowledgeable speakers on topics such as school safety, college preparation and admissions, summer job opportunities, and much more."

I spotted Mr. Holt, one of Pinnacle's three assistant principals and the school official responsible for green-lighting research projects on campus, such as my own. He was dressed in a gray suit, and he asked if I was enjoying the "festivities." Moments later, a message from Deborah, broadcast over the intercom system, instructed parents to head to their child's first-period class. Groups of uniformed cheerleaders were present around campus to direct parents to the appropriate building and classroom, and I made my way to Ms. Quinn's presentation of her first-period AP US history class.

Ms. Quinn greeted me with a smile and a wave as I took a seat in the back row of desks in her classroom. A few parents were already seated and several more arrived in short order. Soon there were twenty-two parents present, sixteen Asian and six White. The lack of Black and Latinx parents was notable, but not surprising given the racial composition of the student body. Ms. Quinn began her fifteen-minute presentation by welcoming all the parents to the class:

MS. QUINN: Hello, good evening, and welcome to first-period AP United States History! My name is Ms. Quinn, and I am your child's AP US history teacher. The first thing you should know is that I am qualified to teach this class and to teach it at a high level. This is my ninth year teaching at Pinnacle, and I've taught this class each and every year. I'm also an official reader for the AP exam, which means that I score some of the essay questions from students across the country. As you might imagine, this means that I have a good sense of what will be asked on the exam and what a strong answer should look like, and my students tend to pass the exam. I've also been at Pinnacle long enough to know that many of you are probably stressed out about your child's performance. In fact, you're probably more stressed out than they are! I want you all to just remember to breathe and relax. Everything will be fine. I don't have any student in here who is throwing up a flag saying they shouldn't be in AP.

Ms. Quinn displayed a few sample AP exam questions on the overhead projector and asked parents to answer them. Many parents took copious notes during the presentation, mirroring the behavior of their children in class.

After fifteen minutes, Deborah's voice came over the intercom system and told parents to move on to their child's second-period class. I remained in my seat as the first group of parents left and the second group began to trickle in for an introduction to Ms. Quinn's AP psychology class. Soon there were nineteen parents present, twelve Asian and seven White. As during the previous period, Ms. Quinn introduced herself, stated her credentials, introduced the course, and presented some sample questions from the AP exam for parents to attempt.

Unlike the first group of parents, who were quietly attentive, the second group asked many questions. One parent asked, "Will we be able to get an indication of how our child is doing during the semester?" Ms. Quinn nodded and mentioned a "parent portal" on the district's online education management system, which gave parents access to grades as soon as they were posted. Another parent asked Ms. Quinn if there were any "supplemental materials for the class" that she would recommend. Ms. Quinn replied that the course materials should be "more than adequate," but that there was a test prep book by Princeton Review that could serve as a good source for additional AP test preparation. A third parent asked when the first test would be. Ms. Quinn replied, with a smile, that the first test had already been given last week. The same parent then asked which colleges were good for students interested in a career in psychology, and Ms. Quinn told her to "do a Google search." The same parent then asked a third question, "Do kids get credit for participation in this class?" "No," replied Ms. Quinn. "This is like a college class. I trust them to take responsibility for their learning."

After the session was over, Ms. Quinn stopped me at the door as I was on my way out. "That mom who asked all those questions needs to just chill and trust the process," she said with a grin. "My experience with these parents is that they are very intense, so as teachers we have to calm them down and reassure them that we know what we're doing."

I said goodbye to Ms. Quinn and headed to Ms. Kitayama's classroom for fourth period. Ms. Kitayama, a Japanese American English teacher, taught freshman and honors classes. The period began with a pre-recorded video message from school leadership. The principal, Mr. Bradley, a Valley View native who was White and in his early fifties, noted that Pinnacle was "consistently ranked among the top 100 schools in the nation," and he thanked all the parents for supporting the school. He highlighted some of the new physical features of the school, such as the solar panels in the parking lots and atop the administration building, and he encouraged parents to help teachers and administrators enforce the dress code. His remarks lasted roughly three minutes.

Ms. Kitayama's presentation to parents came next. Like Ms. Quinn, Ms. Kitayama began by introducing herself and enumerating her credentials, which included a BA from Stanford and a JD from UCLA. She practiced law for six years in Los Angeles as a public defender and considered herself to be an effective attorney, but she had a change of heart along the way and decided to become a high school teacher. Only after this story of her educational and professional journey did she discuss the details of her freshman English class. At the end of the session she told me, "Parents love to hear that I went to Stanford and UCLA and practiced law because they all want or expect their kids to do something similar. That's why I spend a little extra time telling them about my life before I got to Pinnacle. These parents are high strung, and it's reassuring to them to know that I'm a little overqualified."

I left back-to-school night after fourth period, while the event was still in progress. As I walked toward the main parking lot, I saw parents still hustling about, some with campus maps in hand, searching for the right building and classroom. Groups of cheerleaders were still scattered about the campus, helping folks find their way.

When I reached the parking lot it was still full. As I zigzagged between the rows of parked cars, I noticed that two pieces of paper, one yellow and one green, had been wedged into the front windowsill of each car, including my own. These leaflets were advertisements from tutoring agencies. One promised to provide "math and science tutoring at its best from tutors who have Bachelor's, Master's, or PhDs from prestigious universities, and rank in the 95th percentile or higher in math/science aptitude, as measured by their SAT scores." The other offered "in-home tutoring services from elite, screened, and experienced tutors in math, sciences, English, foreign languages, study skills, and SAT prep." These and other tutoring services in Valley View were aware of the institutional success frame at Pinnacle, and they intended to capitalize on it. They knew that

Pinnacle was full of students who would measure success according to which elite colleges they were admitted to, and that most Pinnacle parents had the means to spend thousands of dollars on tutoring to help make it happen.[5] I slipped the flyers into my notebook and headed home.

"TO BE SUCCESSFUL, YOU HAVE TO BE A DOCTOR OR A SCIENTIST"

In 1965, US immigration law changed to favor two broad groups of potential newcomers: those seeking to reunite with family members, and those with higher levels of education. Thus, since 1965, emigration to the United States has largely been characterized by what sociologist Cynthia Feliciano refers to as "positive selectivity"—the fact that most ethnic and national-origin groups who have come to the US in recent decades have had, on average, significantly higher levels of education than those who have stayed behind.[6] Some of these immigrant groups have been characterized by "hyper-selectivity," meaning that they possess higher levels of education than those who remain in their country of origin *and* higher levels of education than the general population in the United States.[7] Chinese and South Korean immigrants are cases in point; over 50% of adult Chinese and South Korean immigrants hold at least a bachelor's degree, compared to 4% of adults in China, 34% of adults in South Korea, and 32% of adults in the United States.[8] For hyper-selected immigrants, their starting point in the quest for upward mobility in the US is relatively privileged, and this privileged position affects how they frame success in school and the labor market.[9] For such immigrants, their "success frame" often includes earning straight A's and a high SAT score in high school, getting into and graduating from an elite college, completing a graduate degree in science, medicine, law, or business, and landing a high-paying, high-status job as a scientist, engineer, medical doctor, attorney, or business executive.[10]

Immigrant hyper-selectivity and the resultant cultural success frames are pertinent to understanding the institutional success frame at Pinnacle High School. Pinnacle's institutional success frame was rooted in the high expectations that Pinnacle parents had of their children. Nearly 50% of Pinnacle students identified as Korean American or Chinese American. The majority of those students were born in the United States as the daughters and sons of immigrants, or they arrived in the US with their parents as young children. For these second- and 1.5-generation youths, their family's immigration story, and the lofty success frame espoused by their parents, were omnipresent sources of motivation and stress that shaped their academic expectations and career goals.

One day in late May, after the annual week of AP exams had passed, I met Ryan, a 17-year-old Chinese American junior, for coffee at the Starbucks near campus. Ryan was born in Maryland, where his immigrant parents met as medical school students. Ryan spent his elementary school years in Shanghai before moving to Valley View at the start of his sixth-grade year. Ryan's parents chose Valley View because of its highly rated schools, and they specifically bought a house within walking distance of Pinnacle because they wanted him to go there for high school.

Ryan was enrolled in a challenging set of classes at Pinnacle: honors pre-calculus, AP US history, AP Chinese, AP biology, and AP chemistry. Though I found it to be common for Pinnacle students to be enrolled in several honors or AP classes at once, Ryan's schedule was notable because he was taking AP biology and AP chemistry concurrently. These were considered two of the most difficult classes offered at Pinnacle, and students who took them both typically only took one at a time. Taking both in the same year was considered "hardcore," even among the most academically ambitious and accomplished students.

Ryan and I were soon joined by his friend Eugene, who was also a junior at Pinnacle. Eugene's parents, who were from South Korea, met in Canada while they were doctoral students in chemistry at the

University of Toronto. Eugene was born in Toronto and lived there until he was ten, when his parents accepted job offers from a California State University and moved the family to Valley View. Like Ryan, Eugene was enrolled in the "hardcore" combination of AP biology and AP chemistry.

During our conversation, Ryan and Eugene spoke at length about the origins of the institutional success frame at Pinnacle and how it was principally driven by the cultural success frame that their immigrant parents championed:

SEAN: Both of you have said that your parents wanted to move to Valley View, and to this neighborhood in particular, so that you would attend Pinnacle for high school. When you were in middle school, did Pinnacle have a certain reputation that you were aware of?

RYAN: It had a reputation as being an amazing school for the academics.

EUGENE: Amazing, but also formidable. Definitely hardcore.

RYAN: Yeah, hardcore and intimidating. I can remember, on the last day of middle school, kids were talking about Pinnacle and how much homework there would be, and how many tests we would take, and how everyone was super smart and studied really hard because the teachers were so demanding.

SEAN: So what's it really been like now that you're about to be seniors?

EUGENE: It's definitely a great school for academics, and there are a lot of really good teachers, but it's not really the teachers that make the school what it is. It's mainly the stress level. The stress level is through the roof!

RYAN: Yeah, it's self-inflicted stress by students. It's about your own expectations and not really your teachers forcing you to study or achieve certain things.

SEAN: Where do those expectations come from?

RYAN: Mainly this area is concentrated with Asian Americans, and so I think it's all about culture. We all grew up thinking that we have to get all A's, and if we don't then we disgrace our families.

EUGENE: Yeah, so true! A is for average, and B is for bottom of the class. That's the mentality; that's where the stress comes from and that's why Pinnacle has this reputation and this environment.

SEAN: Have you explicitly been told by your parents that you need to get straight A's?

EUGENE: Oh yeah, definitely. It's stressful. They bring up examples from their own personal life. It's like, "I had to walk fifty miles in the snow every day, and I was still top of my class!"

RYAN: Yeah, and they'll say, "You're lucky! You're lucky to be here! You're lucky to live in this privileged area. I didn't have these opportunities and I got an A, so you *have* to."

EUGENE: Very often, my dad actually says, "If you don't end up better than me, to me you're a failure." And I'm like, "Dad, you have a PhD in chemistry—that's pretty amazing." And he's like, "No, you have to be better than me."

SEAN: Do you know what he means when he says, "better than me"?

EUGENE: Yeah, he means monetary income and respectability of the job.

RYAN: Which pretty much means doctor, lawyer, engineer.

EUGENE: Exactly! Doctor, lawyer, or engineer.

SEAN: How do you feel about that, given what your interests are?

EUGENE: Chemistry and science have been basically force fed into my mouth, but I don't know if I really like science. I've been told that I like it by other people!

SEAN: And both of your parents are chemists.

EUGENE: Yeah, and they want me to follow the legacy, but I want to keep my options open.

SEAN: How do those conversations go?

EUGENE: It's often in a joking tongue, but there's definitely an underlying truth and seriousness behind it.

RYAN: It's just normal parent talk at Pinnacle.

EUGENE: Yeah, it's kind of insane because it's so routine.

SEAN: Ryan, what's your relationship like with your parents in terms of your schoolwork and beyond?

RYAN: Both my parents are medical doctors, and my mom is also a really heavy chemistry person. Growing up, I've always been taught that to be a successful adult you have to be a doctor or something similar; you have to wear a white coat; you have to be this sort of person. So I really don't see a future of me not wearing a white coat at all. And I don't know if it was forced on me, or if I think I'm fitted for it, but I think I'll be a doctor.

SEAN: And Eugene, you're not so sure?

EUGENE: I'm not sure at all. I'm even getting different inputs from my parents. Sometimes they're saying, "Oh, you could be a chemistry person, Eugene." And then twenty minutes later they're like, "Oh, you could do an MD/PhD in biochemistry and cell biology." They actually forced me to take an internship in a stem cell laboratory last year that I really did not want to do.

RYAN: In Valley View and at this school, parents do a lot of work for the students. Parents find the opportunities and they expect you to go do it and be thankful for it. And if you don't like it, they're like, "You're an ungrateful child."

Ryan and Eugene also shed light on the ways in which parents contributed to a prevalence of academic competition among students at Pinnacle. Parents pushed students to excel by comparing them to their other high-achieving classmates:

SEAN: Is there a lot of competition here between students?

EUGENE: Yeah, a ridiculous amount.

SEAN: How does it play out?

EUGENE: A lot of it comes from parents. Like, I remember I got a pretty high score on my honors chemistry final last year. I think I got a 95 or a 96 or something, and I was like, "Dad, I got a 96 on my chem final!" I was pretty stoked, but my dad said that he already knew about a girl who had gotten a perfect score, so he told me to work harder and do better next time.

SEAN: Is it common for you to hear from your parents about other students here and how well those students are doing?

RYAN: Definitely. Like, there's this kid in our AP chemistry class, and his mom and my mom are friends, and I always have to hear about how high his grades are and how my grades should be just as high.

EUGENE: In this community, we all know each other's families and parents, and then they all talk, and then they're like, "My kid is in this and this and my kid got a perfect score." And with my parents it's all about, "Eugene, why did your friend get a higher score than you? Work harder!" And I'm like, "Oh, sorry dad." So it's this competition between parents that extends down to us and spreads throughout the school.

Ryan's and Eugene's experiences were widely shared among students in Pinnacle's honors and AP tracks. A few weeks later I spoke with Esther, one of their classmates. Esther's parents were born in Seoul and met there as college students. After college they moved to North Carolina, where Esther's father completed a PhD in physics at Duke University. Esther was born in North Carolina but moved to Valley View with her parents as an infant after her father accepted a position as a physics professor.

Now a junior at Pinnacle, Esther was enrolled in a full slate of AP courses: AP calculus, AP chemistry, AP physics, AP French, and AP psychology. She described the academic culture at Pinnacle as "highly competitive, and with a lot of pressure to succeed." She identified Pinnacle parents, including her own, as the primary source of that competitive pressure:

SEAN: Do you feel pressure to get straight A's?

ESTHER: Yeah, I do. But it's not a bad pressure necessarily. It's just pressure to work hard. But yeah, I definitely want to get straight A's.

SEAN: Do you feel pressure from other people to get straight A's other than your parents? Do you feel pressure from anyone here at Pinnacle?

ESTHER: Yeah, it's like a competition here with other people, for sure. Like, whenever we finish a test in class, we always tell each other our scores and compare to see who got what. If I see that someone got a higher score, then it makes me want to do better. But I also hear from my parents about other students who got straight A's because my parents know a lot of other parents from here. My parents will say, "Oh, so-and-so got straight A's, so make sure you try harder." They aren't trying to be condescending in any way. It's to motivate me, but it can be annoying sometimes.

SEAN: What annoys you about it?

ESTHER: They'll call me lazy and say that I don't work hard compared to my friends.

Whereas the conversations about academic success that Ryan and Eugene had with their parents typically focused on the long-term goals of graduate school and a career as a doctor, scientist, lawyer, or engineer, Esther felt more of an explicit parental push toward gaining admission to an elite college or university. In Esther's family, and at Pinnacle High School in general, the bar for what counted as a "good" college was extremely high:

ESTHER: The worst pressure is when my parents talk about colleges and what colleges people got into. This year several seniors got into Harvard, and I heard about it first from my parents. I guess it kind of depresses me because I'm trying to work my hardest, but I probably still won't get into Harvard. Obviously my parents want me to go to a good college, like an Ivy League college.

SEAN: So that's a different pressure than the push to get straight A's?

ESTHER: Yeah, because you can get straight A's and still not get into a good college. Recently my dad told me that he would be okay with whatever college I end up at, but my parents only ever mention the tiptop schools. Those are the schools that are famous in Korea. And also I think they know I would be sad if I went to a crappy school.

SEAN: What counts as a "crappy" school?

ESTHER: I don't wanna to be offensive or anything, but I guess anything below, like, UCLA or UC Berkeley.

Such incredibly high aspirations and expectations were normalized at Pinnacle. The ways in which so many families framed academic success were rooted in their immigrant origins and pre-migration levels of education and socioeconomic status (i.e., their hyper-selectivity). These familial frames influenced and shaped the institutional success frame. Ultimately, Pinnacle's academic culture, identity, and reputation were inextricably linked to the frames of success and achievement that students like Ryan, Eugene, Esther, and their parents lived by and broadcast throughout the school community.

"DON'T BE ALL ASIAN ABOUT IT"

The institutional success frame at Pinnacle was heavily racialized. Exceptional academic achievement was construed as the province of Asian American students, who were openly hailed as the school's academic pacesetters. According to Assistant Principal Holt, the "Korean and Chinese kids" were to thank for Pinnacle's studious classroom culture and ranking as one of the top public high schools in California:

SEAN: What kind of impact do the Korean and Chinese students have on the school?

MR. HOLT: They are what keeps our school rank high. They improve our test scores. If you are a teacher that wants order, and you don't want to have to deal with any problems, and you want the kids that come in and know their stuff—you want the Korean and Chinese kids. They will study probably hours and hours without ever lifting a finger or saying anything.

Asian Americans are often stereotyped as a "model minority" group, whose preternatural intellect and cultural values are responsible for their superior academic achievement relative to other racial groups.[11] The model minority myth, though empirically proven to be deeply problematic and flawed,[12] was ubiquitous at Pinnacle. Some Pinnacle teachers held higher expectations of Asian students relative to their non-Asian peers, which reinforced the stereotype.[13] For instance, in a conversation with me about how the first week of school had gone, Ms. Kitayama candidly admitted: "I don't necessarily look at my classroom and treat a kid differently because they are Asian, but I know that if I have an Asian student in my classroom, I can count on that student. That student will probably work hard and be engaged. I can rely on that kid, and the parents, more so than I can for other [racial] groups."

Pinnacle teachers also leveraged this racialization of achievement as a pedagogical tool. For example, on the first day of school during my second full year of fieldwork, Ms. Quinn distributed a few handouts to her AP psychology class that provided details about the curriculum and news clippings for supplemental reading. Thirteen of the twenty-two students were Asian, seven were White, and two were Latinx. The students, who had been chatting quietly moments before, sorted through the papers and read them silently. Ms. Quinn noticed their change in demeanor, and a grin slowly spread across her face. "Don't be alarmed by all of the handouts," she stated before adding, "It's not like you need to read every word, okay? *Relax*; don't be all Asian about it." Some students smiled, while others chuckled softly at these racialized instructions. The comment was made in jest, but the underlying meaning and intent were no joke. At Pinnacle, there was, it seemed, a nearly universal understanding of what it meant to "be all Asian" about one's study habits: studying for hours on end—and often late into the night—in order to achieve at least a 4.0 GPA, a high SAT score, and admission to an elite college. In other words, to be "Asian" at Pinnacle was to believe in, and abide by, the institutional success frame at all times.

THE RACIALIZATION OF ACADEMIC VALUES

During the two years that I spent at Pinnacle, I found that students in honors and AP classes often drew a racialized distinction between the cultural values of students who took honors and AP classes, and those who did not. For instance, Ryan and Eugene felt that one's selection of classes was indicative of how much one cared about education in a general sense. They were clear about their views on the relationship between race, culture, and academic engagement on campus:

RYAN: The students who don't take honors or AP classes, they always have time to mess around, whereas we don't. It's about how much you care about school, and they just don't care. And it's also by ethnicity and culture. In AP and honors, it's mostly the Asians—mostly all Asians.

EUGENE: And then like two White people! [Laughs]

RYAN: Yeah, it'll be all Asians and then one or two White people.

SEAN: Why is it funny that there are so few White students in the honors and AP classes?

EUGENE: Because it's just funny to think that you're living in America, which is basically White-oriented everything, but then the highest achievers are not all White.

RYAN: The highest achievers are all immigrants.

EUGENE: Exactly—they're all immigrants. And I'm not saying that in a racial standpoint, but I find it kind of ironic because it's not what's expected. You would expect a higher number of Whites to be among the highest achievers. And then, on top of that, you see that even though America has this huge immigration from around the world and all these different types of cultures, you only see these two or three predominant immigrant groups in these AP classes, and it just makes you wonder.

SEAN: What does it make you wonder about?

EUGENE: It makes you wonder why. Why is this? Is this a mentality-driven thing? Is this an ethnically driven thing? Is it genetic? What is it?

As Eugene rightfully remarked, racial stratification in America still sees Whites in positions of ultimate power and authority in nearly all aspects of society. Thus, he found it ironic that Whites were substantially underrepresented among students who were enrolled in the most advanced classes. In light of this disparity, Ryan deduced that Asian students at Pinnacle cared more about education than their non-Asian peers, and Eugene questioned whether cultural or even genetic differences explained why Asian students at Pinnacle were overrepresented among the highest achievers.

This line of reasoning has received mainstream attention from political and cultural pundits in recent years,[14] but the link between Asian achievement and genetics has been thoroughly disproven.[15] The notion of Whiteness as associated with middling academic engagement and achievement has also received scholarly attention of late. In Silicon Valley, which includes several cities that are demographically similar to Valley View, East- and South-Asian immigrant newcomers have replaced the established White population as the academic bellwether in local schools, such that Whiteness connotes academic mediocrity rather than academic excellence.[16]

In a separate conversation with Esther and her classmate, Jolene, who was also the daughter of highly educated Korean immigrants, Esther expressed views on race, culture, and education that were similar to Ryan's and Eugene's:

SEAN: Most of the AP classes that you are in, and honors classes—have they been predominantly Asian students in those classes?

ESTHER: Yeah, especially in math and science. Some of the humanities and language APs have a little more diversity, but the math and science classes are basically all Asian with maybe a couple White people.

SEAN: There seems to be an overrepresentation of Asian students in the AP classes overall. Is that accurate, and why do you think that is?

ESTHER: Yeah, I'd say so. We care a lot about our education and our parents push us a lot to take hard classes and get A's. I guess in other cultures maybe education isn't as important, but, in Asian culture, education is one of the highest things.

Jolene disagreed somewhat with Esther, and instead stressed the importance of family history and immigrant identity:

SEAN: What do you think, Jolene?

JOLENE: I think it's more of the immigration thing. Like, my parents literally worked their entire lives to get me and my sister here [to America]. Their biggest fear is that we're not going to do something meaningful for what they have done for us. I want to help them when they get older and pay them back for what they have done for me their entire lives. So, I think it's an immigrant mentality to work hard, and then later in life you will get your rewards. And a lot of the kids who take the AP and honors classes here, they come from immigrant families and they have that mentality to honor their parents' sacrifices and stuff like that. And more of the kids who don't take AP classes don't have as much of that mentality.

Whereas Ryan, Eugene, and Esther alluded to something inherently cultural and racial about Korean- and Chinese-American students that led to their academic achievement and overrepresentation in high-level classes, Jolene held a different view. She believed that she and most of her Asian peers at Pinnacle pushed themselves academically because they were intent on furthering the American Dream of which their immigrant parents had worked so hard to secure a piece. Indeed, immigration scholars have found that the children of immigrants often express identities that are fundamentally attached to the transnational journeys and sacrifices of their parents, and this sense of self can be a source of academic motivation for the 1.5- and second-generation.[17]

It is also worth reiterating that sociologists of race and immigration have convincingly shown that positively- and hyper-selected immigration plays a significant role in Asian American academic achievement overall. In America, education is universally regarded—by all racial groups and at all levels of income—as being of critical importance.[18] The academic aspirations, expectations, and achievements that Ryan, Eugene, and Esther attributed to "Asian culture" were made possible by the highly- and hyper-selected nature of immigration in their families.

STARTING HOMEWORK AT 10 P.M. ON SCHOOL NIGHTS

I met several Pinnacle parents who were pleased with the academic rigor of the school and how the curriculum prepared students to be strong college applicants, but many of these same parents were also concerned that the level of competition and stress among students was taking an unhealthy toll on their children. Tina was one of those conflicted Pinnacle parents. Born in Taiwan, Tina came to Los Angeles at the age of seventeen because her parents wanted her to attend an American university. She met her husband in college in Los Angeles, and they got married a few months after graduation. Soon they were expecting a baby girl, and they moved from downtown Los Angeles to Valley View because of its reputation for good schools and its steadily growing Asian population.

Tina's daughter, Jessica, who was a sophomore at an elite, private university, had been a standout student at Pinnacle: she maintained a 4.3 GPA, captained the tennis team, played violin in the school orchestra and piano at a Los Angeles conservatory, and was involved with various community service and church activities. According to Tina, her daughter's schedule was so full that, on most weeknights, she did not *start* her homework until 10 p.m. or later:

> SEAN: Did your daughter stay up late to study when she was at Pinnacle?
>
> TINA: Yes! In high school she did not study until after 10 [at night].
>
> SEAN: Did she like to stay up late?
>
> TINA: Oh, no! Not at all, actually. She had no choice, because if she had orchestra or tennis after school then she didn't finish that until probably 6 [p.m.]. And then she needs to come

home and have dinner. And I still remember that during
those years after dinner she will have her own devotion time
at home for probably thirty minutes when she reads her bible.
And then she has to practice piano because she's in the conservatory. So, practice piano, at that level, probably two hours
a day. And then she's playing violin, so sometimes she needs
to practice violin. And she has private lessons. She has piano
private lesson, violin private lesson, and tennis private lesson.
That's a whole lot of things! That takes a lot of time. And so
she usually can't start her homework until 10 at night, and
I think that's very unhealthy.

Thus, though Tina was proud of her daughter's accomplishments,
she was constantly worried about her mental and physical health:

TINA: Her group of friends were all taking those AP classes, too. It's
the competition. I think the competition at Pinnacle is so
stressful, and I can see that she's constantly sleep deprived in
high school. It's unhealthy! I don't like it. And I always had
to tell her, "You need to know how to relax." But it's very
hard. I think a lot of the kids at Pinnacle find it hard to rest
because they have to have things to keep going and going
and be recognized, and that's a problem. Jessica was always
exhausted.

Tina checked in with Jessica often and, at one point, suggested that
she limit her activities or take fewer advanced classes in order to
reduce her stress and fatigue. Jessica resisted, arguing that she did
not want to give up anything as long as she was excelling at everything. Jessica was ultimately accepted at Cal Tech, but Tina worried
that this achievement had come at a cost to her daughter's mental
and physical well-being. This cost was something that I heard about
from many Pinnacle students as well, some of whom were often
so tired from staying up well past midnight to study or finish their
assignments that they had trouble staying awake in class the next day.
    School officials received complaints from several parents, so they
administered a schoolwide survey to assess students' discontents.

Results of this survey revealed that students were most concerned about "stress over grades and college admissions" and "fatigue from lack of sleep." These symptoms were normal for students within Pinnacle's "cutthroat" institutional culture.

"I WISH I WAS MORE INTELLIGENT"

Of course, not all Asian students at Pinnacle were enrolled in the most challenging courses and making top grades. Asian students who did not meet this stereotypical standard often felt like ethnoracial outliers who had come up short. Yuki, a senior, was one such student. His parents emigrated to Valley View from Tokyo the year before he was born, and they owned a popular Japanese restaurant in town. Yuki took several honors level classes as a freshman, but his overall academic struggles that year caused him to reevaluate his choices and adjust his course schedule thereafter:

SEAN: Which honors classes were you taking freshman year, and what was your experience like in those classes?

YUKI: Freshman year I was taking honors geometry, honors world history, and honors English. I think I got an A in geometry. And then in history and English I did okay first semester, I think B's. But then, second semester, I went down to low C's, and then after that I quit honors here.

SEAN: What was it like to struggle in those honors classes?

YUKI: I felt like I was kind of being left back, because everyone was succeeding and everyone was knowing what they were doing. I studied pretty hard, but I felt like sometimes studying wasn't really helping me. It just became a negative cycle; that's what I felt.

SEAN: Were you able to get help or tutoring or anything like that? Did teachers try to help out, or did you just kind of slip down?

YUKI: No, I would say I just slipped down. I wasn't really searching for help that much, but honestly this school is really focused on

> the kids who are at the top of the class and on kind of boosting their opportunities. Maybe if I had been totally failing I would have gotten more help, but I was sort of in the middle, so I just felt that, you know, this is what I have to deal with.

Yuki's grades slid without any intervention from teachers or other faculty, and he felt that the school's inclination to focus on the highest-achieving students enabled and accelerated his drop in performance. As a result, while many of his Asian friends remained on the honors and AP track, Yuki took a total of three honors and AP classes during his sophomore, junior, and senior years combined.

As a junior, Yuki was determined to achieve a high score on the SAT exam since he had taken far fewer honors and AP classes than his closest friends and many of his classmates; he and his parents believed that a strong result on the SAT would offset his modest GPA and lack of AP classes when applying to colleges. Yuki's parents encouraged him to take the SAT again and again until he was satisfied with his score, and he took the test four times. He envied his classmates and friends who took the exam once, scored higher than he did, and bragged that the test was easy:

YUKI: I was able to achieve a 2030 [out of 2400] on the SAT, but I took it four times before I finally got over 2000. Some of my friends took it once and got a 2200 or better. And they were like, "Oh, yeah, it's pretty easy." I thought it was hard!

During senior year, when Yuki heard back from the colleges to which he had applied, his feelings of inadequacy were magnified when several of his Asian friends and classmates gained admission to one or more elite universities. Yuki was not admitted to any, and instead "settled" for a small Jesuit college in Northern California. His academic shortcomings relative to his friends and classmates made him question his intelligence:

SEAN: What kind of colleges were your friends talking about applying to or going to?

YUKI: All the good schools, like Stanford, Harvard, UCLA, UC Berkeley, all the Ivies. A lot of the top-ranked schools.

SEAN: What was that like when everybody's talking about the top-ranked schools in the country like that?

YUKI: I felt like I was kind of left alone and being left behind. But at the same time, I feel like they deserved it, because I know that they studied hard and they worked for it. So I felt good for them, but it was also disappointing that I couldn't be one.

SEAN: Did you kind of wish that you were having that success in those moments? Did you kind of wish that those were your options, too?

YUKI: Yeah, I wish I was more intelligent. I wish I could be smart and that I had the ability to do that, but those kids deserve it. I try to take things positively because not everyone can be like that. I actually think I'd be one of the smart kids at a lot of high schools, but at Pinnacle I'm probably below average.

Pinnacle's institutional success frame was sustained by the students who earned the highest grades and test scores. The highest achievers set the definition of what it meant to be "intelligent" and "smart," and which colleges were considered "good." To be intelligent and smart was to take AP classes and rarely, if ever, earn less than an A. The colleges considered to be good were the top-ranked colleges in the country. Students like Yuki, who fell short of those lofty criteria, could feel like failures even if they were aware that their academic performances would be celebrated at the vast majority of high schools across the state and across the country.

"AROUND HERE, YOU'RE EITHER REALLY SMART, OR YOU'RE JUST NOT"

Ryan, Eugene, Esther, and Jolene were all active participants in Pinnacle's competitive institutional culture of academic excellence. And, though Yuki was not able to reach the soaring achievement levels of his friends and dozens his classmates, it certainly was not for lack of desire or effort. But for many others who had aspirations that did not necessitate such an astronomical conception of achievement, or who were simply struggling to pass their classes, the institutional success frame was a nuisance at best, and, at worst, a source of embarrassment and marginalization. Victoria, a 16-year-old Black junior with a quick wit and an activist's spirit, was one of those students.

Victoria was born in Houston and moved to Los Angeles as a toddler with her mother, older sister, and younger brother while her parents were going through a contentious divorce. They eventually settled in Valley View when Victoria was in middle school, in part because her mother was impressed with the public schools in the area. Her family home was within a short walking distance of Pinnacle, which made it the obvious high school choice for her and her siblings. When Victoria was in eighth grade, her sister, who was three grades ahead, warned her that Pinnacle would be a challenge:

VICTORIA: Pinnacle was really hard for my sister. She told me that the classes moved really fast, so I should make sure to do my homework on time and study hard for everything. She said that it's gonna get hard not matter what, so you have to do your work consistently. She basically warned me to stay on my toes at all times and have a routine, because if you don't, you're screwed.

It seemed as though everyone at Pinnacle knew Victoria. She was a frequent participant in each of her classes, especially when issues of racism and racial inequality were pertinent. Victoria was regularly the only Black student in class, a dynamic that inspired her to speak up so that a diversity of opinions and experiences were presented and considered. But speaking up was often hard:

SEAN: Is it hard to be one of very few Black students at this school?

VICTORIA: Yeah, it is, because the other kids and the teachers can't relate and they don't understand the struggles that we go through as Black people. Like, in my history class we always debate

56

about social issues that happen in America, and I'm the only
Black student in the class. The other students never agree
with me because they can't relate and they don't understand
why I feel the way I feel. They don't know anything about the
world outside of Valley View.

Victoria's willingness to speak up and speak out garnered her the
respect of her peers and friendships from Pinnacle students of all
grade levels, achievement levels, and identities.

Victoria and her friends criticized the institutional success frame
at Pinnacle for its myopic approach to achievement. For example,
one of her friends, Candace, who was Black and a sophomore, felt
that the sheer amount of coursework at all levels of the curriculum
sometimes contradicted the school's goal of preparing as many students as possible for acceptance at elite colleges:

CANDACE: This school is so hard. It's so hard for no reason. Like, they
make it super hard so you can get into these big colleges, but
you can't get into those schools because your grades are so
low because they make it so hard! I'm a pretty good student,
but it's survival of the fittest around here. They need to do
more to support *all* of us, especially the Black and Latino
students because there are so few of us.

Victoria found the institutional success frame to be divisive. She
felt that the prevailing notions of success and achievement in the
school community, both on campus and on social media, fostered a
hierarchical culture in which students in the honors/AP track were
celebrated, while those who were not were denigrated. Eugene and
Ryan alluded to this dynamic during my discussion with them, but
Victoria added more detail and context:

SEAN: Now that you've been here for almost three full years, what's it
been like for you?

VICTORIA: At this school, it's like, if you're not in AP classes, then who are
you? You're not smart enough. The students in AP classes
kind of look down on the people who aren't in AP.

SEAN: How so?

VICTORIA: The AP kids look down on the rest of us on social media. Not all the AP kids because I'm friends with some of them, but definitely a lot of them. They'll post about how many exams they have, and how hard their classes are, and what they're thinking about majoring in at Harvard or whatever. Actually just the other day I had to console my friend because she was sad that she wasn't in any AP classes. She was saying that she wasn't smart, which is crazy because she gets A's and B's.

SEAN: Can you give an example of things that AP students post on social media?

VICTORIA: Yeah. One day on Facebook I was like, "Oh, dude, I'm not ready for this final exam!" And this other kid was like, "But you're not in AP. At least you don't have AP testing like me." And I was like, "But I still have a test. You chose to take AP. You wanted to take the harder class." I was still struggling in my level, but the kids in AP will go on and on about how easy our classes are and how we don't know how it feels to be in AP, but I don't want to know how it feels! They think that everyone is supposed to take AP classes in high school, so if you're not taking APs, then you must not care about school, which isn't true at all. I do care, but I also want to enjoy my time in high school and graduate in one piece.

SEAN: Have you ever felt pressure to take APs?

VICTORIA: This year, everyone was saying "I'm gonna take this AP! I'm going to college for that and this!" I actually had a girl ask me how I expected to go to college if I wasn't taking a certain AP class. And at first I was like, "I should take one!" But I thought about it more and I just know that it's not for me. My friend was in AP psychology for two days, and she was like, "I was in it, and it's not for me. I might have gotten the credit for it, but it was just moving too fast and I was not comfortable in it." So I just don't need that kind of pressure. I'm definitely going to college regardless.

SEAN: Would it be accurate to say that here at Pinnacle it's sort of cool to be in APs and you get status and credibility from that?

VICTORIA: Oh yeah, for sure; it's bragging rights. Kids will be like, "I'm taking a bunch of AP classes. I'm an athlete. I'm involved in this and this. I'm gonna go to this fancy college." They put themselves on a pedestal and they frown upon people who want to go to community college or even a Cal State [California State University]. If you say, "I want to go to V.V.C.C. [Valley View Community College]," AP kids will be like, "You're not doing anything with your life."

Throughout her time at Pinnacle, Victoria and her friends often felt a need to stand up for themselves when students in honors and AP classes attempted to discredit them for avoiding those classes. The institutional success frame fostered this state of affairs by normalizing exceptional achievement and, in turn, alienating those who did not reach that level.

COLLEGE SWEATSHIRT DAY

Pinnacle's institutional obsession with elite college admissions culminated in an annual springtime event. Each year, in late April, Pinnacle held a "College Sweatshirt Day" on which graduating seniors came to school wearing a new sweatshirt from their college of choice. Sweatshirt Day was a celebration of achievement, a way for the school community to bask in the academic success of the student body. Sure enough, sweatshirts representing prestigious colleges and universities were prevalent on this day every year.

As I walked onto campus the morning of Sweatshirt Day, I saw several clusters of students chatting and posing for pictures. Two Asian boys—one set to attend UCLA and the other USC—faced each other, assumed fighting stances, and scowled playfully as onlooked snapped pictures on their iPhones. UCLA and USC are storied rivals in collegiate athletics, and these students were proudly pledging allegiance to their future schools. During a passing period later in the day, I overheard two White students, Megan and Cindy, congratulating each other on their choice of college. "Megan! Hey! Oh my god! You got in at Berkeley?! Amazing!" Cindy's reply was equally effusive—"And you're going to Northwestern?! Nice!" The girls then leaned in together to take a selfie.

The ultimate measure of a student's performance, and of the school's standing as an elite institution, was revealed in these college decisions. Posting scenes like these on such social media platforms as Facebook, Instagram, Snapchat, and Twitter reinforced Pinnacle's institutional success frame and reputation for academic excellence. The message broadcast on social media was clear: students who go to Pinnacle end up at top colleges.

Though college sweatshirt day was meant to be a celebratory recognition of students' accomplishments and a fun way for students to announce their decisions to their classmates and teachers, it also highlighted, amplified, and exemplified the division on campus between higher- and lower-achieving students. Victoria was keenly aware of the ways in which college sweatshirt day was problematic for dozens of senior class members every year, as well as students in lower grades for whom the college admission process loomed on the horizon:

SEAN: When it comes time when colleges are accepting people, do kids often wear the t-shirts and sweatshirts? Is there a lot of participation in that?

VICTORIA: Yeah, the senior sweatshirt admissions day is where everyone wears their college sweatshirt, and you see the seniors walking past with their sweatshirts on. But I feel bad for the kids who aren't wearing anything, because if you're not wearing a sweatshirt, other kids will think it's because you don't want people to know. I mean, if everyone's wearing a sweatshirt in class and there's three kids who aren't, people are gonna be like, "Oh, hey, what college are you going to." They're gonna ask you a question about it, and its gonna get weird. So either you wear your mom's sweatshirt, or—I don't know.

SEAN: Do you think the school should stop have a day for wearing the sweatshirts?

VICTORIA: Yeah, I do actually, because it's the making a day out of it that's the problem. If you want to wear a college shirt one day, or every day, that's cool, go for it. But don't have a day where everyone is supposed to wear one because making it a special day just singles out the kids who aren't wearing anything or who wear something from a college that nobody's heard of.

The tradition was indeed alienating for students who were not set to enroll at a top-ranked college. For example, Anthony, a White, 18-year-old senior who planned to attend Los Angeles City College, participated in sweatshirt day, but felt the need to rationalize his plans to other students when the topic came up:

ANTHONY: Both my parents and my brother went to community college, so that's always been what I wanted to do. But when I'm talking to people here that are going to somewhere like UCLA or NYU, when they see that I'm going to community college, I have to explain why or else it's awkward. I can't just be like, "Yeah, I'm gonna go to community college." I have to explain the practical reasons, and then they get it and it's not as awkward.

Like her friend Anthony, Diana, a senior and the daughter of Mexican immigrants, planned to enroll in community college after graduation. Unlike Anthony, however, Diana chose not to participate in sweatshirt day. I spoke with her the day after the event, at a concrete picnic table outside the math department:

SEAN: What did you think of college sweatshirt day? Did you wear one?

DIANA: Nope! I didn't wear one. I'm going to community college next year, and it's honestly kind of embarrassing sometimes if you're not going to a four-year school. I'm not going to wear something from [Valley View Community College] when there's people walking around with, like, Stanford stuff on.

SEAN: How do you feel about going to community college when you have so many classmates heading off to these fancy schools?

DIANA: I'm honestly okay with it. I have a couple friends going with me, which is cool, and I'll be saving a lot of money. And I like the idea of staying close to home. I know my family is proud of me, so I'm good.

Though Diana did not mention it when we spoke, I later learned from one of her teachers that she would be the first in her family to attend college. But this impressive accomplishment was overshadowed by her friends and classmates who had parents with graduate degrees and were accepting offers from some of the most renowned colleges and universities in the nation.[19] Diana's choice to forego participation in the college sweatshirt ritual was her way of coping with the dissonance between her plans and the institutional success frame.

．　．　．　．　．

An institutional success frame is a consensus interpretation, held by members of an institution, of what constitutes successful individual and group performance at that institution, and what actions are necessary to achieve that success. At Pinnacle High School, success was defined as earning straight A's in multiple honors and advanced placement classes, achieving nationally competitive test scores, and gaining admission to at least one prestigious college or university. That level of achievement was routine and expected, and the school was perennially ranked among the best in California. But Pinnacle's institutional culture was unforgiving and divisive, and its illustrious academic profile masked underlying inequities that ran deep.

Pinnacle's institutional success frame divided the school into two types of students: those who were recognized as successful (i.e., high academic achievers), and those who were not. This division was evident in curriculum tracking at Pinnacle, a practice of within-school segregation in which many students began in honors classes and progressed to AP classes, while many others were tracking into lower-level classes that never led to the honors or AP level. But the chasm between AP and non-AP students at Pinnacle went beyond these spatial and curricular differences to include issues of race, culture, and belonging.

The institutional success frame at Pinnacle was heavily racialized. Academic achievement was construed as the province of Asian students, who were stereotyped as a "model minority" group and widely hailed as responsible for the school's sterling reputation. However, Asian students who did not meet this expectation felt like failures and ethnoracial outliers, and the model minority myth implied that other, non-Asian students of color were somehow flawed in ways that hampered their academic performance. At Pinnacle, Asian students and their parents were regarded as institutional assets, while, as we will see in chapter 2, Black and Latinx students were treated as if they were liabilities and potential problems to be dealt with.

At Pinnacle, the classes one chose to take—and the classes one declined to take—were measured against the expectations of the success frame. Those who took honors and AP classes were said to value their education more than those who did not. Those who achieved the highest grades and test scores were said to value their education more than those who did not. The incessant academic competition among students throughout the school year, and traditions like College Sweatshirt Day, contributed to an academic culture that was congenitally inhospitable to students who struggled to get "good" grades, or who simply had postsecondary plans that did not include an elite, four-year college. These students—who were disproportionately Black, Latinx, or from working-class families—were marginalized on campus, sometimes so much so that they were pushed out of Pinnacle to an entirely separate school nearby. Crossroads High School was the district's school for pushouts.

.   .   .   .   .

Recall Jamal, the Black sophomore and standout athlete at Pinnacle whose transfer to Crossroads led me to expand my research.

Jamal had been struggling academically at Pinnacle in part because his vision was poor. He had prescription glasses, but he usually left them at home or in his backpack at school, so he seldom wore them. This also explained his pattern of academic engagement and disengagement in class, particularly in Ms. Miller's classroom, where his assigned seat was at the back of the room. Jamal had not been diagnosed with a learning disability, but he did have an OHI (Other Health Impairment) on file with the district for his poor vision. His teachers and academic counselors at Pinnacle had access to this information, but I never saw Jamal wearing his glasses at school or heard a teacher remind him to wear them in class.

When he first got to Crossroads, Jamal's comportment in class was much the same as it had been at Pinnacle. Sometime during his second week, however, the academic counselor there reviewed his file and noticed his poor vision. The file also contained a specialist's recommendation that he sit at the front of any classroom and be reminded to wear his glasses at school. The counselor, Ms. Carter, who was Black and had a son about Jamal's age, sent an email to all the teachers at Crossroads to let them know. Her intervention worked; Jamal started sitting in the front row of his classes at Crossroads, and he began wearing his glasses regularly. In class, his levels of engagement and energy were consistently higher than they had been at Pinnacle. His grades improved, and he earned credits rapidly.

Jamal excelled in football and basketball, and he was one of the best players on both teams when he was only a sophomore. Just six weeks after his transfer to Crossroads, Jamal had recovered enough credits that he was eligible to play football at Pinnacle, but he was still barred from taking classes there. From an institutional perspective, Jamal helped Pinnacle on the field, but hurt them in the classroom. He was an athletic asset and a star player on two varsity teams, but he was an academic liability who had no place within the school's institutional success frame. Pinnacle High School used the continuation school system to its benefit, pushing out struggling students to Crossroads to help keep its AP examination pass rates and graduation rate high, as well as the highest possible percentage of graduates who matriculated at four-year colleges. The pushout process, and students' experiences at Crossroads, are the subjects of chapter 2.

2 The Symbolic Criminalization of Failure

A graduation ceremony is a special occasion at any school, but graduation at Crossroads High School is particularly momentous. As a "continuation school," Crossroads was a place where high school students from each of the four comprehensive high schools in Valley View were sent when they had fallen behind on course credits such that they were no longer on pace to graduate with their class. In addition to the academic struggles that all Crossroads students had to overcome in order to graduate, the experience of being sent to the school, and one's status as a Crossroads student, were alone significant challenges. Consider these opening remarks by Mr. Reyes, a history teacher at Crossroads, in his commencement address to a graduating class:

> *Failures!* For a good majority of those graduating today, that is the view that was cast upon you at one time or another while on your journey to this very moment. For some of you, you were branded a failure because of the choices you made academically or socially. Others of you had that label thrust upon you as a result of actions that

were out of your control. Regardless, most of you showed up on your first day here at Crossroads with that same look of, "I can't believe I ended up here," on your face. But the point is not that you were branded a failure; the point is that you took that image the world had of you, balled it up, and threw that image into a proverbial wastebasket. Graduates, you are not failures. You are proof that failure does not define a person.

Mr. Reyes's comments were germane to the experiences of the overwhelming majority of Crossroads students whom I observed and came to know during my time spent on campus. He spoke of a prevailing perception in Valley View that Crossroads was a school for failed students and delinquents who needed to be separated— segregated—from the typically studious and upstanding students of Valley View's comprehensive, "regular" high schools. Ironically, Mr. Reyes's central message to students—"failure does not define a person"—implied that "failure" had, in fact, been an appropriate label for them. At Crossroads, failure was an inescapable theme, even during celebratory ceremonies such as graduation.

As soon as I found out about Crossroads due to Jamal's transfer there, I began to question the school's existence and need in the district. I scrawled the following questions in my notebook: How does a high school like Crossroads, with a student population homogenized as "failures," exist in an affluent neighborhood within a school district known for its academic excellence? Why do students end up there, particularly when the school has an undesirable reputation and the decision to transfer is purportedly left up to the student? Who would choose such a school?

Before I visited Crossroads for the first time, I accessed publicly available data showing that Pinnacle and Crossroads diverged strikingly in terms of the racial composition of their student bodies and their percentages of "socioeconomically disadvantaged" students. I saw that Black and Latinx students constituted just 9.3% of all Pinnacle students, but 47.9% of Crossroads students. Socioeconomically disadvantaged students represented roughly 10% Pinnacle's student population, but over 50% of the student population at Crossroads. These statistics suggested that the district's continuation school model was disproportionately affecting Black, Latinx, and lower-income students.

In subsequent weeks as I spent more and more time hanging out at Crossroads, I began to focus on addressing the following questions: How and why does the Valley View school district's continuation school model disproportionately affect Black, Latinx, and lower-income students? How do students and families experience and navigate the transfer process between their comprehensive neighborhood public high school and Crossroads?

· · · · · ·

Research on school segregation in ethnoracially diverse school districts has primarily focused on within-school segregation and inequality. Researchers have highlighted the ways in which "tracking" disproportionately assigns White and Asian students to rigorous honors and advanced placement college preparatory courses while funneling Black and Latinx students into a schedule of less rigorous remedial courses.[1] Students in honors and advanced placement classes benefit from the wealth of social and cultural capital available to them in higher academic tracks due to the presence of more highly motivated classmates and more highly qualified teachers in those classes.[2] Meanwhile, those in lower-level, remedial courses lack access to the same valuable resources and experiences,[3] and they often finish high school ill-prepared for postsecondary coursework.[4] Tracking is infrequently meritocratic, and is instead influenced by parental resources and teacher recommendations. Since tracking often reflects racial inequality, different academic tracks come to be associated with different racial groups in ways that mirror common racial and cultural stereotypes.[5] The transfer of students of students from Pinnacle and other comprehensive high schools in Valley View to Crossroads is a severe form of tracking that happens between schools rather than within them. This between-school tracking is harsher because it detaches students from the academic, extracurricular, and socioemotional resources that are far more abundant at comprehensive high schools such as Pinnacle.

The demographic disparities between Pinnacle and Crossroads were rooted in distinct aspects of the transfer policy and process that placed Black, Latinx, and lower-income students at risk. Transfer to Crossroads was voluntary, but students often faced coordinated pressure from school counselors and administrators to transfer, and those from more privileged backgrounds were better positioned to resist and avoid a move to Crossroads. Students who were recommended for Crossroads and ended up transferring often lacked the social or economic capital to pursue viable alternatives, and they did so with tremendous reluctance and anxiety. Once the transfer was complete, students' experiences at Crossroads were predominantly punitive in nature: they encountered restrictive metal fences and gates, supervision by an armed police officer, limited bathroom privileges, and no off-campus privileges during the school day. Crossroads students were also prohibited from visiting the campus of any comprehensive high school in the district, including the one from which they had been transferred. Moreover, and crucially, the curriculum at Crossroads was so sparse that it disqualified graduates from matriculating at a four-year college. Pushing struggling students to Crossroads stigmatized these students as "failures" and fostered a student climate of academic apathy that was counterproductive to Crossroads's stated purpose as an academic rehabilitation center.

. . . . .

When compared to the four comprehensive, college preparatory high schools in Valley View, Crossroads High School stood in sharp relief as a separate and unequal institution. As a member of the Pinnacle Parent Teacher Association (PTA) put it to me in the first week of my fieldwork, "There are the four regular high schools, and then there's Crossroads. Crossroads is the outlier." Some of the most striking examples of this inequality were evident in the differences between Crossroads and the comprehensive high schools in terms of campus layout and amenities, and the privileges that students had while on campus. Among all the high schools in Valley View, Pinnacle and Crossroads offered the most startling differences between them.

In chapter 1, I described the wealth of facilities and opportunities, both curricular and extracurricular, that Pinnacle High School provided for its students. Crossroads High School offered none of these features and opportunities for its student body, which typically swelled throughout the school year from around 150 in September to between 200 and 250 in June, as small groups of students were transferred in multiple waves throughout the year. The privileges that Pinnacle students experienced, and the air of competitive ease that most of them displayed,[6] presented a stark contrast to the experiences and outlook of most Crossroads students. While Pinnacle students enjoyed the trappings of a flagship high school, Crossroads students' high school experiences were typified by limitations and disadvantages, which were evident in the paucity of extracurricular activities, enrichment programs, and courses available to students. For example, at back-to-school night during the fall of my second year of fieldwork, the school was selling t-shirts that read, "Crossroads Athletics: Undefeated Since 1974." The shirts were intended to be humorous because Crossroads had no sports teams. Crossroads also had no drama program, no music program, no student clubs, and no PTA. The lack of a PTA at Crossroads was emblematic of a lack of parental participation overall. In fact, parental involvement was such an issue at Crossroads that the school instituted a back-to-school night policy that students could earn course credits if a parent or guardian showed up to the event.

Crossroads also lacked material academic resources: there was no library, there were not enough textbooks for students to take them home from school, and the limited curriculum was based on the minimum standard for obtaining a high school diploma in California. This truncated curriculum was especially consequential. Regardless of their academic record at Crossroads, even if they earned straight A's there, graduates who pursued postsecondary education were ineligible to enroll in a four-year college or university, and thus could only turn to trade school, the military, or, more often, community college to continue their education. This was significant given that less than 30% of students seeking degrees at California's community colleges either attain them or transfer to four-year universities within six years, and over 80% of California community college students who do not graduate within six years drop out of college altogether.[7] Crossroads students could return to their home institution once they had recovered enough credits, but return was rare. For example, during the 2014–2015 school year, only 17% of Crossroads students transferred back at the end of the school year, which is when most such transfers occurred.

I stated the following in the introduction and chapter 1, but it is worth reiterating here: Pinnacle and Crossroads differed markedly in the racial composition of their student populations, particularly in terms of students of color. While Asians comprised 39% of Valley View's population, they constituted 52.2% of the student body at Pinnacle and only 7.5% at Crossroads. Black and Latinx students were grossly overrepresented at Crossroads: they comprised 1.9% and 9.2% of Valley View's population, 2.1% and 7.2% of Pinnacle's student body, and 11.4% and 36.5% of the student body at Crossroads, respectively. These disparities illustrate the extent to which academic apartheid disproportionately impacted Black and Latinx students.

The arrangement between Crossroads and the district's four comprehensive high schools specified that students were to be transferred to Crossroads strictly due to academic underperformance and not behavioral problems. In fact, there was a separate "education

Figure 4. Crossroads High School from the street

Figure 5. A section of Crossroads High School's perimeter fence and one of its two gates

Figure 6. The main quad at Crossroads High School

center" in Valley View for students who repeatedly broke rules or the law. Nevertheless, and though the school was nestled well within the boundaries of an affluent suburb, the physical space had multiple features that are common of schools in low-income neighborhoods plagued by violence and illicit activity: the grass beside the school was uncut and growing wildly; the school's administration and classroom buildings were rectangular with low ceilings and flat roofs, such that they resembled a series of trailers; three floodlight poles lined one row of classrooms; an imposing black metal fence ran around the school perimeter. Crossroads was the only high school in the district with a perimeter fence.

The fence, campus buildings, floodlights, and interior courtyard were configured for the panoptic surveillance of students. The classroom buildings and main office comprised three sides of a rectangle that insured students were always visible when they were outside of a classroom or the main office. The only openings in the seven-foot fence were at two gates that were swung open by staff at the beginning and end of each school day but otherwise remained closed and locked at all times.

CONFINEMENT AND SURVEILLANCE

For many Crossroads students, their school day was an experience of being confined and surveilled. The near constant surveillance of students was enhanced by the unique positioning of the Valley View police officer stationed at the school. A squad car from the Valley View Police Department was often parked out in the parking lot in front of each high school in the district, but police presence at other Valley View high schools was quite different than police presence at Crossroads. At the four mainstream high schools in Valley View, the police officer assigned to the school could most often be found in or around the main office, near the front entrance of the school. The officer would occasionally venture to other parts of the campus, but this was rare and typically happened only when there was a need to monitor a particular event or scene, such as a pep rally before a football game against a crosstown rival. The Pinnacle police officer hung out near the front of the school at the beginning and end of each school day, but because the school was large and students had the freedom to enter the school from a variety of locations, most students entered and exited the school without encountering the officer at all. Most of the time the police officer was out of sight and out of mind.

Just a mile away, down an inviting street lined with palm trees, past an upscale apartment complex that bordered a well-manicured golf course, Crossroads High School had a highly visible police presence, a presence that contributed significantly to the punitive climate there. Unlike their peers a Pinnacle, students at Crossroads entered the school through a gated portion of the perimeter fence, and all students arriving to school had no choice but to walk directly past a Valley View police officer and one or two security guards stationed at the opening. Once the first bell sounded to start the school day, I seldom saw the police officer in front of the school, though an SUV or squad car from the Valley View Police Department remained conspicuously parked next to the front curb during business hours. Instead of hanging out in the main office or near the main entrance

Figure 7. Police car position at Crossroads High School

as at other local high schools, the Crossroads police officer observed and patrolled the courtyard during the lunch period and breaks between classes.

This difference in police posture and positioning between Crossroads and each of the mainstream high schools signaled a corresponding difference in the perception of the student populations at each school. At the mainstream high schools, police tended to stay near the main entrance, which suggests that police presence was meant to protect the school community from outsiders. At Crossroads, police placement and movement in the spaces between classrooms suggests that this conspicuous presence of law enforcement was meant to protect students from their classmates and to protect teachers from students. Moreover, the police officer at Crossroads sometimes randomly searched backpacks, bushes, and other potential hiding places for illicit drugs and drug paraphernalia, often without any credible reason to believe that such substances or items would be found. At Pinnacle and other comprehensive high schools in the district, such searches were, as the officer at Pinnacle put it to me, "evidence-based" and "exceedingly rare."

"We Are Not a Disciplinary School!"

I encountered a constant institutional contradiction at Crossroads. On one hand, administrators like Mr. Johnson, the school principal, fervently proclaimed that, "we are *not* a disciplinary school!" On the other hand, multiple features of the school—a perimeter fence to keep students on campus, low-slung classroom buildings, limited curriculum, lack of extracurricular activities, and conspicuous presence of local law enforcement—communicated a very different reality. This reality compelled dozens of students to use words like "prison," "jail," "incarcerated," "criminal," "punishment," and "ashamed" when I asked them what it felt like to attend school at Crossroads.

Many students felt that the noticeable police presence at Crossroads, coupled with the perimeter fence and locked gates, signaled an overall lack of trust from teachers and administrators. Students interpreted this lack of trust as unjust since Crossroads purported to be a school for students with academic problems, not disciplinary problems. Janet, a Filipina sophomore, compared Crossroads to Pinnacle and expressed views that I found to be representative:

> JANET: Over at Pinnacle, you see the cop just a little bit here and there, mostly up at the front of the school. That school has trust in students. Here [at Crossroads] it's just way too overprotective. The cop is here and he's armed with a pistol and always watching us, and it shows that they don't have trust in us. And, on top of that, we're fenced in all day. This school is like a prison or a jail. It makes us feel like we're bad kids or something, but we're not.

For Janet and dozens of her classmates at Crossroads, the combination of an armed police officer vigilantly observing students between classes, and a perimeter fence with locked gates that kept students on campus all day, was demoralizing. Students did not feel respected; they felt like delinquents.

During one of my early morning visits to Crossroads, I stood with Mr. Johnson and Officer Williams, the Valley View police officer assigned to Crossroads, on the asphalt of the courtyard just outside Mr. Johnson's office. They were making small talk and surveying students arriving for first period classes. During our brief conversation, I made a comment about the uniqueness of the fence at Crossroads. Mr. Johnson responded with a pointed criticism of the campus layout:

> SEAN: I think Crossroads is the only high school in Valley View with a perimeter fence like this.
>
> MR. JOHNSON: That's right. The district built this school according to a prison model, which is unfortunate. Quite frankly, I don't think it's appropriate as a high school setting. In fact, I'd love to take that damn fence down. It sends a message that these are bad kids, and our students get that message. It looks bad from out there [*Mr. Johnson pointed to the busy intersection beyond the far corner of the courtyard*], and it feels bad from in here. It's an eyesore.

Officer Williams agreed with this sentiment. He blamed a general culture of high achievement in Valley View for the features of Crossroads that made it feel like constant detention for most students:

> OFFICER WILLIAMS: All the security stuff here is a little over the top, but this is Valley View so they freak out easily around here. These aren't bad kids that go here. Trust me! I deal with bad kids and these kids aren't bad! This would be like a normal high school in most places, just not in Valley View. These kids are only bad because Valley View sees them that way.

Taken together, and particularly when compared to the comprehensive high schools in the district, Crossroads's physical features contributed to an unwelcoming and punitive atmosphere of confinement, panoptic surveillance, and control. Furthermore, the school infrastructure was problematic to a broad range of institutional actors, including students, administrators, and even police. The perimeter fence was a deeply unflattering distinction, an "eyesore" that added considerably to the disciplinary vibe on school grounds.

To be sure, many schools sit on grounds delineated by fences, bars, and locked gates. However, these elements of the school campus at Crossroads were criminalizing when considered within the broader context of Valley View's high schools. All comprehensive high schools in the district had an "open campus" layout and policy; students at each of Valley View's comprehensive high schools were free to leave campus during lunchtime and free periods, and they did so with regularity. Crossroads students were denied that privilege. Administrators at both Pinnacle and Crossroads insisted that Crossroads was "not a disciplinary school," but it sure felt that way to be on campus.

In sum, while Pinnacle students enjoyed a wealth of academic resources, extracurricular opportunities, and spatial freedom, Crossroads students' high school experience was one of relative deprivation and disadvantage. Researchers have amply documented such carceral characteristics of schools and criminalizing treatment of students in lower-income, racially segregated neighborhoods, such as in East Oakland, California[8] and on Chicago's South Side.[9] The Valley View case demonstrates that this racialized tenor of surveillance and inequality is also present in districts that are far more affluent.

"I DON'T WANT TO BE TERRORIZED":
THE STEREOTYPES AND STIGMA ASSOCIATED
WITH CROSSROADS AND ITS STUDENTS

At Pinnacle High School, Crossroads was widely believed to be a place for students who were "lazy," "delinquent," or whose parents "don't care about education as much as they should." Some teachers held such views. For example, Ms. Reynolds, a blonde substitute teacher in her mid-twenties who often taught at Pinnacle, told me that despite never having set foot on the Crossroads campus, she refused to teach there because she did not want to be, "terrorized by a bunch of bad kids."

Crossroads had a decidedly negative reputation among Pinnacle's students. During a conversation about Crossroads with Eugene and Ryan, the AP students whom we met in chapter 1, they summarized what I found to be the predominant perception of Crossroads held by Pinnacle students regardless of which academic track they were on:

> SEAN: What do you know about Crossroads High School?
>
> EUGENE: Crossroads is like the penitentiary for students. If you go to Crossroads, you have failed miserably as a student and a person, basically.
>
> RYAN: Yeah, Crossroads is the bad school. It's almost like, if you mess up, then you go there, so it's almost like a prison. Because if you mess up here [at Pinnacle], then you go over there, and you're done for life, pretty much.

For students at Pinnacle, Crossroads was a place to avoid because it was strongly associated with deviant behavior and failure. Furthermore, Pinnacle students understood the potential long-term consequences of enrolling at Crossroads, a comprehension exemplified by Patrick's comment that students who ended up at Crossroads are "done for life, pretty much." Crossroads's reputation was so unfavorable that, in Patrick's estimation, students who attended or graduated from the school would carry that stigma with them for many years thereafter.

These beliefs were not lost on students who were set to transfer to Crossroads from Pinnacle or another high school in the district. Students expressed feelings of dread at the thought of attending a school with such a lousy reputation. For example, Celia, an eighteen-year-old senior who emigrated to the United States from Mexico with her parents at the age of four and began high school at Pinnacle, was "terrified" of being transferred to Crossroads:

SEAN: What was it like for you when you knew you were coming here [to Crossroads]?

CELIA: When I found out that I was being transferred I started asking around at Pinnacle and I heard that the kids at Crossroads are all drug addicts, and you might get assaulted in the bathroom, and there is always smoke in the bathroom. I got so terrified I went home and cried. Even the first day here, I came through the office and I didn't wanna come inside because I was so scared. It looked like a place where that stuff might happen, with all the bars and stuff. It didn't look like a school at all.

In addition to fear, Crossroads students often expressed a great deal of shame and embarrassment in their predicament, feelings that were frequently echoed by other family members. In a conversation during lunch with Juan, a seventeen-year-old Mexican American junior, he told me that his father, a local real estate agent, was dismayed when he found out that Juan was being transferred to Crossroads. "My dad believed that Crossroads was a school for bad kids who do drugs and make trouble. He felt that me being here would downgrade our family name." Juan also mentioned that his father feared for his real estate business, worrying that if his clients found out that his son was a student at Crossroads, they would not want to do business with him:

JUAN: I usually go with my dad to look at houses with his customers. They'll ask me, "Where do you go to school," and I used to say, "Crossroads," but my dad was like, "Don't tell them that." He thought it would be bad for his business and the family. So now I just say I go to Pinnacle still.

Similarly, Miranda—a seventeen-year-old junior whose parents were originally from Colombia—said that she and her immediate family were ashamed that she was a Crossroads student, so they kept it a secret from extended family:

SEAN: When people ask you what high school you go to, what do you tell them?

MIRANDA: It's so embarrassing to go here, to Crossroads. My parents don't tell anyone I go to Crossroads, not even family members. My dad is really good friends with a lot of people in our community, and everyone thinks that kids that go to Crossroads must be drug addicts. So, if my dad were to tell people I went to Crossroads it would probably have a bad image on me. Like, if people knew I went here they would all think that I did something really bad, but I didn't.

Miranda was reluctant to tell even her closest friends out of fear that they would judge her harshly and that she might fall out of favor with them:

SEAN: Did you tell your friends?

MIRANDA: Not at first. I thought that if I didn't say anything they would just assume I moved schools or something. So I just didn't say anything, and the day I left I had to return all my books and it was in the middle of the semester, and someone was like, "oh, what are you doing?" I was like, "I'm returning all my books because I'm switching schools." They were like, "oh where are you going?" I'm like, "oh, Crossroads," and I never heard from that friend again, and I was like, "oh my god, this is awful." Even my good friends, obviously they know I go to Crossroads, and they are always like, "are you okay?"

SEAN: How did they find out?

MIRANDA: Because I told my good, good friends. And I still hang out with them a couple times a month, and whenever they see me they are like, "you look skinny, are you on drugs?" They are always like, "how are you surviving? Oh my god, I heard it's terrible there!" I have to reassure them every time that

I'm alright, that I'm not strung out or something crazy like that.

The overwhelmingly negative perception of Crossroads in the local community embarrassed students, and the experiences shared by Celia, Juan, and Miranda epitomize the anxiety and humiliation that students so often felt when making the switch from Pinnacle. Parents were embarrassed, too; they sometimes worried about negative impacts to their careers and the dishonor that an association with Crossroads could bring on their families. As a result, students and parents lied or told half-truths to other family and friends to save face and minimize the shame.

"I'm Chinese, So I Guess I'm Not Supposed to Be Here"

Of all the students whom I came to know during my time hanging out at Crossroads, the Asian students consistently expressed the most profound sense of shame in their transfer to Crossroads. I received a heads-up early on that this might be the case when, on my very first day of observation, one of the school counselors, Ms. Clarke, remarked that, "Coming here can be hard on all students, but the Asian students seem to take it the worst. I've had Asian students tell me that they are the shame of their family. It's like they are dishonoring their proud immigrant families."

A few weeks later, Jessie, a Chinese American sophomore at Crossroads, spoke to me about the relationship between his identity as a Crossroads student, as his ethnoracial identity as a Chinese American:

JESSIE: It's hard to be one of the only Asian kids here. When I first got here, I felt like everyone was staring at me like, "why is that Asian kid here?" I'm Chinese, so I guess I'm not supposed to be here; I'm supposed to be a top student, so it's very shameful in our [Chinese] culture for me to be here. But I'm doing good here in all my classes, so I should be able to go back to Pinnacle at the end of the year.

Michael, a Korean American junior at Pinnacle, had an experience that echoed Jessie's. He told me that other Crossroads students seemed surprised to see him when he first arrived on Campus:

MICHAEL: I came here to Crossroads because my anxiety made it hard for me to be at Pinnacle. Pinnacle is such a big school, and the counselor thought I would do better if there were less people around. But it was weird when I first got here [to Crossroads] because all the other kids looked at me funny. There aren't many Asian students here, obviously, so I think people were just surprised when they saw me. I actually felt okay about coming here but then I started to have second thoughts when I saw how everyone was looking at me all the time.

Jessie, Michael, and other Asian students at Crossroads had fallen short of the positive academic stereotypes associated with Asian students in Valley View and in other districts across the country.[10] These stereotypes were rampant in Valley View's high schools due to a combination of the large size and predominantly middle-class status of the Asian community in the district. Asian students at Crossroads had not lived up to the exacting standards of success that their immigrant families, and the general Valley View community, had of them. They felt like ethnoracial outliers because they did not meet the perceived group norm.[11]

THE ACADEMIC APARTHEID PROCESS

Sociologist Victor Ray argues that most organizations are "racial structures—cognitive schemas connecting organizational rules to social and material resources."[12] According to Ray, one of the common characteristics of racialized organizations and institutions is that rules are often decoupled from formal practices in ways that reproduce racial inequality. The Valley View Unified School District's continuation school model, and Pinnacle High School's interpretation and execution of that model, provide compelling examples of this racialization and how institutions bend rules to suit their interests in ways that can inadvertently harm those they serve.

An Arbitrary Threshold

Pinnacle High School had a "threshold of credit deficiency" that a given student had to reach before they were deemed a candidate for transfer to Crossroads. Students typically approached or reached the threshold after failing two courses in the same semester, failing the same course twice, or if their cumulative GPA dipped below 2.0.

This credit deficiency policy, and the low bar for reaching the threshold, disproportionately affected Pinnacle's Black and Latinx students. At Pinnacle, Black and Latinx students' GPAs were, on average, considerably lower than those of their White and Asian peers. Table 4 displays schoolwide data on Pinnacle students' GPAs for the 2014–2015 school year, my first full year of fieldwork. The data are disaggregated by race and GPA quartile.

Black and Latinx students at Pinnacle were roughly twice as likely as White students, and four times as likely as Asian students, to maintain a cumulative GPA in the bottom quartile. These substantial racial disparities in GPA indicated that Pinnacle's Black and Latinx students were far more likely to approach or reach the threshold.[5] Furthermore, it was standard practice at Pinnacle for school officials to push for the transfer of students who had not met the threshold and, therefore, were not yet "credit deficient."

Mariah, a Black, sixteen-year-old junior at Pinnacle, was one of several students I met who faced this early pressure. Mariah experienced a dip in her grades during sophomore year, though she never failed a class, and her GPA stayed above 2.0. Nevertheless, during that period of academic struggle she felt that counselors and

Table 4   *Pinnacle High School grade point average by racial group and quartile, 2014–2015*

Race	Total, All Grades	0–1.99 GPA	2.0–2.99 GPA	3.0–3.99 GPA	4.0+ GPA
Asian	1,430	5.0%	15.0%	57.6%	22.4%
White	1,017	10.3%	27.6%	51.9%	10.1%
Latinx	224	18.8%	40.6%	37.5%	3.1%
Black	73	23.3%	43.8%	30.1%	2.7%

assistant principals pushed her to transfer to Crossroads instead of trying to help her improve her grades:

SEAN: What's your experience been like at Pinnacle?

MARIAH: Honestly? I don't want to say this, but I hate it here. Everyone thinks it's a great school, but they don't care about anyone. All they do is all for looks. The teachers don't care about you. They just care about the students that started off good and are the top students. You could be all the way behind and they don't try to catch you up, you're just left back there. I mean, when I first came here it was really hard for me, and none of my teachers cared.

SEAN: What do they care about?

MARIAH: They only care about the students who are already doing well. And with me, when I was struggling, they were trying to find a way to get me out of the school instead of helping me.

SEAN: How so?

MARIAH: They were like, "Ok, well, you can go to Crossroads." From what I heard, Crossroads wasn't a good school, so I really didn't want to go there. So I felt like, instead of trying to send me to Crossroads, they should help me get back up to speed and stay here at Pinnacle. But they don't care. They don't want to help that much.

Mariah never reached the threshold of credit deficiency, yet she faced this pressure just the same. With the option to stay or go, Mariah resisted the pressure and chose to stay, hoping that her subsequent teachers would be more helpful.

My conversations with several Pinnacle administrators and teachers corroborated Mariah's account and confirmed a customary institutional practice of recommending students for transfer to Crossroads even when those students were above the credit threshold. Mr. Bradley, the principal at Pinnacle, lamented a recent change in philosophy at Crossroads regarding the acceptance of transfer students from Pinnacle:

SEAN: When you recommend a student for transfer to Crossroads, does Crossroads just automatically accept them?

MR. BRADLEY: Usually they take them, but not always. There were a couple instances recently where we saw a kid that maybe wasn't totally at the threshold, but we knew that their grades had been slipping. Last year we had a handful of sophomores that we wanted to send because we wanted to kind of do it sooner rather than later. Our assistant principals and counselors went back and forth on the issue with their colleagues at Crossroads, but ultimately the kids had to stay here until they met that threshold. The new principal over there is really strict about the threshold stuff.

Coordinated Pressure to Transfer

Though a transfer to Crossroads High School for "credit recovery" was optional for students deemed credit deficient, Pinnacle administrators actively pushed for the transfer of students by pressuring parents and students to make the switch, especially in cases where the family was leery or otherwise resistant. Assistant Principal Holt described this process as a joint effort between assistant principals and counselors to persuade reluctant families to leave Pinnacle for

Crossroads. Guidance counselors typically made initial contact with students and their parents regarding a potential transfer, but assistant principals were always in the loop and often played a central role later on:

> SEAN: Do you make decisions about which students should go to Crossroads or not, or is it more of a counselor thing?
>
> MR. HOLT: It's actually more of a counselor thing because it's based on credits and not discipline. But I'll get involved if the parents need the hard sell, like if the parents are blocking the move or saying no. For example, I dealt with parents last year who went over to Crossroads to take a look, and they came back here and they were like, "It's got fences around it and it looks like a prison. I don't want my kid there." I told them that our rigorous environment is just bad for some kids. I told them that Crossroads had a system where you can get more credits quicker. They ultimately made the switch, but they didn't go quietly.

Institutional actors at Pinnacle believed that Crossroads was the appropriate setting for students who were struggling academically, but they also knew that Crossroads was deeply undesirable. Therefore, administrators leveraged the institutional success frame during the transfer decision process, referencing the academic "rigor" at Pinnacle to legitimize and "sell" a transfer to Crossroads to students and parents. Administrators justified the transfer recommendation and process to parents and students by arguing that Pinnacle's environment was simply too difficult for some students, and that students who had fallen behind were hopelessly off track to graduate.

Students and parents needed to be sold on the move because they routinely questioned the merits, legitimacy, and consequences of making the switch. Of the fifty-nine Crossroads students whom I interviewed, fifty-eight told me that they did not want to transfer to Crossroads, and fifty-one mentioned repeated attempts by faculty to convince them to transfer despite their consistent objections and pleas for more support. For example, Tremont, a Black senior who began high school at Pinnacle, expressed disappointment in the lack of options presented to him as a "credit deficient" student and denounced the abruptness of the transfer process:

SEAN: How did you find out that you were coming to Crossroads?

TREMONT: One of my teachers told me to go to the office, and then the [assistant] principal said that I didn't have enough credits so I might be going to Crossroads.

SEAN: Was the transfer an abrupt thing, or did they warn you that you were behind on credits?

TREMONT: It was very abrupt; it was just a week in advance. They said I was low on credits and they said, "you're probably going to Crossroads." Then I was here [at Crossroads] a week later. They didn't really give me a chance to improve first.

SEAN: And did they give you a choice to stay at Pinnacle?

TREMONT: It was a choice, but it was like a false choice. I was told that I could stay at Pinnacle and fail, or go to Crossroads. I wish I had stayed because I think I could have picked my grades up, and I told them I could, but they convinced my mom that I had to come here. I'm still mad about it.

Pinnacle counselors and principals would also often attempt to reassure students and parents by telling them that a high school diploma from Crossroads was the "same level" of diploma that students received from Pinnacle:

SEAN: Is it hard to persuade kids to make the switch to a school that's so different?

MR HOLT: Well, the schools are certainly different, but the diplomas are the same, and that's what we tell families. Whether you graduate from here or Crossroads, you get the same diploma issued by the Valley View Unified School District. The only difference is the name of the school. It's not a lesser degree from Crossroads. It's not a GED or a certificate.

This statement, though true on its face, omitted the key fact that the Crossroads curriculum was limited such that graduates were unable to directly enroll in four-year universities. Though graduates from Crossroads and Pinnacle both received diplomas that appeared to be equal, the institutions were so dissimilar that a diploma from Crossroads was worth considerably less to those who wished to go to college. Thus, the potential ramifications of a transfer to Crossroads could easily extend well beyond high school.

Some Crossroads students did not become aware of the limitations of Crossroads diploma until they began the college application process. Consider the experience of Dominique, a Black, seventeen-year-old senior who was set to enroll at Valley View Community College after graduation:

SEAN: Why did you decide on V.V.C.C.?

DOMINIQUE: The decision was pretty much made for me. I went to [the guidance counselor] and told her that I wanted to apply to Long Beach State because my cousin goes there, but she said that my only option for next year was to go to community college. And that was, like, shocking to me because I've been doing well in all my classes here.

SEAN: Did she say why?

DOMINIQUE: Yeah, because we can't get all the classes we need here so I wouldn't even qualify for a state school.

Dominque had a perfect attendance record at Crossroads and passed all of her classes. She was popular among her peers and praised as "hardworking," "focused," and "going places" by her teachers. Unfortunately, the places she could go after high school were constrained by Crossroads's skeletal curriculum. Dominque felt the alienation of seeing that her hard work and achievements did not amount to much, at least not as much as she thought they would or should.

The transfer process from Pinnacle to Crossroads provides clear examples of how a racialized organization can legitimate the unequal distributions of resources.[13] Institutional actors at Pinnacle did this explicitly. The consistent and coordinated efforts of administrators to "sell" a plan to transfer from Pinnacle (a school with copious curricular and extracurricular resources) to Crossroads (a school with far fewer resources and opportunities for students than any other high school in the district) are examples of school officials perpetuating and legitimizing segregation and inequality.

RELYING ON SOCIAL, CULTURAL, AND ECONOMIC CAPITAL TO RESIST THE PUSH TO CROSSROADS

During the 2015–2016 school year, 11.2% of Pinnacle students were designated by the school district as "socioeconomically disadvantaged," compared to a district average of 16.5%. Meanwhile, at Crossroads, 51% were socioeconomically disadvantaged. These data are evidence of a socioeconomic disparity between Pinnacle and Crossroads students, and they suggest that the district's continuation school model disproportionately impacted the most disadvantaged students in the district. I wanted to find out why and how this was the case.

Education researchers have documented robust links between family resources and students' academic engagement and achievement. For example, an abundant body of sociological research has shown that school officials recognize and reward students and parents who exhibit "middle-class cultural capital"—habits of behavior and speech, as well as expressed knowledge of how educational opportunities are distributed, that signal a privileged class status to institutional actors and help secure valuable resources.[14] Social capital—a constellation of social ties that yield institutional resources and support[15]—is also vital for academic engagement and achievement.[16] In high school, for instance, students who struggle academically often have fewer upwardly mobile adult relatives, neighbors, or family friends than those who succeed.[17] In more dire circumstances, a lack of available social capital can contribute to high school dropout.[18] In terms of school enrollment decisions, parents draw upon their social networks when making decisions on where to enroll their children in school,[19] and middle-class parents are often better equipped to navigate these decisions because their social networks provide valuable information that is not equally available to lower-income parents.[20]

I found a similar set of social processes at work at Pinnacle. Once labeled "credit deficient," some Pinnacle students were able to avoid the move by drawing on their family's social ties, intimate knowledge of the local public school system, or monetary wealth. For example, at Pinnacle's back-to-school night during my second year of field-work, I met Ms. Bright, a Spanish teacher who was White and in her late twenties. Ms. Bright and her younger brother both graduated from Pinnacle. Her brother fell behind on his coursework during sophomore year, reached the threshold of credit deficiency, and was pressured to transfer to Crossroads. But Ms. Bright's mother was a teacher at another comprehensive high school in Valley View, and she was skeptical that a transfer to Crossroads would help her son. Making use of her district connections, she called a friend who taught at Crossroads and asked for advice. The friend told her to keep her son at Pinnacle no matter how bad the assistant principals or counselors made his situation sound. Ms. Bright said that her younger brother did indeed remain at Pinnacle, and her parents challenged Pinnacle teachers and administrators to do more to help him stay on track. Her brother eventually graduated from Pinnacle and enrolled at a nearby California State University, where he earned a degree in economics and then began a career in local politics.

Ms. Bright's story was not unique; I found that parents of credit deficient students relied on a combination of social, cultural, and economic capital to prevent a transfer to Crossroads. Before a junior varsity soccer game at Pinnacle, I met a Korean mom whose daughter had failed two classes at the school as a freshman. When the school recommended that the girl begin her sophomore year at Crossroads, her parents withdrew her from Pinnacle and enrolled her in a nearby private school. They did this after consulting with fellow members of the Pinnacle Korean Parent Teacher Association,

a Korean arm of the Pinnacle PTA that provided social and academic
support for Pinnacle's Korean families, particularly those who were
recent immigrants and possessed limited English language proficiency. With the social and cultural capital provided by the Korean
PTA, and the economic capital to pay the $40,000 private school
tuition, these parents kept their daughter out of Crossroads.

When Thomas, a White, sixteen-year-old junior at Pinnacle, fell
credit deficient, his parents did not want him to be transferred to
Crossroads. According to Thomas, his parents, who were both law-
yers, had heard from other Pinnacle parents that Crossroads was
"a place to avoid," and they spent "thousands of dollars on private
tutoring" to improve his grades. Thomas's grades improved with
the extra help, and he went on to graduate with his class, on time,
from Pinnacle. He was able to avoid a demoralizing and stigmatizing
transfer to Crossroads because his parents had the means to spend
thousands of dollars to supplement his high school education and
ensure that he graduated from a prestigious school.

I spoke with several teachers and administrators at Pinnacle on
the issue of why the school was unable to persuade some students
to transfer to Crossroads. Mr. Thompson, an assistant principal
at Pinnacle for nearly a decade, expressed views that were characteristic among the Pinnacle faculty. Crossroads was, according to
Mr. Thompson, "so unpopular that no student wants to transfer
there." As a result, the decisions that credit deficient students and
their parents made about whether or not to transfer to Crossroads
often reflected socioeconomic differences:

> SEAN: Do most students end up accepting your recommendation
> for them to transfer to Crossroads?
>
> MR. THOMPSON: Yes, most of them do end up going, but it's like pulling
> teeth to get them to agree to the transfer. I've never seen
> a student who was excited about going to Crossroads.
>
> SEAN: And for the students who end up staying at Pinnacle and
> not transferring to Crossroads, what are some of the
> reasons why they end up staying?

MR. THOMPSON: Well, all of them want to stay, but the ones who end up staying—from what I've seen—are the ones who have parents who can just throw money at whatever the problem is. They'll enroll in expensive online classes or hire expensive private tutors. We've also had credit deficient kids withdraw from Pinnacle and enroll in private school rather than switching to Crossroads.

Social, cultural, and economic capital were critically valuable assets for credit deficient students in their desire to avoid Crossroads despite attempts by school leadership to compel them to transfer.

THE DISPROPORTIONATE PUSHOUT OF DISADVANTAGED STUDENTS

Pinnacle administrators were more likely to prevail over students who lacked the resources to successfully resist. As such, the practice of pressuring students to transfer placed students of lower socioeconomic status at risk. For example, Savannah, a Black sophomore, moved to Valley View after attending her freshman year of high school in North Carolina. She described herself as a "good student in North Carolina," but she fell behind on her coursework immediately at Pinnacle because Pinnacle did not recognize all of her freshman credits from her North Carolina school, and she found the workload and pace of classes at Pinnacle to be much more demanding. When Savannah was told by a Pinnacle assistant principal that she "would probably be going to Crossroads," she assumed that she had no choice:

SAVANNAH: They told me that I could come back to Pinnacle if I got my credits up, but they didn't have a plan for me if I stayed [at Pinnacle]. They said I had a choice to stay, but that I would fail if I stayed! So, the choice was to basically stay and flunk out, or go to Crossroads. But I was scared to go to Crossroads because I had heard bad things about it, but I felt I had no choice.

A few months after Savannah was transferred, I spoke with her mother, Tanya, who had recently landed a job as a waitress at a local diner. Tanya expressed frustration that Pinnacle had not done more to help Savannah remain there, and that she was not able to do more to help her daughter:

SEAN: What do you think led to Savannah enrolling at Crossroads?

TANYA: Well, we moved here from Charlotte after I divorced my husband. The divorce and the move were expensive, and we were living with extended family when we got here because I hadn't found a new job yet. And then Pinnacle says that they're going to send Savannah to this Crossroads school when she had barely had time to get settled in. I wanted to get her a private tutor so she could maybe stay at Crossroads, but I don't have the money for that. So now she's at *Crossroads*, which is extra disappointing because we moved here to Valley View partly because of the good schools! I don't think we would have moved here if I'd known she would end up where she is right away.

Without an established social network in the community to turn to for guidance, or the financial means to supplement her daughter's education, Tanya felt as though she had no choice but to acquiesce to Pinnacle's recommendation that Savannah enroll at Crossroads.

Like Savannah, Edson, a seventeen-year-old Latino junior at Crossroads, moved to Valley View from the East Coast with his mother, who earned a modest income as a bus driver. After struggling academically during his sophomore year at Pinnacle, Edson showed up at Pinnacle in August before his junior year to enroll in another year of classes. He was determined to, as he put it, "right the ship," but Pinnacle had other plans for him:

SEAN: How did you find out you were coming to Crossroads?

EDSON: I showed up for orientation in the summer, and the lady in the office was like, "Oh, I don't think you're coming back to Pinnacle this year. You need to go see the assistant principal."

> Nobody told me or my mom anything, not even a phone call or an email about it. And so the next day I went to the assistant principal with my mom and he said that my credits were bad and I wouldn't graduate if I stayed at Pinnacle, even if I passed all my classes. My mom got pretty upset over that.

SEAN: Did she try to prevent it, prevent the transfer?

EDSON: Yeah, she was arguing with him, but he had made his mind up that I should go and that I would just fail if I stayed. And then her plan was to sign me up for this tutoring thing so I wouldn't have to go to Crossroads, but it ended up being too expensive.

Out of options, Edson reluctantly enrolled at Crossroads.

The transfer policy and process that sent students to Crossroads placed Black, Latinx, and lower-income students at risk. The "threshold of credit deficiency" policy, and the arbitrary way in which the policy was exercised, reveals how racial inequality was reproduced through the continuation school system. Moreover, the voluntary transfer policy, and the process of pressuring students and parents to transfer, reveal how social class affected who ended up at Crossroads. With a choice to stay or go, but under pressure from administrators to transfer, students from more privileged backgrounds could rely on their family's social, cultural, and economic capital to secure additional academic support, typically through expert advice and private tutoring. Some students from well-to-do families even withdrew from Pinnacle and enrolled in a nearby private school to avoid Crossroads. These attractive alternatives were prohibitively expensive for lower-income families.

"DUMPING" STUDENTS TO CROSSROADS

Once a family made the decision to leave for Crossroads, that decision was final; when a student enrolled at Crossroads they had to remain there until they recovered all of their credits and were no longer credit deficient, at which point they had the option to stay and graduate from Crossroads, or transfer back to Pinnacle. Fourteen Crossroads parents raised this and other issues during a meeting with four members of the local public school accreditation commission. The meeting was held on a Saturday in a multi-purpose classroom at Crossroads. The commissioners listened intently and took extensive notes as parents voiced unanimous frustration with the transfer process and the overall relationship between Crossroads and the comprehensive high schools. They perceived the transfer of a student to Crossroads as a way for high schools like Pinnacle to "protect their elite status" and "sidestep the need to support all students." Several felt that Crossroads was a school for students who, as one dad in attendance put it, had been "outcasted." A mom remarked that Crossroads was a place for students that schools like Pinnacle "don't want to help directly because helping struggling students would require more time and effort than convincing them to leave for Crossroads."

Many students at Crossroads also shared these beliefs. Hassan, a sixteen-year-old junior at Crossroads who was tall, slender, and the son of Somali immigrants, began his high school career in San Diego. He enrolled at Pinnacle when is family moved to Valley View midway through his freshman year after his parents separated. He had been a good student in San Diego—"A's and B's," he said—but he struggled with the move to a new city. His mother, an administrative assistant at a Toyota dealership, had a new work schedule that left him with far greater responsibilities in caring for his three younger siblings, one of whom was a toddler.

Hassan found the academic culture at Pinnacle to be extremely fast-paced and competitive, especially compared to his prior high school in San Diego. "My high school in San Diego was pretty ghetto," he told me one day on the blacktop that stretched between classrooms. "It was basically all Black and Mexican kids, and the school needed a lot of repairs and stuff. The neighborhood was a little rough at times, but not too bad. I knew some people that was in a gang, but I wasn't involved with anything like that."

Hassan did well in his classes at Pinnacle until midway through spring semester, when the pressure and workload eventually overwhelmed him. He failed a class, which was "shocking" to him because he was used to earning good grades. Counselors at Pinnacle subsequently pressed him to transfer to Crossroads, and he felt as though they did so hastily to protect the school's reputation:

> SEAN: Do you have any ideas for why Pinnacle was leaning on you to go to enroll at Crossroads?
>
> HASSAN: I think Pinnacle cares a lot about its reputation. I heard stories from my friends who came here from other schools, and they say that when they're having that meeting about coming to Crossroads, the other schools are more lenient, and you have more of a choice to stay or go. But at Pinnacle, if they see you are slipping up even a little bit, they want you to go to Crossroads right away. They just care about their reputation so much; they don't want their reputation to be ruined by students like me who need more help.

Hassan's experiences led him to conclude something very similar to what Mariah had come to believe: Institutional actors at Pinnacle appeared to care more about the school's reputation as an academically elite high school than they did about helping students with lower GPAs. Hassan was disappointed in this approach because he had shown the ability to earn A's and B's in high school.

Crossroads teachers agreed. The prevailing perception among Crossroads teachers was that Crossroads played a direct role in helping comprehensive high schools like Pinnacle manage their academic rankings and reputations by serving as a "dumping ground" for struggling students, even if those struggles were nascent and addressable at the comprehensive site. Mr. Gregory, who taught math and science, expressed views that were representative among his colleagues:

> SEAN: What role do you think Crossroads plays in the district?

MR. GREGORY: I think that, for the district and the comprehensive high
schools like Pinnacle, Crossroads is about getting rid of
the students that don't fit in at their school. My feeling is
that we are just this dumping ground for the other high
schools. A lot of these kids here, for whatever reason, just
aren't fitting in at the comprehensive schools, and those
schools don't have as much time for the struggling
students.

Mr. Gregory's sentiments were common among teachers and faculty
at Crossroads; nearly all felt as though the school's stated purpose
of credit recovery was undermined by the way in which the school
was used by the neighboring comprehensive high schools as a place
to jettison low-achievers whom those schools did not want to be
responsible for.

ACADEMIC APATHY: THE RAMIFICATIONS
OF CLUSTERING "CREDIT DEFICIENT"
STUDENTS IN ONE SCHOOL

Due to its status as a continuation school, Crossroads was a place
where nearly all students had faced academic challenges and were
behind on their coursework. This characteristic undoubtedly contributed to its reputation as a school for "bad kids," but there were
other aspects of the district's continuation school model that may
have hindered "credit recovery" for Crossroads students.

Many students began their time at Crossroads motivated to
work hard and make up credits, but gradually lost focus and slid
into a pattern of academic apathy and defiance. Coleman, a Black,
eighteen-year-old senior at Crossroads, saw this pattern as the
school's primary dilemma:

SEAN: Have you seen kids changing while they're here in terms of
their approach to school in general?

COLEMAN: I definitely see kids changing while they're here. Most kids come here just for credits, and then they get connected with other connects and all the plugs for the drugs, and then they have everything that they need right at their fingertips. That fucks their whole mind up and their mentality changes. Instead of, "I'm just trying to chill with my homies," it changes to, "I'm trying to get fucked up with my homies." Instead of doing the work, it's "fuck the work." It's a complete contradiction. They send you here to restore your credit, but there's actually a lot more distractions in a worse way here. It's a complete contradiction.[21]

Jeremiah, a Black junior at Crossroads who was good friends with Coleman, spoke about how his behavior as a Crossroads student had changed over time:

SEAN: When you first got here, were you motivated to make up your credits?

JEREMIAH: Yeah, most definitely. I was really scared the first time I came here because I'd heard that it was a place for degenerates. I wanted to just do my work so I could get out of here and get back to Pinnacle.

SEAN: But now you're planning to stay and graduate from Crossroads. Did something change along the way?

JEREMIAH: To be honest, I kind of fell into some of the bad things that I heard about Crossroads before I got here. This school is really easy [academically]; there's not much work and a lot of kids don't really do it. My friends weren't doing the work so I stopped doing it. I could still pass the classes without doing much work, so I stopped trying.

After speaking with Coleman and Jeremiah about this issue, I followed up by asking teachers if they noticed changes in the comportment of their students over time, for better or worse. I found that Crossroads teachers noticed an alarming trend of gradual disengagement and willful "laziness,"[22] corroborating Coleman's and

Jeremiah's assessments. Consider the following exchange I had with Mr. Davis, a twenty-nine-year-old history teacher who had been at Crossroads for three years:

SEAN: Do you see kids come in a certain way and then they're here for a long time and they change?

MR. DAVIS: Yes, and typically in bad ways. For instance, we have a student who, when she first showed up, she came in and did all her work and tried to catch up on credits. Now, within a year, she has fallen way, way down to the point where she's failing and she doesn't even care. She got mixed in here with the wrong people and basically had continuous opportunities to connect with kids who don't make smart decisions.

This sort of gradual assimilation into a prevailing student ethos of academic apathy was typical at Crossroads.

Indeed, the disappointment and shame that many students felt in being sent to Crossroads, and an institutional culture void of intellectual curiosity, resulted in a sizeable minority of students who were defiantly apathetic about their schoolwork and more interested in socializing with their classmates during and after school. This dynamic created challenges and distractions for students who *were* motivated to recover credits and return to their comprehensive high school, or those who were simply striving to graduate on time from Crossroads. Students who successfully recovered credits had often developed strategies to avoid Crossroads's social pitfalls and remain focused on their work, such as doing assignments during the lunch period or getting permission from teachers to listen to white noise while working on assignments in class.

Ironically, the student body culture of academic apathy at Crossroads was compounded by aspects of the school schedule that were implemented with the goal of increasing the likelihood of successful credit recover for all students. First, Crossroads had a shorter school day than the comprehensive high schools in Valley View; first period began at 8:20 a.m. instead of 8:00 a.m., and the final period ended at 1:00 p.m. instead of 3:05 p.m. Second, Crossroads assigned no homework in any of its classes, which meant that students did all of their coursework, including special projects, in class. The combination of a short school day and no homework, as well as no extracurricular activities such as clubs or sports, meant that students left school each day with no school-oriented work to do and many hours of daylight to find something else to do instead.

DREAMS DEFERRED

In the following paragraphs I introduce two Crossroads students, Miguel and Francine, whose cases challenged the pervasive stereotype that Crossroads was a school for deviant and troublesome youth who lacked ambition. Miguel transferred to Crossroads after failing two classes at Pinnacle. He struggled with traditional subjects like math and science, but he had a passion for culinary arts and a goal to become a chef and open his own restaurant. As a young girl, Francine and her family fled a brutal civil war in the Democratic Republic of the Congo. They eventually settled in Valley View, but she soon fell behind in school and enrolled at Crossroads.

Miguel Loses a Career Path

Some Crossroads students encountered difficulty at their comprehensive high schools because they were not interested in traditional subjects like math and science. Miguel, a seventeen-year-old Mexican American junior at Crossroads, was one such student. Miguel began his high school career at Pinnacle. He was affable, a good soccer player, and popular among his classmates, but he did not enjoy the academic aspects of school. He put very little time into his studies, and his grades reflected his lack of effort. At the end of his sophomore year, after failing two classes that spring semester, he

1

was summoned to the counseling office and told that he would need to begin junior year at Crossroads

During his orientation at Crossroads the next fall, one of the academic advisors asked Miguel about his plans for the future. He told her that he loved to cook for his family at home, and that he wanted to be a chef and open his own restaurant someday. She informed him that the school district offered several vocational classes, including "culinary arts," as part of a "career technical education program" (CTEP). CTEP training was popular among Crossroads students because it counted as course credit toward graduation. Miguel took advantage of the opportunity and eagerly enrolled in the program. He enjoyed it because, as he put it, "I get to learn and practice stuff that I'll need when I get a real job. I know I'll never use the shit we're doing in my other classes, so what's the point? I really don't see the point for me."

Things were looking up for Miguel despite his disinterest in the core curriculum, but his auspicious start in CTEP would not last. Early in Mr. Johnson's tenure as principal, several teachers complained during faculty meetings that too many students were consistently showing up late to first period. In response, Mr. Johnson developed a plan, with district support, to compel more students to arrive on time each morning. He enacted a policy that students who were late eight times in a single semester would face a series of penalties, one of which was that they would be pulled from their first period class and any CTEP classes they were taking.

Miguel was chronically late for first period. I asked him why, and he explained that Crossroads was much farther from his home than Pinnacle was, and that his mom was no longer able to drop him off at school in the morning due to a change in her work schedule. As a result, he said, he took the city bus each morning, but he complained that the bus service in Valley View was slow, with long intervals between buses. This combination of factors meant that he was often late for the first bell of the day. (I can confirm that bus service was sporadic over the duration of my fieldwork, so much so that I avoided taking it.) Mr. Johnson did not accept Miguel's explanation.

I asked Mr. Johnson why involvement in CTEP was at risk for students who arrived late to school, citing Miguel's case as an example. "Participation in culinary arts is an extracurricular privilege that is earned," he responded, "so it can also be taken away." But for students like Miguel—students interested in learning a trade that would help them launch a career—culinary arts and other similar courses were much more than "extracurricular."

Miguel was soon expelled from the program, a move that alienated him and frustrated Mr. Gregory, his pre-algebra teacher. I had a brief conversation with Mr. Gregory outside of his classroom the day after Miguel had been dropped from CTEP, and he was disappointed in that outcome:

MR. GREGORY: Culinary arts was the one thing that Miguel liked in terms of school. It was the one thing that he was really engaged in, and now it's gone. We want these kids to find their passion, and we urge them to find their passion, and so I don't think we should punish them by taking that away, which is what happened with Miguel. He's a good kid and we need to support him.

No longer in the program, Miguel began skipping school altogether, only showing up occasionally to turn in assignments or when he wanted to see his friends. I caught up with him just after school one day about a month after he lost his spot in CTEP; he was on his way to a park across the street to hang out. I asked him about getting pulled from culinary arts: "Oh, it totally sucks, man," he said, shaking his head. "It was the only reason I was coming here [to Crossroads]. Now I don't really have a reason to be here." He dropped out a few weeks later.

I found it common for Crossroads students to be interested in and committed to vocational education, only for the district to make clear that vocation training should not be a priority for any student.

Miguel's case is an example of how interest in learning a specific job skill or trade was devalued and easily dismissed because such goals did not align with prevailing notions of school success. Part of the institutional success frame at Pinnacle was that a successful Pinnacle graduate was one who enrolled in a four-year college or university, and preferably a prestigious one at that. Students like Miguel, who wished to pursue vocational training in lieu of a bachelor's degree, did not comport with this success frame; they struggled to fit in with Pinnacle's institutional culture, which contributed to their transfer to Crossroads. One might imagine Crossroads as a place where vocational education would be championed, especially given the widespread interest in it among students. However, paradoxically, vocational education was viewed at Crossroads much that same way as it was at Pinnacle—as an extracurricular privilege rather than an important step toward a job or career.

Francine's Arduous Road to Crossroads

Many students ended up at Crossroads through no fault of their own; they had been unable to overcome a series of trying circumstances in their lives that affected their academic engagement and achievement. Francine, a seventeen-year-old junior, shared her the story of her path to Crossroads with me, and it was an especially vivid example of the dislocation and turmoil that many Crossroads students had dealt with prior to their enrollment.

Francine was born in the Democratic Republic of the Congo during the Second Congo War. Her earliest memories were of the sounds of gunfire and bombs every night and taking shelter under her parents' bed. When Francine was five, her father, a medical doctor, was killed by crossfire. After his death, the family fled to a refugee camp in neighboring Rwanda, where they stayed for nearly five years. The camp provided safety and basic shelter, but school was not available to children there. Francine's mother applied for a refugee visa to bring the family to the United States, and they eventually settled in Las Vegas when Francine was twelve. Francine enrolled in the sixth grade in Las Vegas, her first experience with formal schooling of any kind. She said that school was difficult because, "At the age of twelve, I could not read, write, divide, add—anything." She studied hard in and out of school, watching movies and television shows to learn English more quickly, and taking a full slate of summer school classes each year to accelerate her learning.

After three years in Las Vegas, when Francine was set to begin ninth grade, her mother decided to enroll in community college in Valley View and she moved Francine and her four younger siblings there. Francine did well in high school as a freshman, earning "a mix of A's and B's" in her classes. However, Francine started to have problems with her mother at home, which she attributed to the lasting familial trauma and stress of surviving a brutal civil war. Francine missed five weeks of school during freshman year for family therapy and a brief hospital stay, and this time away from school caused her to quickly fall behind on credits. Her high school counselor suggested that she transfer to Crossroads and maybe graduate early, but Francine did not want to go to Crossroads; she had heard from other high school students that Crossroads was "all about bad kids, fights, gangs, and drugs." She saw teachers use the threat of Crossroads to warn misbehaving and low-achieving students by saying things like, "keep this up, and we're going to send you to Crossroads." But Francine knew she was behind, and the chance to graduate early was a chance that she reluctantly took.

Francine was an exemplary student at Crossroads, and I frequently observed her studying at a picnic table during the lunch period. When I asked her why she always worked through lunch, her answer was direct: "Because I really shouldn't even be at Crossroads! I'm trying to get ahead, stay ahead, and get out of here." Her approach paid off, as she recovered all of her credits in one year and graduated early, at the end of her junior year. After graduating she immediately enrolled in classes at Valley View Community College. Francine—and many of her classmates—were proof that the

prevailing stereotype of Crossroads students as lazy, juvenile delinquents was inaccurate and unfair.

The continuation school model in Valley View displaced and
penalized students like Francine—students who were highly motivated and capable but encountered significant obstacles in their lives
that were beyond their control. Francine summed this up well when
she told me:

FRANCINE: When I struggled I just needed extra help. Maybe tutoring or
            something like that, or extensions on assignments so I could
            complete my work. I've always been good at school, but there
            was just so much going on in my life. So I don't think I should
            have been sent here to Crossroads because coming here is like
            a punishment, but I didn't do anything wrong! I'm a good
            person and I'll be successful because I've overcome a lot.

For most students in America, the tremendous danger, hardship,
and loss that Francine and her family endured on their journey to
a better future in the United States is the stuff of nightmares. Yet,
despite these hardships, Francine achieved incredible success: she
survived a civil war that killed her doting father; she made it safely
to America with her mother and brothers and sisters; she entered
American middle school in the sixth grade and made enough progress to start high school on time in Valley View. But the accumula-
tion of severe obstacles that she encountered in her young life left
her unable to avoid Crossroads. Francine's case is an example of how
even students who had beaten the longest of odds could wind up at
Crossroads.

· · · · ·

The continuation school model in Valley View, which involved the
explicit pushout of "credit deficient" students, plainly exacerbated
racial and socioeconomic inequality in the district. This was no
secret; the district gathered racial and socioeconomic statistics each

year on each of its high schools and made this data publicly available online. Why, then, did the Valley View Unified School District maintain this model? Whose interests did it primarily serve?

My findings suggest that, despite the inequality that it promoted, the system was maintained because it aligned with the district's reputation as academically elite. At Pinnacle High School, where exceptional achievement was commonplace, students who fell behind were framed as misfits who did not belong. Many current and former Pinnacle students, like Mariah and Hassan, felt that the school catered to the highest achieving students and was quick to give up on and push out students who fell behind.

The most salient threat that Crossroads students posed was not one of violence or other illicit behavior. Instead, students who struggled academically threatened the academic ethos of exceptional achievement at comprehensive high schools like Pinnacle. For Pinnacle administrators, the fact that some students struggled at Pinnacle was proof that the school's "rigorous environment" was "just bad for some kids." This way of framing credit deficiency was useful for Pinnacle because it worked to justify the hidden inequities in the transfer process, and the glaring inequality between the two schools.

Simply put, Crossroads served the interests of academically elite, comprehensive, college preparatory high schools like Pinnacle. Rather than seeking to modify the Pinnacle environment to be more inclusive of all students, or implementing and sustaining additional academic support for students who had fallen behind, institutional actors at Pinnacle could conveniently shepherd lower-achieving students to Crossroads. The presence of a continuation school in the district gave Pinnacle the option of sending struggling students to Crossroads while focusing their considerable educational resources on high-achievers. These high-achievers enhanced the school's reputation by scoring top marks on standardized tests and gaining admission to the most selective colleges and universities in the country.

Structuring Crossroads according to a "prison model" had the unintended consequence of criminalizing students and, in effect, punishing them for struggling. Previous research has shown that punitive school policies and surveillance tactics, such as those of Crossroads, frame students as problems, troublemakers, and threats to public safety.[23] This framing and treatment often backfires by marginalizing students and alienating them from their teachers and school work.[24] At Crossroads, many students began their tenure highly motivated to get back on track, but the academic culture at Crossroads routinely left them feeling disaffected, and they gradually succumbed to a pervasive culture of academic apathy.

Students were not the only district community members who felt such discontent; Crossroads teachers were frequently dispirited by the inordinate amount of class time that they had to devote to classroom management and discipline rather than teaching subject matter. Meanwhile, Pinnacle teachers were unburdened by issues of discipline, and could consistently count on their students to be de facto teaching assistants and reliable classroom helpers. It is to these student-teacher interactions, and the contrasting classroom climates at Crossroads and Pinnacle, that we now turn.

3 The Segregation of Teaching and Learning

One spring morning during my first year of fieldwork, I arrived at Ms. Quinn's classroom during the morning snack period. I found this twenty-minute break in the class schedule to be invaluable, as it was one of the few times that I could speak one-on-one with teachers during regular school hours. Sometimes these snack period discussions could extend well beyond twenty minutes if the teacher had a free period afterwards.

On this particular day I wanted to talk to Ms. Quinn about Crossroads. I had not seen her in a few weeks, and she asked me how my project was developing. I told her that I was expanding the scope of my work to include Crossroads, and she replied with somewhat of a warning:

MS. QUINN: Oh. Well, you should know that Crossroads is a very different sort of school than we are here at Pinnacle. I don't think you'll get a great sense of what things are like in Valley View schools over there at Crossroads because it's so radically different than any other school in the district.

SEAN: How so? *[I did not tell Ms. Quinn that I was already aware of the glaring demographic differences between the two schools, and that I had been engaging in non-participant observation at Crossroads for several weeks.]*

MS. QUINN: Well, I think literally everything is different. But, as a teacher, one thing that jumps out to me is the difference in the actual job of teaching and what that entails. At Pinnacle we're driven by points, so everything we do as teachers is really geared toward the academic achievement of our students. Crossroads teachers are prison guards. There isn't a focus on education because they have to keep control. So I feel very fortunate to have a crowd here that doesn't need controlling.

As I listened to her comparing and contrasting the two schools, I wondered whether she had ever visited Crossroads.

SEAN: Have you ever been to Crossroads?

MS. QUINN: No, but I drive by it all the time and it looks like some sort of correctional facility. It honestly looks like a little prison or something.

I was struck by the strength of Ms. Quinn's opinions on teaching at Crossroads given that she had never been there even for a visit, but I soon discovered that the mere mention of Crossroads elicited strong opinions from a variety of Pinnacle teachers. For instance, later that day as I was leaving campus, I had a brief conversation with Ms. Reynolds, the young substitute teacher. She grew up in Valley View and graduated from Valley View High School. I asked her if she had ever been to or taught at Crossroads. She frowned and shook her head. "I've never been. I refuse to teach there," she said with a chuckle. "I don't want to be terrorized."

Prison guards. Little prison. Terror. These comments by Ms. Quinn and Ms. Reynolds, and the images and emotions that they evoked, piqued my interest in comparing the day-to-day realities of teaching at each school. I became especially curious about any slippage between what Pinnacle teachers were describing and what it was actually like to teach at Crossroads.

What I ultimately found was that the classroom culture at Crossroads did not match the pervasive, widespread dysfunction and unrest that Pinnacle teachers like Ms. Quinn and Ms. Reynold's suspected. In fact, most Crossroads students were quiet and respectful during class periods, focused on completing their assignments and getting back on track toward graduation. However, nearly every Crossroads class contained a small handful of students who disrupted the classroom learning environment by talking loudly during quiet activities, telling profane jokes, or engaging in random outbursts of raucous teasing and horseplay. These behaviors distracted the rest of the class and forced the teacher to intervene in an attempt to restore and maintain order. Previous research has shown that disruptive behavior in class, even from just a few students, can impede learning and contribute to teacher dissatisfaction and burnout.[1] Indeed, the Crossroads environment presented various challenges to teachers, who were constantly managing their classrooms to keep recalcitrant students focused and on task. Crossroads teachers strived to be effective and to "get by" despite the challenges.

In contrast, the academic culture at Pinnacle was one in which students were, more often than not, steadfastly studious and academically engaged. Classroom interruptions were few and far between. When class was in session at Pinnacle, teachers had the freedom to teach unencumbered by distractions. As a result, Pinnacle teachers expressed satisfaction in their jobs and spoke of their good fortune to be teaching at such a school. Consider these comments from Mr. Jefferson, a history teacher in his mid-forties who had previously taught at a private high school in Los Angeles:

SEAN: What's it like to teach at Pinnacle?

MR. JEFFERSON: The kids here are really focused, I would say. They pay attention and they do the reading, which means that in class we can have wide-ranging discussions and go into

more depth on the topics that interest them. I can present complex arguments and they get it, and their written work is pretty thorough and enjoyable to read most
of the time.

Though Pinnacle and Crossroads were located in the same school
district in the same affluent suburb, they diverged sharply in terms
of the social and academic culture of a typical class in session. In the
following pages, I present data drawn from hundreds of hours of
observation in classrooms at Crossroads and Pinnacle. I highlight
the classroom experiences of teachers at each high school to show
the ways in which academic apartheid created separate and unequal
teaching and learning environments in the district. Furthermore,
I show how a teaching job at Crossroads stigmatized teachers due to
the school's substandard reputation, and how this stigma affected
teachers' opportunities to advance in their careers.

PINNACLE HIGH SCHOOL
AND THE FREEDOM TO TEACH

At Pinnacle, academic excellence was the norm and had been for
decades. Most Pinnacle students approached class time focused and
determined to learn the subject matter so that they could perform
well on any upcoming homework assignments, class projects, or
exams. Pinnacle teachers often told me that the best part of their
job was how committed to academics their students were. This, they
said, made their jobs easier and more rewarding. Ms. Potter, whom
we will now meet, was one of those teachers.

AP Chemistry Class at Pinnacle

Emily Potter was a White, middle-aged chemistry teacher and
basketball coach at Pinnacle. Her AP chemistry class provides a

representative example of a classroom setting at the school. The classroom culture that I observed during my first time hanging out in Ms. Potter's class was consistent with my numerous visits that followed. On that initial visit, during the spring of my first year of field work, there were thirty-two students present, and the racial composition of the class was as follows: twenty-four Asian (75%), seven White (22%), and one Latina (3%). Ms. Potter weaved between the desks, stopping briefly at each one to check students' homework assignments. Some students corrected the mistakes that Ms. Potter pointed out, while others chatted quietly with a classmate or two. Ms. Potter did not appear bothered by the abundance of talking; students were speaking quietly, and almost all were discussing the homework.

After she finished checking all of the assignments, Ms. Potter exited the room through a door at the rear. She left without informing the class that she would be stepping out. Many students raised or turned their heads to watch her leave, but their behavior did not otherwise change; they continued to talk with those seated around them, and the volume of these conversations remained at a low hum. Students did not use this period of unsupervised time to mingle sociably; to the contrary, many helped each other on class work. A girl helped a boy with his lab assignment. Another boy was struggling with a certain problem on the same lab assignment, so he asked a boy seated next to him what that student got for an answer and how he arrived at that answer. Pinnacle teachers often received assistance from their students in this fashion because Pinnacle students frequently acted as teachers' aides.

Crossroads teachers did not have this resource at their disposal. In fact, teachers at Crossroads often struggled simply to keep students on task. Classrooms at Crossroads tended to become unruly when they were not supervised. Students often became loud and boisterous when teachers were not speaking to the class, or when a teacher stood in their doorway to speak with a student or another faculty member outside.

Ms. Potter returned to the room roughly one minute after leaving. She approached the front of the room and, in a loud voice, asked students for their attention so that class could begin. The class quieted down immediately and fell completely silent, save for the sound of clicking pens and notebooks flapping open on desks. She asked students to take out their notebooks, though most had already done so. She told the class that they would be "starting a new unit" of study, and she stressed the importance of this unit. "This new unit will repeat itself, in different ways, for the rest of the year, so an understanding of it is critical to your success in this class from here on out." The class was intensely focused on the lecture, and nearly all students took copious notes.

At the conclusion of the lecture, which lasted about fifteen minutes, Ms. Potter distributed a thin packet of review problems. "Ok, take the next ten minutes or so to work through page one. Refer to your notes if you get stuck." A few moments later, Ms. Potter noticed a boy working on his lab assignment, which was supposed to be for that night's homework. She advised him to stop and to focus on the lecture. "Now is not the time to be working on your lab assignment." He responded right away, putting away the assignment and retrieving a notebook and pen from his backpack. Ms. Potter moved to sit with two girls who were working at one of the lab tables on the side of the room. With her back to the rest of the class, she helped them work through some of the review sheet problems. She had the freedom to focus on those two students without worrying about the behavior of the other thirty students over her shoulder, a luxury that teachers at Crossroads did not have.

Ms. Potter taught two sections of AP chemistry, and I visited her other section for the first time the following week. There were twenty-nine students in class that day—twenty-one were Asian (72%), six were White (21%), one was Latino (3%), and one was Black (3%). Students who had turned in their homework assignments were socializing quietly at their desks, laughing and joking. It was the last week of April, so college decisions were a hot topic among students. Two

Korean American boys chatted about their college choices, excited that one would be attending UC Berkeley and the other UCLA. The boys smiled and loudly high-fived each other.

Ms. Potter began passing back graded homework assignments, and many students spun around in their seats to compare scores with their classmates. An Indian American boy chuckled about the way that Ms. Potter had written "100%" on his homework. "Ok, let's get started" said Ms. Potter in a calm, commanding voice. A hush fell over the room, as if she had flipped a switch to turn off all sound except that of her own voice. Students retrieved a pen or pencil from their backpacks, opened their notebooks, and set their eyes on Ms. Potter.

Ms. Potter could count on her students to focus once she began the day's lesson. She did not need to spend any time quieting the classroom before beginning the lesson, or in maintaining her students' attention during the lesson. These luxuries allowed her to spend nearly all her time and energy on teaching. Indeed, students who paid close attention during class sometimes still struggled with certain concepts and needed extra instruction, but this fact underscores a core benefit of the common classroom culture at Pinnacle High School—the presence of students who assisted their teachers by casually helping classmates with challenging course material, both during class and during office hours. During my ethnographic observations at Pinnacle High School, I witnessed this type of informal peer tutoring daily in a variety of classes, and it constituted a tremendous pedagogical resource for Pinnacle teachers and students alike.

Ms. Potter was quick to express her gratitude for Pinnacle students' ability and willingness to help each other. These students made her job easier and more enjoyable:

SEAN: What's it like as a teacher to have students who help each other with the course material?

MS. POTTER: It's awesome! They help each other during class, which you've seen. But sometimes, particularly during office hours, if there are several students there and maybe they have different questions, I can call over another student like, "Hey, come help them with this," and it's great. I can't always anticipate what they'll have trouble with, but their classmates get it. It makes my job so much easier.

Ms. Potter's chemistry classes were representative of the normal, everyday classroom culture at Pinnacle. This classroom culture was calm and orderly, a state of affairs that promoted an acceptance of responsibility for studious behavior and attention to detail.[2] Education researchers have described the management dynamic of such classrooms as "person-centered" rather than "teacher-oriented":

> A person-centered classroom creates a balance between the wants of the teacher and the efforts and needs of the students, forming a collective classroom, including all persons in the classroom. A person-centered classroom is balanced between the needs of the teacher and the learner . . . a gradual progression of building trust and developing shared responsibility for the management of the classroom.[3]

In Ms. Potter's chemistry classes, she and her students worked together to manage the classroom. If a student was struggling with a concept or simply had a question about the material, a classmate was often close by to lend a helping hand. Ms. Potter counted on this help when class was in session and during her formal office hours, when students often received impromptu tutoring from one or more of their classmates. Crossroads teachers could not count on their students to function as pedagogical resources and partners in this way.

Although classes were typically much larger at Pinnacle than they were at Crossroads, Pinnacle teachers could afford to provide their students with far more individual attention than Crossroads teachers could because Pinnacle students often monitored and managed their classmates' behavior as well as their own. Students at Pinnacle helped each other and learned directly from each other during class, which decreased the pedagogical burden on teachers. Pinnacle teachers spent very little time managing student behavior in their classrooms whereas Crossroads teachers spent a significant portion of a typical class period managing student behavior.

Though the environment in Ms. Potter's classroom was the norm at Pinnacle, I did encounter a handful of exceptions—classes in which students' general level of focus was relatively inconsistent. In the following paragraphs we will meet Mr. Ventura and take a look inside one of his classes in session with a group of students who were not among Pinnacle's academic elite.

"The Students I Get Aren't Going to an Elite College": Marine Science Class at Pinnacle

Mark Ventura was a White science teacher in his mid-forties who had been at Pinnacle for seven years. He taught freshman biology, AP biology, and marine science. I became interesting in his marine science class because I had heard from several students that marine science was considered an "easy class" at Pinnacle. Prior to observing the class, I met with Mr. Ventura during the snack period, and he provided a brief overview of the course and its students:

MR. VENTURA: The class is mostly juniors and seniors who are looking for an interesting and fun class. It's not an honors or AP course, so most of the students I get aren't going to go to an elite college after they graduate. In fact, I usually have a few kids every year in marine science who end up over at Crossroads. So, it's a bit of a mixed bag in terms of the students I get in here, which is a bit different than most of the classes at Pinnacle where the achievement is so high. But most of my marine science kids do just fine.

As a lower-level course with a subject matter and workload that many students considered "fun" and "more relaxed," marine science was not the typical class at Pinnacle. These characteristics provide a useful comparison to the everyday classroom settings and demands on teachers at both Pinnacle and Crossroads.

My first day of observation in marine science came in November during my second full year of fieldwork. I arrived in the classroom just before the bell sounded to signal the start of the period. Mr. Ventura was standing at the front of the room with students seated in front of him in several rows of desks. There were thirty-four students in class that day: seventeen White (50%), eight Asian (23%), six Latinx (18%), and three Black (9%). The classroom was large enough to accommodate each of these students at desks and still have plenty of room for four large, island counter spaces behind the desks, each equipped with a sink and faucet in the center for cleanup during and after lab work and demonstrations.

Mr. Ventura grabbed a stack of graded homework assignments from his desk. He turned and faced his students, holding the papers up in front of his chest to call attention to them, and addressed the class:

MR. VENTURA: I'm going to pass these back, and I want you to take some time to look it over and see what you missed. Some of you did a poor job on this or didn't turn it in at all. Some of you turn things in late and put them on my desk, but don't put your name on it. Consequently, some of you received very low scores. Julia, you do this more than anyone else in my career.

Students chuckled at Julia's expense, but I did not know which student Julia was, so I could not make note of her reaction.

Mr. Ventura started walking up and down the rows of desks to return the assignments, but he soon paused to acknowledge the laughter around him. He was not amused:

MR. VENTURA: I was actually laughing just like all of you as I was grading these because some of you didn't think and just wrote down an answer. Maybe you're doing this in your other classes, too. But you can do a better job, and you *should* do a better job. Now, I see only one person doing what they're supposed to, and that's Sharon. Go over what you

got wrong. No one should be just sitting here staring off
into space.

Mr. Ventura finished distributing the assignments and told students
to quiet down. He instructed students to retrieve a recent, graded
lab assignment from their binders. Many students did not follow
directions on this assignment, he said, and he admonished the students collectively for generally sloppy work by comparing them to
another section of marine science students:

MR. VENTURA: You're missing easy points, and it's because you aren't
                doing all the work. You aren't caring. It's frustrating. You
                guys take longer [to complete lab assignments] than
                second-period—every time. It makes me want to take
                second-period to the aquarium next month and not you,
                ok? Bottom line, I don't want you to get a C or a D in this
                class if you don't need to.

The class then shifted gears to continue a California map assignment that they had been working on for the past two weeks. They
spent a few minutes labelling distances on the map, and then they
used the finished map to work through a set of word problems based
on the distances between various locations. Mr. Ventura called on
a different student to answer each question. Andy, a White junior
sitting near the back of the room, was not paying attention; he was
swiping and tapping at the screen of his iPhone, which he had con-
cealed beneath his desk and out of Mr. Ventura's sight. Andy's map
was not on his desk where it should have been. Mr. Ventura spotted
his map-less desk and called on him to answer the next question.
Andy was caught unprepared; he quickly slipped his phone into the
front pocket of his hoody and glanced up at Mr. Ventura, then turned
to face a nearby classmate and mumbled for help.

Mr. Ventura saw an opportunity to call Andy out in front of the
class, and he took it. "That's why you have a poor grade in this class—
because you look to your friend and say, 'you do it,' because you're

too lazy to do your own work." Andy bent down to flip through folders in his backpack, looking for his map. Mr. Ventura watched Andy fumble around in his backpack with a slight smile on his face, as if amused at the boy's disorganization. After a few seconds in this dubious spotlight, Andy pulled the map from his backpack. "Ok," said Mr. Ventura. "Now open up your map and focus."

Although he was clearly frustrated with the class that day, Mr. Ventura never raised his voice in anger and he smiled frequently. Mr. Ventura was not managing a rambunctious classroom, as was often the case for teachers at Crossroads. He was not trying to motivate students to do their work. He was not worried that some students would distract others. Rather, he was addressing a lack of attention to detail, urging his students to do a better and more thorough job on assignments by getting organized, paying closer attention, and following directions. Students did not talk back when Mr. Ventura lectured them about their academic engagement; they sat quietly and listened. In contrast, when teachers admonished a student or an entire class at Crossroads, one or more students typically argued with the teacher and questioned their authority or expertise. During such moments, students' verbal responses were occasionally laced with profanity, behavior that would have been exceedingly abnormal and unpopular among students at Pinnacle.

CROSSROADS TEACHERS AS CLASSROOM MANAGERS

On a cloudless Friday afternoon just before winter break, I arrived at Crossroads as the bell rang to signal the end of the lunch period. As I stepped out of the main office and into the courtyard, students were gathering their backpacks and trudging toward various classrooms, fanning out across the asphalt.

I spotted Ms. Owens, the assistant principal, sitting in a green golf cart on the opposite side of the courtyard. She had been driving the vehicle from one group of students to another, giving instructions as needed. She pulled up on a group of boys walking slowly toward one of the classroom buildings as they laughed with each other and shuffled through a small patch of grass. "Get to class on time, guys! Move faster!" she yelled. She stopped the cart next to the concrete table from which the boys had just left and noticed a candy-bar wrapper on the ground. "I don't like this trash. Who's gonna pick up this trash?!" Isaiah, a Black senior, turned around and replied: "Not me! I already did my slavery time!" Ms. Owens frowned and shook her head before bending down to pick up the wrapper. She then drove around the grass to park beside the main office. We exchanged hellos, and I asked her about student discipline on campus:

SEAN: Would you say that discipline is a large part of what goes on here and the job here?

MS. OWENS: Yeah, but I don't know that it's just direct discipline as opposed to more interventions to keep the kids on track. I mean, the discipline is horrible here, don't get me wrong. There's a lot of disrespectful, defiant behavior going on. There's not fights here or stuff like that, but the defiance and the disrespect from students can get pretty bad.

Crossroads was not supposed to be a disciplinary school, in the sense that district policy dictated that students were to be sent to Crossroads because they were credit deficient and not because of behavioral problems. But classroom disruptions were a common component of the academic culture at Crossroads, and I routinely observed teachers managing their classrooms and keeping students on task. These disruptions and provocations undermined teachers' authority and shifted the focus from teaching to keeping and restoring order. Thus, although most students in each class were quiet and respectful of each other and the teacher, nearly every class had a small handful of students who lacked academic focus and caused frequent disruptions in class. Such students were a source of frustration for the Crossroads students who were motivated to improve.

During a discussion at one of the outdoor picnic tables, Stacy, who was White, and Francine, who was Black, expressed frustration with some of their classmates' in-class antics:

STACY: I don't like how kids talk shit to their teachers here. It's so disrespectful!

FRANCINE: Yeah, totally! Did you hear that girl today in English?! She was just arguing and talking so much shit. That's why I could never be a teacher at a school like this, because if I'm a teacher, and a kid talked to me like that, I might smack them! I would get fired on my first day! It's hard to get work done when kids talk shit all during class. That's why I do a lot of my work out of class.

The students at Crossroads who recovered the most credits often had to develop special strategies to avoid distractions caused by their classmates. Those who were engaged—the ones who followed their teachers' directions on assignments, took notes, and completed their work thoroughly and on time—were business-like in their approach to recovering credit. The higher-achievers at Crossroads made a conscious effort to insulate themselves from the constant distractions coming from their classmates. Francine did coursework at an outdoor picnic table by herself during lunch or in an empty, quiet classroom. This strategy allowed her to get ahead and avoid disruptions. Others, like Stacy, obtained permission from teachers to listen to white noise on headphones during class to block out extracurricular antics around them. The state of affairs, then, was that Crossroads, a school established so that students behind on their coursework would be able to catch up on that work, featured a classroom culture rife with distractions that made credit recovery more difficult.

In the following pages we will go inside the classrooms of three Crossroads teachers: Mr. Reyes, Ms. Turner, and Mr. Gregory. The challenges that they faced were typical of what I observed in a variety of classrooms at the school, and their comments echoed those that I heard from many of their colleagues.

"Does It Smell Like Weed to You?": History Class at Crossroads

Mr. Reyes taught history at Crossroads. I arrived at his classroom one morning after the snack period, with enough time to have a brief conversation with him before the bell sounded to signal the start of class. There were eighteen students in class that day—seven Latinx (39%), six White (33%), four Black (22%), and one Asian (6%). I began talking with Mr. Reyes at his desk. Then, just as he was telling me how pleased he was with the progress that his students had made so far that year, a faint smell of marijuana filled the air, as if a tiny skunk were loose in the classroom. Mr. Reyes stopped abruptly in mid-sentence, with a look of incredulity on his face. "Does it smell like weed to you?" he asked. I nodded.

Mr. Reyes rose from his chair and walked slowly around the room between the rows of desks. Other students begin to pick up on the smell. "It smells like kush, for real!" someone shouted from the back of the room. A White boy named Jessie, whom I recognized because he had recently been transferred from Pinnacle, scolded the anonymous offender: "You gotta package it appropriately, bro. Use a vial or a zip-lock bag. C'mon!" Students laughed, because the implication of this comment was that it was fine to bring to school marijuana and other substances that were prohibited on campus as long as one took necessary steps to avoid getting caught.

Mr. Reyes arrived at Tobias's desk and looked down at him and those around him. Tobias was a short, slender boy, the son of Portuguese immigrants. He described himself as "Afro-Latino" because, as he put it, "some people think I'm Black and others think I'm Mexican." Tobias was a frequent disruptor in all of his classes. He looked up at Mr. Reyes and raised his hands, as if surrendering. "You can search my bag," he said. "I ain't got nothin' on me. I don't do that stuff at school." Mr. Reyes shook his head. "I don't want to search your bag," he replied. "I'd like to trust you." Mr. Reyes's brief investigation turned up no leads, and the smell hung in the air for the rest of the period.

"Goofing Around": English Class at Crossroads

Ms. Turner, a White English teacher at Crossroads in her late forties, had taught middle school for twenty years before coming to Crossroads. Now in her third year of teaching at the school, she had grown frustrated by her inability to cover as much material as she wanted in her classes due to the constant, unwelcome task of maintaining order. After a handful of brief conversations with Ms. Turner about students in her classes whom she described as "disruptive" or "class clowns," I started spending more time in her room so that I could see for myself the classroom culture that she was describing and the ways in which it affected her pedagogy.

One morning, in early October, I arrived at the school just in time to hear the bell signaling the start of third-period classes. I hustled across the courtyard, entered Ms. Turner's room, and sat down in the plastic chair at the edge of her desk. As I looked up to see who was present, Ms. Turner was circling the room, walking from table to table to check on each student. There were thirteen students in class that day: four Latinx (31%), four Black (31%), three White (23%), and two Asian (15%).

Ms. Turner arrived at a table near the front of the room and noticed that one of the boys there, Carlos, a Latino senior, was not working on his research paper assignment. She asked him what he was working on, and he replied that he had to give a speech the following day in one of his other classes and that he was way behind on that assignment and needed to work on it now. Ms. Turner responded by telling Carlos that he, and all other students, were only allowed to work on assignments for her class while they were sitting in her class. Carlos refused to accept this rule and argued with her about why he should have been able to work on an assignment for another class. She countered that he needed to manage his time more efficiently and responsibly so that he could complete all of his work on time without using class time inappropriately. He eventually acquiesced after she reminded him that he was behind on his work in her class, and therefore might not earn any credits in the class if he did not get to work.

Ms. Turner turned her attention to Eric, a White sophomore who had been at Crossroads for about two months. He was wearing a red t-shirt and basketball shorts that extended below his knees. He wore earrings in both ears and listened to rap music loudly through his headphones. He usually only used one ear bud to listen to the music, strategically placing it in his left ear so that Ms. Turner could not see it while she was sitting at her desk. On that particular day, however, Eric had given himself away; he had inserted both ear buds, one in each ear, and he was bobbing and swaying to the music as he sat at his desk.

"I'm tired of the music, Eric," said Ms. Turner as she approached his table near the back of the room. "Turn it off. It's been two weeks and you haven't done a thing in here." Eric looked up at her in disbelief. "But I've been working! I've been turning stuff in! Right?!" She told him to follow her to her desk, and he rose laboriously to shuffle across the room, dragging his feet on the carpet with every step. She pulled up his "grade report" on her desktop computer. The scores indicated that Eric was behind on his work and had a few assignments that he had yet to turn in. Ms. Turner tried to convince Eric that, with a few days of concerted effort, he could make up all of his work and be back on track. "You can still earn credits in this class," she said. Eric agreed that he could make up the work, nodding repeatedly and saying "ok" when Ms. Turner encouraged him to focus on his classwork. Eric walked slowly back to his seat and sat down in a heap.

Meanwhile, Matthew, a Black sophomore, was also listening to music as he surfed sports websites on a computer at the far end of the room. Ms. Turner asked him to stop listening to the music, but he replied that he should be allowed to keep listening because he was done with his work. Matthew and Eric were good friends, and Eric repeatedly left his seat to approach Matthew. He tapped Matthew in the back of the head, and Matthew spun around in his seat and cursed at Eric: "Ey, fuck you, bruh!" Eric cursed back at Matthew and they giggled in unison. Matthew cranked up the music volume, and he and Eric engaged in a constant back-and-forth of insults. The crude language used by the pair seemed to grow louder and more profane with each invective.

Ms. Turner was at her desk, helping another student with a portion of their paper. She was aware of Eric and Mathew and their disruptive behavior, but she did not intervene right away. After about thirty seconds of roughhousing, Eric and Matthew had an audience of several classmates watching them. Ms. Turner, again, asked Matthew to turn his music off, and she asked Matthew and Eric to refrain from "goofing around" with each other and disrupting their classmates. Eric walked slowly back to his seat while Matthew reminded Ms. Turner that he had finished his work for the day. She asked him to show her his finished work, and he told her where to find it near his backpack. "No, Matthew, *you* need to show it to *me*."

Matthew found a few papers in his backpack and brought them to Ms. Turner, who instantly determined that he was nowhere close to being finished with the assignments that he claimed to have completed. Shaking her head slowly, she told him what he needed to do, suggested a task for him to get started on, and sent him back to his usual seat at a table near her desk, far away from the computers. "You are so off task," she said to him as he slumped down heavily into his chair. "Why are you insulting me?" he replied. "It's not an insult; it's an observation," she returned in a kind, patient voice.

Eric asked to go to the bathroom and Ms. Turner excused him. A few minutes passed and Eric had not returned. Then, a booming voice reverberated around the main quad, clearly audible because the classroom door was propped ajar. *"Eric! You've got one minute!"* It was Mr. Johnson, the principal, who often stood observing outside the rear door to his office, which opened onto the courtyard. Ms. Turner left her desk to stand in the doorway and wait for Eric. He soon returned, and she reminded him to go straight to the bathroom and straight back next time, and not to disrupt and distract other teachers and students. Eric took a seat next to Matthew, and the two of them instantly resumed their relentless, profane banter. After several fruitless attempts to refocus their energy on the task at hand, Ms. Turner threatened to send Matthew and Eric to the main office.

Near the end of the period, Ms. Turner noticed a girl sleeping at her desk. She walked over to the girl and woke her. "You're behind," she whispered to the exhausted student. "I want you to get ahead and be the student you can be." Meanwhile, Eric and Matthew continued to playfully insult each other, and Ms. Turner was now fed up with them. She told them that she was going to send them to the front office and email Mr. Johnson to report their misbehavior. They responded by pleading with her to let them work and talk quietly until the period ended. Their pleas were interrupted by the bell, which saved them; Ms. Turner let them go with no punishment.

After class, when the room was empty, Ms. Turner explained to me that this had been a particularly difficult class period for her. Matthew and Eric had been "unable to leave each other alone." As such, they had accomplished very little in terms of coursework and impeded their classmates' progress. I witnessed dozens of class periods like this at Crossroads, periods in which a couple of rambunctious students set the tone with their disruptive displays.

"I Think You Should Work at a Library, Where Nobody Talks"

The following day brought more of the same for Ms. Turner's English class, this time during fourth-period with an entirely different group of students. I entered the classroom a few minutes after the bell, and students were working at the computers along the back wall. Ms. Turner was sitting at her desk and scrolling through the gradebook. She saw me as I passed through the doorway, smiled, and shook her head. I walked over and pulled up a chair to the edge of her desk. "I'm pretty frustrated today," she said. "I've been abused by students all morning." Joey, a White junior, asked if he could use the bathroom, and Ms. Turner said that he could not. She had been reading a novel, aloud, with her fourth-period students that week, but they had not made nearly as much headway as she had hoped and planned for.

Ms. Turner constantly managed her fourth-period English class that day, telling a small group of students to "quiet down," asking a girl to "please put your phone away," and frequently deriding the entire class for their lack of "maturity" and "focus." Tobias—the boy who had been suspected of bringing marijuana into Mr. Reyes's class—was often involved in these episodes. He questioned Ms. Turner's choice of profession: "I think you should work at a library, where nobody talks," he said with a straight face. Several students laughed at this suggestion. Ms. Turner smiled. "Maybe you're right," she replied as her smile faded.

Ms. Turner continued her attempt at facilitating a productive discussion of the novel, but her progress was mired by constant interruptions from a few members of the class. She moved a Latino boy, Alejandro, with whom Tobias had been constantly talking. A few minutes later, now sitting at a table on the other side of the room, Alejandro was still talking to those seated around him. Ms. Turner stopped the attempted class discussion to address Alejandro directly. "You talk everywhere, don't you? Unbelievable." He stared back at her and replied, "I told you [moving me] wasn't going to do anything." Alejandro turned and looked over his shoulder at Tobias and called out to him: "Yo, Toby! Wassup, bruh!" Tobias smiled and turned up the volume on his mp3 player; he had been listening to music for the past fifteen minutes or so, concealing his headphones under his sweatshirt hood, which he had pulled up over his ears.

I was back in Ms. Turner's fourth-period English class two weeks later. Students were taking a quiz on a documentary film that they had just finished watching in class. After about ten minutes of the quiz, Ms. Turner informed the class that they had one more minute to finish up. She began circling the room to collect the quizzes, finally arriving at David's desk. David, who was a fifteen-year-old sophomore, was one of two Filipino students at Crossroads that year. He told her to wait because he was not finished. "Hold up! I'm not done!" David turned away from Ms. Turner and continued writing an answer on his paper, but she had seen enough. "You need to leave class, David," she said, sternly. "I'm going to have someone pick you up."

She headed to her desk and emailed the front office to notify them of David's behavior. She then marched back across the room to find David hunched over his exam. "You're done! You! Are! Done!" she snapped as her frustrations boiled over. She snatched his paper off the table, crumpled it up into a tight ball, and dropped it into a nearby recycling bin. Scowling, David got up from his chair, put his backpack on, and stood quietly next to his table. He knew that Roberta, the lead security resource officer (SRO), would soon appear in the doorway to escort him to the office.

Tobias was watching closely, and he questioned David's response, egging him on. "Aw, c'mon, David! You're just gonna let her punk you like that?! That ain't right, bro!" David glanced at Tobias and his scowl deepened as he stared back toward to door. Roberta soon arrived, and David walked out of the room as soon as he saw her in the doorway. He had been through this before and he knew the drill—go speak with Ms. Owens, the assistant principal, in her office to determine if he should return to class, spend the rest of the day in the front office doing worksheets, or be sent home.

"At Least Act Like You're Listening"

The following week, I visited Ms. Turner's second-period English class for the first time. The class was watching a short video about Native American culture. Ms. Turner told me that the video was meant to serve as the introduction for the day's lesson. Groups of students were turned sideways, conversing noisily and ignoring the video. Ms. Turner shook her head, sighed heavily, and smiled—a sequence of expressions that communicated a lighthearted sense of resignation.

She paused the video to move a particularly disruptive student. The boy, a White student whom I did not recognize, was speaking loudly and profanely to the classmates sitting around him, alternating his gaze between his peers and his phone, which sat on his desk in plain sight. Cell phone use was quite common during class time despite the fact that cell phone use was prohibited in class. Students who used a phone during class tended to keep the device in their lap and partially under a desk or table, hidden from view. As such, this boy's open use of his cell phone was a flagrant expression of intentional rule-breaking and defiance.

Ms. Turner was now standing over the boy at his desk. "Look, I'm trying to help you. Listen!" He ignored her. "Ok! That's enough!" Ms. Turner looked up to address the class. "We're going to be moving to assigned seating if the disruptions continue! Some of you need to learn basic behavior so you can accomplish something in here!" Ms. Turner addressed the boy who had his phone on his desk. "Take your hood off and your hat off and put your phone away. You know the rules." The boy did as he was told. Ms. Turner sat back down at her desk and turned toward me with a smile. "They are such a chatty little class," she said, with a cheerful sarcasm that undoubtedly helped her cope with the unwelcome challenges of her job.

Ms. Turner walked to the front of the room as the video concluded. Students were sitting at long, rectangular tables, two to each table, facing the front of the room. Ms. Turner distributed copies of a magazine that contained an article that complemented the video. Students were supposed to work through a series of questions listed at the end of the article. "Ok, class. So now you have some tools to answer the video discussion section. Let's do a little warm-up before we work from the article. What's the mood of the video?" Students blurted out the following responses: "sad," "informative," "boring." Several were in constant conversation with each other, even when Ms. Turner was addressing the entire class. Some students asked questions about the video or the article, while others shouted out comments about some completely unrelated topic. Students did not raise their hands to speak, so they were constantly talking over one another. Ms. Turner attempted to read a portion of the article aloud, but the chatter continued as she read. She got through two sentences before she stopped and closed her magazine. "When the teacher is reading, please at least *act* like you're listening. *Please.* It makes me feel good. It makes me feel like a teacher. I want to feel like a teacher, alright?"

. . . . .

I want to feel like a teacher. Those words epitomize the experience of teaching at Crossroads. Whereas class time was highly structured at Pinnacle, with a clear set of objectives for the class period and often a PowerPoint presentation and lecture from the teacher, the lion's share of class time at Crossroads was loose and unstructured. The lack of structure at Crossroads was meant to give students greater flexibility to work at their own pace, and to give teachers opportunities to tailor coursework to students' specific needs. But this approach backfired; the chaotic nature of class time at Crossroads often left students to decide which worksheets and other assignments to complete, and it quickly exposed the students who were less dedicated to their credit recovery. Students who had trouble getting started on their work, staying on task, and completing their work struggled in the Crossroads environment since they were often expected to choose what to work on during class. Students who were less assertive academically tended to lean heavily on the teacher for help, which pulled the teacher away from others who also needed assistance. Crossroads's smaller class sizes were supposed to allow students to receive more individual attention than was possible at any of the comprehensive high schools, but this was often inhibited by the need for teachers to spend a considerable amount of instructional time deal with deviant classroom behavior.

Ms. Turner's experience with Tobias is a case in point, as he could hardly begin a class assignment without repeatedly asking her—or any of his other teachers, for that matter—for help. For instance, during one class period I observed Tobias wondering, aloud, how to revise an autobiography assignment. "Tobias, I emailed your autobiography back to you with comments and suggestions, so check your email," replied Ms. Turner. "You need to look at the directions because you didn't even give me a full draft." Tobias lowered his head in disappointment. "She's the teacher," he sneered to a small audience of classmates around him. "She's supposed to help me."

Ms. Turner, who had been at the computers assisting students on revising their autobiographies, walked across the room to her desk, where I was sitting. She shook her head and described to me how Tobias's behavior affected her job:

MS. TURNER: Tobias needs *so* much attention, both directly from me but
                      also from his peers. He takes up so much oxygen in here
                      that it's hard for me to help other students unless I ignore
                      him or just decline to help him with every little thing.
                      Sometimes I can't teach because I have to sort of contain
                      him and refocus him.

Tobias was up out of his seat now, complaining that he should not be expected to get anything done in the class if he was not getting help. He threw his arms up, looked toward the ceiling, and mumbled a few expletives. A few students were entertained by Tobias's outburst, but others appeared to be growing tired of his incessant calls for help. Two girls asked Tobias how Ms. Turner could help him write his autobiography, given that he knew his own life better than anyone else. "*You* know the most about *you, right?* So just get it done, dude. I did mine in, like, 20 minutes," one of them said. Ms. Turner overheard this conversation and others around the room. "Class! This is individual work! If you need help, I can help you, but please be productive!" When the bell sounded a few minutes later to signal the end of the class period, several students had already packed their bags in anticipation.

A MISMATCH BETWEEN STUDENTS' GOALS
AND THE CROSSROADS CURRICULUM

Mr. Gregory, the thirty-year-old math and science teacher at Crossroads, had taught at a comprehensive high school in another Southern California district for one year before moving to Valley View and starting at Crossroads. I met Mr. Gregory when he was in his second year at Crossroads, and he felt as though the job of teaching there was fundamentally different than teaching at a comprehensive high school, particularly in an affluent, high-achieving suburb like Valley View. For Mr. Gregory, this difference was tied to his perception of Crossroads's primary purpose in the district:

SEAN: What do you see as Crossroads's mission as a school, its purpose?

MR. GREGORY: I think Crossroads as a whole is about teaching students simple facts of life. The biggest question I get from students in math or science is, "When will I ever use this? How will this help me at a real job?" And I'm like, "It's not about what we're learning in the book; it's about how your *behavior* is. You're learning how to act in the adult world." For us here, it's much more about getting you prepared for life right after high school. At the end of high school, you should be college- or career-ready. And I think that, based off of our curriculum, you could go to a two-year college if you focused, because we are going to give kids the skills that they need for that, but I just don't think that a lot of our kids are going to go that route; I think they're gonna go into the workforce. And right now, with a lot of them, if they came and I was their boss, they wouldn't last very long.

SEAN: Would you hire them?

MR. GREGORY: Good question. Probably not, just based off of what they have to offer. But I also know them because I teach them. If they sat down and did the right things in an interview, and I didn't already know them, then maybe. But if I did hire them, they would not last, because if they actually have to work, they just don't have that strong work ethic. And students always say, "Well, I'll get paid at a job. I'll get my money. Here, you don't give me anything." And it's one of those things where I'm like, "We do give you something; we give you credit every day. That is your paycheck. Did you get your credit today, or not?"

SEAN: So these students aren't particularly prepared for post-secondary education.

MR. GREGORY: Right.

SEAN: But you're also saying that they're not particularly prepared for the workforce?

MR. GREGORY: Exactly, and that's tough. I come in here every day and I do my job. "Here's your work. Here's how you should behave. You should be sitting down," and all that good stuff. So, I guess I'm preparing them for how to behave as employees, but we don't have a full college-prep curriculum and we don't have a lot of options for them to build specific job skills.

Mr. Gregory believed that the district was "setting up Crossroads kids for failure," and that dozens of Crossroads students were out of place at the school. He felt that students were out of place because the curriculum neither prepared them well for college or a job directly after high school. Moreover, the job required him to teach college-prep material to students who often aspired to get a full-time job after high school in lieu of college enrollment. The following exchange that I had with Mr. Gregory further illustrates these points:

SEAN: When I talk to the school leadership at Pinnacle about Crossroads, in the context of a decision to try to send a student here to Crossroads, I hear a lot about what's similar about the two schools. But it seems as though there are way more differences than similarities.

MR. GREGORY: Yeah, definitely way more differences! But, from what I've heard, the district expects the Crossroads curriculum in any of our classes to be the same as the curriculums for the other high schools in the same class. Like, my earth science class isn't supposed to be different from the other earth science classes [at the comprehensive high schools]. We're going over all of the academic vocabulary and ideas about how the earth works, and we're doing all of this universe stuff, and it's very abstract and it's very hard for the students to comprehend, like the size of the Milky Way and stuff like that. And that abstractness is what they have a real tough time understanding, but those are the standards for the earth science curriculum—that students understand how big the Milky Way Galaxy is, and this proportional relationship with the universe, and how many galaxies there are, and so on. So . . .

[He paused, searching for the right words to make his point.]

. . . So, what we have here is these kids who aren't academically inclined who are still being held to those same academic standards that they've already been failing at this whole time, and yet we're still spinning the same wheel over and over. As a teacher, that's frustrating because it's hard for me to be effective with that approach.

SEAN: How do you deal with that—with the apparent mismatch between many of these students' aspirations on one hand, and what is being asked of them on the other?

MR. GREGORY: You know, you try to be creative with it, and you try to show students the academic progress that they're making. But, when you just have flat out refusal to do anything, it's mutiny. What do you do? One against nineteen when they're all saying, "We're not doing any work." Or maybe three will commit to doing work that day and the other sixteen won't. I mean, at the end of a given day, maybe four or five out of nineteen will earn their credit for that day. And I don't like that portion of it. I don't like that aspect of teaching at Crossroads. And I try to think, "What can I do differently to make things a little more interesting?" That's a tough part, because [students] ask, "Do you really like this science thing? Do you really care about how big the Milky Way Galaxy is?" And I say, "Yeah, I find it interesting." At the end of the day, is that knowledge helping me do anything? Not really, but I just find it

interesting. I like to learn little tidbits and I like to gain
knowledge for knowledge's sake. For kids over at
Pinnacle, learning about this abstract stuff might present
an opportunity to do well on an exam. But many of these
Crossroads kids are hungry for knowledge that they can
apply right away and use in the real world. We don't really
offer that here so they aren't focused, which makes it
really hard to teach them anything.

Which students benefit from acquiring "abstract" knowledge in
a class, such as the size of the Milky Way Galaxy? Such information
helped the majority of Pinnacle students because most Pinnacle students were preparing for the next step in their academic careers—
enrollment at a four-year college or university. Learning and being
tested on abstract concepts, or concepts that they may never use
again in school or their careers, was part of that journey, and many
Pinnacle students approached all of their classes with a sense of purpose to learn the material regardless of their interest in the subject
or career goals. They knew that they needed to do well no matter the
material so that they could move on to the next phase of their education. Their path was stressful, yet straightforward.

The path forward for Crossroads students was uncertain and the
final destination was often in doubt. Their options for postsecondary
education were limited. They asked Mr. Gregory if he cared about
how big the Milky Way Galaxy was because they asked the same
questions of themselves. For most students at Crossroads, gaining
academic knowledge for the next step as a means to an end had far
less relevance than it did for Pinnacle students since the goals that
Crossroads students were working toward were so often undefined,
unclear, or undesirable.

For Mr. Gregory and many of his colleagues, this mismatch between
demands of the curriculum and students' interests and aspirations
presented profound challenges to teaching. One such challenge was
the issue of discipline. Like Ms. Turner, Mr. Gregory identified discipline and behavior problems as his greatest professional challenge,

which was telling because Crossroads was, first and foremost, a school for students who were behind on their coursework and not a school for those who had previously engaged in deviant behavior. Mr. Gregory saw a direct connection between the concentration of struggling students at Crossroads and the persistent behavior problems that teachers at the school dealt with. This meant that the job tasks when teaching at Crossroads were unique in the district:

MR. GREGORY: Compared to the teachers at the comprehensive high schools, I have a lot more discipline stuff that I have to deal with. And some teachers here say, "Oh, teachers wouldn't put up with this behavior at a comprehensive school." Well, teachers don't *have* to put up with this at comprehensive schools! At those high schools, you might have a class of thirty-five and thirty-four of them are working hard, and you can deal with that.

SEAN: But it's not that simple here.

MR. GREGORY: It's not that simple here. It would be nice if it were, but it's not.

SEAN: So, here, if a student has an issue in the class and they start acting up, what happens most of the time?

MR. GREGORY: Most of the time I try to go, "Ok, that's not acceptable behavior and you need to correct it in whatever manner is appropriate." You're out of your seat? You need to sit down. You're talking out loud? You need to stop talking. Until it gets to the point of outright refusal and disrespect. And, again, even teachers here at Crossroads say, "This behavior just wouldn't be tolerated at Pinnacle! They don't do it like this at the other schools!" But, at the same time, I'm like, "We're not the other schools; we're continuation school, so we have a different population than everybody else." Some of our students don't necessarily want to be here. We have the students that are going to be disruptive and they're all funneled to us here. So, yes, shouting in class at Pinnacle might be an immediate two-day suspension for a kid. Here, shouting in class, if I did that to every single student, suspended them, pretty soon I wouldn't have a class.

SEAN: And I've seen things here where one student will start acting up in class and then three more will jump in.

MR. GREGORY: Oh yeah! Happens all the time. It snowballs really fast.

SEAN: Why do you think that happens? Because it seems like it's
almost contagious in those moments.

MR. GREGORY: It is, it is. It's that mentality where, "Well, he's doing it, so
I can do it." And there's a higher threshold for that behav-
ior stuff here because of our unique student population,
so that snowball can happen really fast.

SEAN: Is that one of the hardest things about teaching here?

MR. GREGORY: Yeah, the discipline just never ends. We have teachers
that have been here for two decades and still kick people
out for behavior stuff. I mean, I don't feel that there's
some trick with how to deal with students. It's the system
we're in. It's the environment that has been created and
the cards that all of us, teachers and students, have been
dealt.

It's the system we're in. It's the environment that has been created.
Mr. Gregory blamed the behavior problems at Crossroads on the
continuation school model and its segregation of credit deficient students. In trying to address the problem of credit deficient students,
the district had "created" other challenges.

· · · · ·

As these snapshots of classroom culture at Pinnacle and Crossroads
show, the district's continuation school model resulted in separate
and unequal schools with disparate teaching and learning environments. At Crossroads, teachers spent considerable time managing their students instead of teaching them. In-class disruptions,
which were frequent at Crossroads, undermined teachers' authority and shifted the focus from teaching to a persistent need to keep
and restore order in otherwise disorderly classrooms. Consequently,
teachers frequently expressed frustrations in their inability to teach,

and described their jobs as fundamentally disciplinary in nature. Many, like Ms. Turner, reported that on many days they did not feel much like teachers at all. Some, like Mr. Gregory, recast their jobs as helping students "prepare for life."

In the credit recovery environment at Crossroads, all students were behind on their coursework. As a result, teachers constantly reminded students of their progress—or lack thereof—and referenced students' credit deficiency as leverage when they felt the need to motivate students to stay on task. The behavior of students in Ms. Turner's class demonstrates how difficult it often was to keep students on task in such an environment. Research has shown that teachers have greater success in managing student behavior when students feel a strong connectedness and belonging to their classmates, classroom, and school.[4] But this sense of community was difficult for teachers at Crossroads to cultivate due to the school's status as a continuation school and the stigma that was attached to that label. It was hard for teachers to inspire feelings of community and belonging in their students when most of those students did not want to be there at all. Being there made them feel like castaways and failures.

THE STIGMA OF TEACHING AT CROSSROADS

In chapter 2 we saw how Crossroads's status as a continuation school supported various negative perceptions of the students who went there. For students and parents throughout the district, Crossroads was widely stereotyped as a place for "bad" kids who engaged in "risky behavior," and whose families did not place enough value on education. These stereotypes were undoubtedly stigmatizing for Crossroads students, who often felt dejected and embarrassed to be there.

Crossroads teachers also had to confront the stigma associated with continuation school in a district as academically competitive as Valley View. Hints of the stigmatization of teachers emerged in the job application process. When a prospective teacher applied to a teaching position in Valley View, they submitted to the district a single application that was then forwarded to any schools that were hiring. Mr. Gregory recalled a conversation he had with Mr. Johnson's assistant, Louise, during his application process. Louise called Mr. Gregory to offer him an interview for an open position. According to Mr. Gregory, Louise asked if he was clear that Crossroads was a continuation high school, if he had any questions about the ways that a continuation high school was different from a comprehensive high school, and if he were willing to interview for a position at a continuation school. Louise added that a lot of applicants turned down offers to interview at Crossroads because they did not want to teach at a continuation school. A popular opinion among teachers throughout district was that Crossroads teachers were "pigeonholed" and stereotyped as less competent than their counterparts who taught at comprehensive sites, as this belief helped render teaching jobs at Crossroads as unattractive. Crossroads's administrative staff members were aware of these negative perceptions, which is why they made sure that any teacher they booked for an interview was committed to teaching in a continuation school setting. They wanted prospective teachers to be fully aware of what they were signing up for.

Jonathan Angulo, a former history teacher at Crossroads who recently accepted a job as an assistant principal at a nearby comprehensive high school, corroborated the notion that Crossroads teachers were viewed as less competent than their peers at comprehensive schools. Mr. Angulo felt disrespected and devalued at district-level meetings and conferences, where teachers from comprehensive high schools would avoid sitting with him and his Crossroads colleagues, or easily dismiss his comments and suggestions on various pedagogical issues. He began looking for another job just a few weeks after he was hired at Crossroads because he did not want to "get stuck" teaching there:

MR. ANGULO: I didn't want to be labeled as a continuation-school teacher and get stuck teaching at an alternative school for the rest of my career. I had to get out, and a lot of new teachers at Crossroads felt that way when I was there. And I still talk to a couple of the new teachers over there and they still feel that way. Even if they stay a few years, they're always looking for a way out at the first good chance.

Two years prior, Mr. Angulo had nearly landed an assistant principal job at a neighboring high school. He made it through the first round of interviews and was one of the finalists, but he was not offered the position. Determined to leave Crossroads, he arranged a meeting with the principal of that high school to receive detailed feedback on his application, and he candidly recalled their conversation:

MR. ANGULO: The principal was very blunt with me. She told me that the biggest reason I'm not getting the job was because I'm coming from Crossroads, and they were concerned about my ability to adjust to their environment. And the other thing is that they were very, very worried about what their school community would think to have a teacher from Crossroads come in. How would she explain that to the parents? She didn't feel that she could explain it, so I didn't get the job. I understood, and I appreciated her honesty, but that was tough to hear because I knew that I could do the work.

Mr. Angulo's opportunities to teach elsewhere in the future were limited because of the negative stereotypes and assumptions about Crossroads and its teachers that circulated throughout the district. He felt a sense of urgency—that if he did not get out as quickly as possible, he might have to teach at Crossroads or another continuation school indefinitely. This and other similar concerns made it hard for Crossroads to recruit and retain teachers, especially those whose skills were in demand elsewhere.

. . . . .

Research on pedagogy has found that teachers in public schools consistently mention "classroom management" and "student discipline" as among the most important issues that they face,[5] but Pinnacle High School and Crossroads High School present important exceptions. Though both high schools were located in the same affluent, suburban school district, the day-to-day job of teaching and classroom management differed drastically between them. The institutional success frame at Pinnacle—stellar grades on a challenging course schedule, impressive test scores, and eventual acceptance into a highly ranked four-year university—set a schoolwide standard that supported teachers in their work. Pinnacle students were, by and large, studious and focused during class time. I rarely observed Pinnacle teachers attempting to quiet their students during class or otherwise refocus them on the task at hand, and I did not observe a single case of a Pinnacle teacher struggling to maintain order and decorum in the classroom. When one or more students became disruptive in any way during class, as teenagers are wont to do from time to time, it was almost always other students who called the behavior out, typically with a brief and discreet comment. The result was that behavior problems were rare, and Pinnacle teachers had the freedom to teach without the burden of keeping students on task or disciplining them.

Meanwhile, at Crossroads, teachers were compelled to spend considerable instructional time managing student behavior so that those who were committed to credit recovery could complete their work in an environment where distractions were minimal. In fact, I found that Crossroads teachers frequently spent just as much time managing their students and preventing classroom disruptions as they did teaching course material. As a result, accomplished and experienced teachers tended to avoid taking jobs at Crossroads. Researchers have suggested that such avoidance may limit the quality of instruction that students receive in schools that teachers avoid.[6]

A position as a Crossroads teacher marked one as less capable than their counterparts teaching at comprehensive high schools. This transfer of stigma from the institution to the individual worked against Crossroads teachers at district staff development meetings, where they often found themselves isolated and ignored. Thus, Crossroads's young teachers, and those that were early in their careers, usually kept an eye out for other teaching gigs to apply to.

The situation was quite different for Pinnacle teachers, who frequently expressed to me their sense of accomplishment in landing a job at Pinnacle, how it was an ideal professional setting for them, and that they hoped to remain there for many years. This contrast dovetails with extant research showing that teacher turnover is roughly twice as high at under-resourced schools as it is in highly resourced schools,[7] and that the primary reason why young and new teachers seek to leave under-resourced schools is job dissatisfaction.[8] Past research has also revealed a negative relationship between rates of teacher turnover and student achievement.[9] In other words, higher rates of teacher turnover are associated with lower student achievement. This was a concern at Crossroads, given that students were frequently taught by teachers who were on the job market and looking to teach elsewhere.

The most capable students at Crossroads succeeded, in part, because they were able to ignore the provocations of their classmates and maintain a singular focus on their work. Though provocateurs were a small minority of Crossroads students, they were highly influential in creating distractions during class time. As such, and in vivid contrast to the general classroom culture at Pinnacle, high achievers at Crossroads rarely interacted with their peers during class time, and there was not an organic culture of peer tutoring and support. Such a culture did exist at Pinnacle, and both students and teachers benefited from it.

When struggling students are funneled to one school, the result is a set of classroom environments that do little to motivate apathetic students. Class periods are challenging and distracting for students who are motivated, and detrimental to the pedagogical freedom and efficacy of teachers. The distinction between Crossroads and Pinnacle was startling in this regard.

Over the course of my field work I found that the public education system in Valley View worked best for those who had access to resources that could help them achieve their goals. This was true for students, teachers, *and* parents. In chapter 4, I will introduce you to a group of Pinnacle parents who provide a striking example of the utility of co-ethnic community resources.

4 The Institutionalization of Ethnic Capital

One morning during spring break, I met Wendy, a Korean mother of two teenage daughters, to discuss her decision to move from South Korea to Valley View and enroll her kids at Pinnacle. Wendy explained that academics were "highly competitive in Korea," and the school day was long and exhausting for her children—"from sun-up to sun-down," she said. She and her husband worried about the stress that their daughters were constantly under as a result of the academic culture and schedule in Seoul, South Korea, so they decided that she would leave for America with the girls while he stayed behind temporarily to continue his job as a software engineer with Samsung. They considered New York City and Seattle because they had friends or extended family in those cities, but they eventually chose Valley View with some help from local Korean media:

SEAN: How did you choose Valley View?

WENDY: Valley View is well known in Korea, especially in Seoul. Valley View is in the newspapers and magazines and on television

shows advertised as the best place to live in America because
of the public school system and the large number of Koreans
here. And actually Pinnacle is known in Korea, too. Korean
families move to Valley View and want to live close to
Pinnacle so their kids can go there.

Wendy's move to Valley View was reflective of a pattern of migration to Valley View in recent decades. Not long ago, Valley View was
a mostly racially White suburb known for its balmy weather and stellar public schools. The weather and schools are still highly regarded,
but, in recent decades, the city's ethnoracial landscape has changed
considerably as a result of contemporary immigration. Valley View
is, today, recognized as a destination city for East Asian immigrants,
particularly those from South Korea and China. Asian population
growth in the city has significantly outpaced that of other groups[1];
between 2000 and 2010, the Asian population nearly doubled, from
43,042 to 83,176 individuals—an increase of over 93%. The overall
share of Asians in Valley View also increased markedly during that
time, from 29% in 2000 to 40% in 2010. In 2010, Chinese- and
Korean-Americans comprised the majority of Valley View's Asian
population, at 22% and 32%, respectively, and over 20% of the total
population combined, regardless of ethnic or racial background.
Meanwhile, though the overall number of Whites also increased
during this period, the percentage of Whites fell from 61% to 50%
amid a wave of new non-White residents. The Los Angeles Times and
other local newspapers closely tracked these demographic trends
and the public response to them, publishing articles and op-eds
about how Asians had become the "dominant group" in Valley View
and what this surge of Asian residents meant for the future of Southern California's suburban communities.

Part of my motivation for this project was a desire to understand
how this sort of ethnoracial change affected suburbs like Valley
View. In what ways has the steady increase of Asian residents in Valley View affected local schools and districts? To what extent have

Asian immigrant families had to adjust to existing school cultures, and to what extent has existing school culture changed in response to an increase in Asian students? What factors influence the nature and direction of these adjustments?

IMMIGRANTS, ETHNIC RESOURCES, AND ACADEMIC ACHIEVEMENT

Immigration scholars once posited that immigrant incorporation into a new society followed a steady trend of boundary dissolution in which immigrants become increasingly like natives in their way of life.[2] However, this theory of immigration was limited in applicability because it was based on the upward mobility of White, European immigrants and their American-born children in the early twentieth century. Subsequently, other scholars contributed important theoretical modifications to our understanding of immigrant incorporation, noting that immigrants of various ethnic and racial backgrounds settle into various social and economic strata in the United States. These varied trajectories of incorporation are based on a combination of a group's pre-migration social class status and the social and political climate in the receiving country.[3]

Additional studies indicate that immigrants often conform to and adopt certain aspects of mainstream society in the receiving country while purposefully preserving key elements of their ethnic and immigrant cultures and identities.[4] Moreover, a large body of research indicates that, for ethnic minority immigrant populations, the adaptation and preservation of longstanding cultural customs within co-ethnic communities can be advantageous for the academic engagement and achievement of the second generation.[5] The consistent underlying premise linking this immigration canon is that immigrant incorporation is an overwhelmingly one-sided process in which new immigrants gradually absorb and adopt essential elements of the American mainstream.[6]

Few have considered that immigrants—rather than conforming to prevailing ideas, values, and customs—can also greatly influence dominant cultures[7] and institutions[8] in a new land. For instance, some Asian immigrant groups have altered mainstream conceptions of academic achievement in American schools. Asian American students are vastly overrepresented among those attaining the highest grades and test scores at all grade levels, and those enrolled in elite public and private universities.[9] In Silicon Valley, sociologists Tomás Jiménez and Adam Horowitz found that East- and South-Asian immigrants' widespread academic success led to a reshuffling of the racial hierarchy in schools, such that White students and "Whiteness" came to be associated academic mediocrity.

Asian cultural traits and values are often cited by social and political pundits to explain why Asian Americans, on average, exhibit the highest levels of academic achievement of any racial group. For example, in 2015, prominent *New York Times* op-ed columnist Nicholas Kristof wrote an editorial on the subject,[10] an essay so popular that it was later translated into Korean and Chinese for its readers. Kristof pointed to "East Asia's long Confucian emphasis on education," and Asian Americans' "hard work, strong families and passion for education" as primary reasons for their overrepresentation on the top rungs of academic achievement. In so doing, he reduced Asian American achievement to cultural traits and values, and hailed Asians as a racial group that other groups—Blacks, Latinos, and, in some cases, Whites—would be wise to emulate. Other best-selling authors have made similar culturally-based comparisons that juxtapose Asian success against the cultural deficits and failings of other ethnic and racial groups.[11]

Social scientists have interrogated such comparisons for decades, arguing that they perpetuate problematic stereotypes of Asians as a homogenous, "model minority" group.[12] Some scholars have challenged strictly cultural explanations for racial achievement gaps by highlighting the far more influential role played by factors such as pre-migration socioeconomic status and education levels. For example, the average Chinese citizen emigrating to America has, on average, more years of education and higher levels of wealth than both the average Chinese citizen living in China and the average American.[13] Sociologists Jennifer Lee and Min Zhou have found that, for many East Asian immigrants, a combination of favorable pre-migration socioeconomic status and a strong immigrant work ethic in the United States have led to the adoption of an exacting cultural "success frame," in which excellence in school and a prestigious professional career are standards to live by.[14] Indeed, the most empirically rich and rigorous studies of recent years convincingly demonstrate that cultural expressions of achievement among Asian Americans have deep structural roots.[15]

The Utility of Ethnic Capital

For immigrant youth, skill development is influenced by the strength of co-ethnic networks in the United States, and the co-ethnic support system of resources, or "ethnic capital," that these networks provide.[16] Ethnic capital is particularly crucial for immigrants' educational attainment,[17] and immigrant groups often access educational resources through co-ethnic community organizations.[18] For instance, South Korean and Chinese families in Valley View made use of several co-ethnic educational resources throughout the city, such as community centers, churches, and standardized test preparation services. These neighborhood resources provided reliable social and cultural capital for South Korean and Chinese families. However, while social scientists have amply shown how sources of ethnic capital *external* to schools can promote educational attainment among the children of immigrants, far less is known about ethnic community resources that may exist *within* public schools and other mainstream institutions.

Over the course of my fieldwork in Valley View, I found that Korean immigrant parents partnered directly with schools and school districts to facilitate the academic success of their children.

Specifically, I found that Korean parents were able to embed their ethnic community resources *within* institutions such as Pinnacle High School. Nesting these resources within schools promoted Korean parental involvement and provided distinct advantages for Korean students. I refer to this state of affairs as the *institutionalization of ethnic capital*—ethnic community resources that are embedded within an institution. The institutionalization of ethnic capital provided Korean families with continuous access to a support system that helped them navigate the local school district and reap maximum benefit from it.

. . . . .

Like most public high schools, Pinnacle had a PTA that facilitated communication and collaboration between parents, teachers, and students. The PTA raised money for technology enhancements and classroom supplies, helped coordinate various special events, and hosted a series of invited speakers to address pertinent topics such as applying to colleges and summer internship opportunities for students. The group was open to all parents and always intent on recruiting new members.

The Pinnacle PTA was active and influential, but it was not the only parent group on campus. In 1997, South Korean parents of Pinnacle students established the Korean Parent Teacher Association (KPTA). Only Korean parents were eligible to join the KPTA. The KPTA held its own group meetings and hosted its own events. The group typically had between forty and fifty active members and held its monthly meetings in the school's multi-purpose room. Pinnacle was the only high school in Valley View with an ethnically-segregated parent organization.

The KPTA was a reliable source of ethnic capital for Korean American students and their parents. According to the Pinnacle KPTA website, the organization's primary functions were as follows:

"[We] reach out to our Korean community to create a better understanding of the public school system and to bridge the cultural gap between parents, students and teachers. We also focus on establishing the Korean identity among the Korean students coming from various cultural backgrounds and helping those students adjust to school life, as well as raising funds to improve the educational environment and promoting awareness of Korea among other ethnic groups in our school communities."

The KPTA framed Korean culture as exceptional and thus responsible for the impressive academic achievements of Korean students at Pinnacle. Raising substantial sums of money for the school enhanced the reputation and status of Korean students and families on campus. Moreover, the KPTA was engaged in a perpetual campaign to increase teachers' knowledge of important Korean cultural customs, and to encourage teachers to spread that knowledge to colleagues. These pursuits aimed to facilitate school participation among Korean parents and to boost the educational opportunities and achievement of Korean students.[19]

"LANGUAGE SHOULD NOT BE A BARRIER"

Wendy, whom we met at the start of this chapter, was a proud member of the KPTA. She was thankful for her membership because it provided the social support that she and her children needed while her husband was still overseas in Seoul. Immigration scholars refer to transnational immigrant families like Wendy's as "astronaut families"—families in which one parent emigrates with the child or children ("satellite kids") to settle abroad, while the other parent stays behind in the country of origin to work and support the family financially.[20] In the cohort of East Asian families who came to American in the 1980s and 1990s, both fathers and mothers were likely to emigrate together with the family, and both were likely to be in the American labor force. Stay-at-home motherhood has been more common in recent cohorts of East Asian immigrants.[21] The rise of the astronaut family—particularly middle-class and upper-middle-class Taiwanese, Chinese, and Korean immigrant families—happened around the turn of the twenty-first century, coinciding with the increase in stay-at-home motherhood among that cohort in the United States.[22] Such families are sometimes referred to as "wild-geese families" in the Korean case, and many of the Korean families at Pinnacle were living in this transnational manner.[23] The "wild-geese" arrangement allows families to maintain and reap the financial benefits of an established career in the country of origin, but also tap into the educational advantages of raising children in the United States.[24]

Among wild-geese families in the United States, parents often lack the language proficiency or local knowledge about American schooling that would enable them to participate fully in their children's education.[25] Hannah Kim, president of the KPTA, recognized these challenges among co-ethnic members of the Pinnacle community. Hannah was born in Seoul and moved to Valley View with her parents in the early 1980s when she was in middle school. Hannah was a Pinnacle alumna and, when I met her, had two sons enrolled at Pinnacle. She pursued the position of KPTA President—an elected position that came with a two-year term—because she felt as though her three decades of residence in Valley View, as well as her understanding of Pinnacle as both a former student and current parent, left her uniquely qualified for the position.

In her conversations with me, she described the KPTA as a "bridge" for Korean parents between the way things are in Korea, and the institutions and cultural customs in American that may be unfamiliar and confusing to them:

HANNAH: A lot of these parents that join our organization are recent immigrants. So, number one, they're not familiar with the educational system here in America because they did not go to school here. Number two, they join for resources and information because of the language barrier. Number three,

> they come for more of a social aspect because they might not know anyone or have friends here when they come from Korea. They can talk to other moms and see what going on and meet people. So those are the three things that we try to do, and the bottom line is that language should not be a barrier to participation.

She added that this was particularly important for Korean families in which one parent had stayed behind in Korea:

HANNAH: We have several families where the mom is here with the kids and the dad is still in Korea. In those cases where the family is split up like that, it's good because we can support those families and those moms because they need the extra support to adjust to Valley View and the Pinnacle community.

The KPTA provided new immigrant Korean families with an educational network that was a valuable source of the social and cultural capital for Korean students and their parents,[26] particularly satellite kids from astronaut families.

Much of the cultural capital came directly from the "general PTA"—the name used on campus for original parent teacher association that remained open to all who wished to join. Hannah attended all general PTA meetings and events, and then relayed that information to Korean parents at the separate KPTA meetings. She spoke to the KPTA group in English, but there was always a translator present to repeat her words in Korean. For Hannah, this was a critical aspect of her job as president: "My vision is that I am basically a huge interpreter between the general PTA and the KPTA. I help to keep our Korean parents informed and engaged."

Hannah also saw her role as that of a motivator and facilitator of Korean parent participation—a credible source of inspiration for Pinnacle's Korean parents to become informed and engaged members of the Pinnacle community. Indeed, building and maintaining consistent participation from the Korean parent community was a key objective of the KPTA. For example, in wake of the news that the school principal was set to leave Pinnacle at the end of the 2015–2016 schoolyear, the district's main office sent an administrator to several general general PTA meetings to gather information from parents on the qualities that they desired in a new leader. And, to increase transparency in the hiring process, the district opened an online survey for all Pinnacle parents to provide feedback on their preferences for a new head of school. Hannah viewed this as a "tremendous opportunity" for KPTA members to be heard when they might otherwise have very little input:

HANNAH: I told all my members, "Here is your chance to get involved! This is very important! It's a tremendous opportunity for us to be heard, so fill out those surveys." Because a lot of the Korean parents will ignore those emails because they are in English. So, I've been actively telling my members to fill those surveys out because I want them to be more a part of the Pinnacle community. See, in the past, a lot of these moms kind of just dropped their kids off and that was it. They didn't get involved because of the language barrier. I think we're changing that.

One of the benefits of the KPTA for Korean immigrant parents was that the organization supported their acculturation by easing the burdens of linguistic assimilation. The KPTA strived to minimize the language barrier between Korean immigrant parents and school faculty, and thus supported the incorporation of Korean parents at Pinnacle from passive observers to influential institutional actors.

SUPPORTING PINNACLE'S KOREAN STUDENTS ACADEMICALLY AND SOCIALLY

The KPTA was also directly involved in promoting the academic well-being of Korean students. For example, the group organized information sessions to help guide Korean parents through enrolling their children in various standardized test preparation courses.

Consequently, it was not uncommon for the sons and daughters of KPTA parents to begin SAT tutoring as freshmen on advice from other parents in the group. There were many standardized test prep centers in Valley View that catered specifically to Korean students and families; they hired Korean students at nearby colleges as tutors and offered classes in Korean as well as English. Local test prep centers were places where Korean students could sharpen their test-taking skills, and where their parents—particularly those who were recent immigrants—could be part of a co-ethnic community in Southern California.

Keeping Korean Students Out of Trouble

The bulk of KPTA activity involving students concerned subject tutoring, all manner of test preparation, and the college application process. But the KPTA also intervened when Korean students ran into academic or behavioral difficulty at school:

SEAN: Other than tutoring and test prep, what are some other services that you facilitate or provide that directly affect Korean students?

HANNAH: If a student has a problem at school, we'll try to step in and we'll try to help out that student and that family.

SEAN: What kind of problems do students have where they can come to you and you can intervene?

HANNAH: So, we had an issue with this Korean boy being caught cheating. I think it was plagiarism. The parents, who hadn't been in America for very long, called me and they didn't know what to do because that kind of thing [plagiarism/cheating] is a big deal here [in America]; it's a huge deal. So, the parents called and said, "We have to have a meeting with the principal and we need help with the meeting." And so we sent somebody from our group to help them prepare for the meeting and then to participate in that meeting and be a mediator and a translator, if necessary, during the meeting.

SEAN: You arranged for someone from the KPTA to prepare them and then be present with them in their meeting with the principal?

HANNAH: Yes, for interpretation and counsel. And so, in that plagiarism case, we were able to resolve it nicely and it didn't end up on that kid's record.

Sarah, a current Pinnacle parent and KPTA member, served as KPTA president before Hannah assumed the role. Sarah told me that, in addition to relaying information back and forth between the general PTA and KPTA meetings, she also worked with Korean parents to assist when their children got in trouble academically or socially. This was especially important for Pinnacle's Korean "astronaut families," in which the father stayed overseas for work while the mother moved to America with one or more children:

SARAH: When I was president, I had several instances when parents called me for help. This is a really unbelievable story, actually. On a Thursday night, I get a phone call from a mother in the KPTA that I had never met before. She called me frantically in regards to her son, who she said was about to get expelled. I asked her what happened and she said that he was caught smoking on campus and it was his second or third time. She asked if I could do her a favor and talk to the administration about the likelihood of an expulsion. She mentioned that an expulsion would affect his college admissions, and she started making excuses about why her son was misbehaving.

SEAN: Excuses to you?

SARAH: Yes, to me. She said that the reason was because the father is still in Korea and the son is here feeling stressed and without the discipline of the father. As a result, he started smoking and there's nothing much she can do about it. I thought, "no, that's not gonna fly!" I told her to be sure to talk to them and tell them that he needs help rather than a harsh punishment. And I helped her write a letter to the school.

SEAN: So he wasn't expelled?

SARAH: He wasn't expelled, but just suspended instead. He ended up
         getting three days of suspension and he had to go to school
         on Saturdays for a few weeks. And six months later I ran into
         the mom and she told me that it was the best thing that had
         ever happened to him and that her son had matured a lot. So
         it ended up being a great experience for me as president
         because we resolved the issue so nicely. The boy learned a
         lesson without getting punished too harshly.

Taken together, these episodes underscore the influence of the
Korean Parent Teacher Association on the Pinnacle administration
and its broad benefit to the Korean community. They show how
the KPTA marshaled resources on behalf of parents and students
who needed assistance. The group offered advice and encouragement to parents and students, as well as translators to accompany
parents in all manner of meetings with school administrators. The
group linked students to co-ethnic standardized test preparation
services, and advocated for students who faced disciplinary action
due to academic, social, or behavioral transgressions. The KPTA's
support of its members was broad, yet purposefully targeted to the
most pressing needs of the Korean community—both on and off
campus.

CULTIVATING AN EXCEPTIONAL REPUTATION

One morning after class, Ms. Quinn, the history and psychology
teacher who was always willing to engage me in conversation and
give her opinion on a wide range of issues, asked me if I was going to
attend the upcoming "Teacher Appreciation Luncheon" hosted by the
KPTA. She did not mince words when describing her disapproval of
the luncheon, as well as her unease about the presence and motives
of an ethnically-exclusive parent group on campus:

SEAN: What's your opinion of the luncheon?

MS. QUINN: I think the luncheon is bribery by the Korean parents so
            we'll treat their students better. It's a safe bribe. I refuse to go
            to it. The culture in Korea is that it's the norm for parents to
            gift their children's teachers for the child's benefit. I'm very
            American and I find it offensive. Why can't they just be part
            of the general PTA? Why do they need their own separate
            group?! And also the school day is modified every year for
            the luncheon, so the class periods that bookend the event are
            shortened. This is frustrating because it eats into instruc-
            tional time that our students need. The AP exams are com-
            ing up and we have a lot of ground to cover.

A safe bribe so we'll treat their students better. Ms. Quinn certainly
understood how such an event might be advantageous for the Korean
community at Pinnacle. Rather than viewing these and other activities as the honest efforts of a non-White immigrant community to
adjust and participate within an education system that was entirely
unfamiliar to them, Ms. Quinn interpreted their actions, and their
very existence on campus, as "offensive" and un-American.[27]

I asked Ms. Quinn how the lunch was structured and what typically happened during the event. She replied that the KPTA would
"give a few thousand dollars to the school and feed everyone." She
added that most of the teachers who attended the annual event did
not understand why the KPTA was necessary at all when the school
already had a PTA, but that they went "for the free food, which, I'll
admit, is quite good." I asked her if I could attend the luncheon and
she replied that I should go. "Here's the flyer," she said as she dug
through the small, blue recycling bin under her desk to retrieve her
copy. She had crumpled it into a ball before tossing it into the bin.
She smoothed it out on her desk before handing it to me.

Her disdain for the event increased my excitement to attend;
I was curious to see what all the fuss was about. Moreover, in light of
Ms. Quinn's opinions about the KPTA, I also made a note to follow

up with Hannah and others regarding any backlash that they might have faced as members of the group.

The Teacher Appreciation Luncheon

The KPTA's annual Teacher Appreciation Luncheon was a special occasion on campus. The event was held in the Pinnacle multi-purpose room, a rectangular space large enough to comfortably accommodate about two hundred people. Colorful paper ornaments hung from the ceiling, and more were arranged clustered together on the wall like giant paper flowers in full bloom. Tables were spread throughout the room, and each was decorated with a white tablecloth, candles, and a vase overflowing with large, white tulips. The KPTA served the lunch as a buffet with twelve different dishes in a robust display of Korean culinary culture. A group member stood behind each dish along the buffet line, smiling and eager to serve a teacher or staff member. A large and colorful banner on the wall behind the food greeted guests with a message of gratitude—"THANK YOU Teachers & Staff." Three additional tables ran perpendicular to the buffet line, presenting an assortment of pastries, fruit, coffee, and tea.

Each seat was accompanied by a program that included a brief statement of thanks from Hannah, and a lunch menu organized into "appetizer," "entrée," and "dessert" sections. Business sponsors and the names of all KPTA members and their children enrolled at Pinnacle were listed on the back of the program. This list was a clear signal to teachers, who checked to see if they recognized any names of students who were in one of their classes. After taking a seat at one of the tables, I asked Ms. Kim, a Korean-American Spanish teacher in her mid-twenties, if there were other luncheons like this at Pinnacle during the year. She said that there were a "handful" of similar events, but that this was the only "ethnic luncheon" and "by far the most extravagant."

"Excuse me! Hello, everyone! Welcome!"—my conversation with Ms. Kim was interrupted as Hannah got everyone's attention with the help of a microphone. She and four other members—the KPTA "leadership team"—were standing at the front of the room, and they proceeded to thank teachers and staff for "making this the best school." They also acknowledged their fellow Korean parents:

HANNAH: And a special thank you to all of the passionate and dedicated Korean parents for all of their hard work in making this special event possible. We [Korean parents] will continue working hard for our students and the school. Thank you!

Everyone in the room applauded enthusiastically.

Next, Hannah announced a donation of $5,000 from the KPTA to Pinnacle, as well as an additional $1,500 of classroom supplies. These declarations were met with exuberant whoops and applause. The luncheon ended with a raffle, and a teacher sitting next to me won a stainless-steel cookware set from Williams Sonoma valued at over $500. Other prizes included movie tickets, $100 gift cards, small kitchen appliances (e.g., a coffee maker), and an overnight stay and spa treatment package at the luxurious Pelican Hill Resort in Newport Coast. When the raffle was over, Hannah announced that all gifts were donated by KPTA members and that all food was prepared by KPTA members. These comments were met by more applause.

The luncheon served at least three important functions for the KPTA. First, it was a chance to publicly praise faculty and staff with an impressive assortment of food and prizes, and to publicly declare a large donation of money and supplies to the Pinnacle community. Second, the luncheon was an opportunity to reaffirm a commitment to working with the school to support a shared vision of academic exceptionalism through fundraising and partnerships with local businesses. This objective was reflected in comments made by KPTA members during the lunch about continuing to "work hard for our students and the school."

Third, and maybe most importantly, the luncheon served to increase the profile of Korean parents and students on campus by underscoring their commitment to academic excellence. The event presented Korean parents as members of the Pinnacle community

Figure 8. The Annual Teacher Appreciation Luncheon hosted by the Korean PTA

who were steadfastly invested in the success of their students and the school more broadly. The luncheon reified the "model minority" stereotype that Asian achievement outpaced that of other racial groups because Asian students and families cared most about education—a view that was prevalent among members of the KPTA. A few weeks after the luncheon I spoke with Vivian, a member of the KPTA leadership team, and she referenced culture and values to explain Asian students' academic success at Pinnacle:

> VIVIAN: Culturally, Asians are very school-oriented. Education is the number one priority. So, wherever you have a good school district, you'll find that there will be a lot of Asians, right?

For Vivian, the fact that, in the US, East Asian immigrants tend to settle in middle-class neighborhoods that are zoned for highly resourced schools was proof that Asians valued education more than other racial groups. The luncheon only provided more evidence of this for many members of the Pinnacle community who did not have a full grasp of the socioeconomic factors that supported academic opportunity and achievement for Asian immigrant students and families on campus and beyond.

Additionally, and more to the point, the luncheon supported the notion that Korean students and their families, and Asian families more broadly, were largely responsible for Pinnacle's stellar academic reputation. Pinnacle teachers witnessed their Asian students outperforming their non-Asian students in terms of grades and test scores, and they often wondered why this was the case. Was it cultural? The KPTA luncheon suggested a convenient answer because it featured Korean parents as deeply devoted to the success of their students. Using the back of the official event program to list the Korean students whose parents were members of the KPTA signaled to teachers that each of those students came from a family that put education first. The implicit message was that these were the students who were most likely to succeed and who deserved the benefit of the doubt in class.

.   .   .   .   .

In the days immediately following the luncheon, I kept thinking about the identity work that such an event did for the Korean community at Pinnacle. I certainly interpreted it as a conspicuous signal to the broader school community that its Korean families were important partners of the institution, but I wondered whether this was an explicit goal of the group in planning and hosting such events. Were they purposefully trying to project a certain favorable image of Korean families, or were they strictly focused on thanking teachers and staff?

A few weeks later I spoke with Hannah about the image of Korean students and families that the KPTA promoted on campus:

SEAN: Do you think that the KPTA enhances the image of Korean students at the school? Is that an explicit goal of the group?

HANNAH: Yeah, for sure; that's why we all do it. As moms, we want our kids to be proud of who they are. A lot of these moms, even the ones who don't speak much Korean, they want their kids to be proud that they are Korean. And we want to have a voice at our school and we want to contribute and be involved in the community, but, because of the language barrier, many feel like they can't. But I really encourage them and I tell them, "You are a stakeholder in this high school community, and you have every right and every voice, and you should be proud." And we want to show that to the school and to our kids as well.

SEAN: Do you think that Koreans have a good reputation at Pinnacle?

HANNAH: I do think we have a good reputation. A lot of the teachers come up during our luncheon and they'll seek out certain parents because they want to meet so-and-so's mom. And I get a lot of that, too. Teachers will come and seek out me or other moms and they'll tell us how wonderful our kids are at school and how hardworking they are, and that says it all. After all the work that we put in, having teachers tell us that is very gratifying.

SEAN: Why is that reputation so important?

HANNAH: Because it affects the way we're treated. If teachers respect our students and respect our community, then they can do better at supporting them academically and socially. If Korean parents are participating, then the school will work better for us and what we want for our kids.

As Hannah's comments made clear, enhancing the status of Korean students and parents was one of the KPTA's primary goals, and it inspired nearly all of their activities in the Pinnacle community. The Teacher Appreciation Luncheon was a prime example of this ethnic identity work.

ACHIEVING SOLIDARITY WITH THE GENERAL PTA

One morning after class, the week after the luncheon, I commented to Ms. Quinn, jokingly, that I had not seen her at the event. She laughed and reiterated her critique:

MS. QUINN: Ha! That's funny! Well, that lunch is a bribe. It's bribery. The general PTA already does a lunch and I think that's enough. We really don't need separate parent groups and separate luncheons. It's unfair to all of the parents and their kids who can't be in the Korean PTA.

I did not encounter or hear of any students who felt this strongly about the KPTA, but a few White students told me that they thought the group was "weird" or that they were not sure what the purpose of the group was. Max, a White student whose mother sometimes attended general PTA meetings, told me that he thought the existence of the group was "interesting because there's a PTA already. I have a friend whose mom is really involved in the Korean group, and he used to get embarrassed because she would show up randomly at school with other Korean moms." These comments connote curiosity, not outright opposition.

In light of the apparent diversity of opinion on campus regarding the KPTA, I asked Hannah whether she or other members had experienced any backlash from the wider Pinnacle community in response to KPTA events, or simply due to the group's presence on campus:

SEAN: Do you feel that the KPTA has a good relationship with the general PTA and with the Pinnacle parent community as a whole?

HANNAH: Yes, I'd say it's very good now. But in the beginning, the early years when the KPTA was new, a lot of the general PTA didn't approve, or they weren't sure why we needed a separate Korean PTA, and they wanted us to just be a part of the general PTA. And there were a lot of people who said, "Why are you making your own group? Why are you doing your own thing? Why are you trying to make our community more segregated? Why segregate yourself like that?" So, I think that in the beginning there was a lot of misunderstanding and miscommunication. But now that the years have gone by, they [general PTA members] know why. And I make it clear, "We're not trying to distance ourselves from you. Actually, we're trying to help you. We want to work with you. We share your goals. Whatever you want to advertise in the general PTA, I go straight to my members and I use translators and I relay that message to them." That's my vision; I am the mediator between these two groups. I don't want ours to be a separate thing, away from them. And also, we have our own fundraising. We contribute every year. We do a cash donation of $1,000 to the general PTA. So, I want to convey the message that we work side-by-side with the PTA. We work together.

SEAN: Do you still get people who don't understand?

HANNAH: I'm sure that there are still people who don't understand. They don't approach me and they don't tell me that, but I'm assuming. Actually, it's kind of funny, because whoever the general PTA president is, the KPTA president works directly with that person. It's case by case because everyone is different, so with some of the PTA presidents there has been some friction between our groups, and some of them really love us. This year I am having a great relationship with Linda [president of the general PTA]. She is very supportive of us. We are in constant communication, and I tell her what's going on, and she tells me, "Go ahead and do that," and so forth. I try to keep that relationship tight.

Hannah's response indicated that, for Korean families at Pinnacle, the institutionalization of their ethnic capital was not always widely accepted by other (mostly White) parents, particularly those in the general PTA who wished for Korean parents to fall in line and incorporate themselves into the existing institutional channels of parental involvement. For the KPTA, acceptance by the broader parent community at Pinnacle had to be earned; it had to be cultivated through public and private demonstrations of shared commitment to the institution.

OPPORTUNITY SEEKERS

In diverse societies, dominant racial groups customarily seek to maintain their privileges by monopolizing resources.[28] This is certainly the case in the education sphere; sociologists Amanda Lewis and John Diamond have found that, in racially diverse, suburban school districts, White parents often engage in "opportunity hoarding" by taking advantage of "the material, cultural, social, and symbolic resources that enable some to translate their care into more advantages for their children . . . These resource differences interact with school policies and practices that enable White and middle-class parents' resources to pay off."[29] In the same study, Lewis and Diamond found that White parents' commitment to diversity and racial integration in the schools their children attend was often "shallow" in that many White parents were only interested in racial diversity to the extent that it exposed their children to kids from a variety of racial backgrounds. These parents saw this exposure as beneficial to the development of their children as long as such exposure was limited; they feared that too much racial diversity (i.e., too many Black and Latinx students in the honors and AP classes that their children took) could dampen the academic rigor in those classes. White parents' fears of diverse schools in their neighborhoods have been consistently reported in newspapers of record such as the *New York Times*, which, in 2020, published a podcast on the topic titled *Nice White Parents*. These parents worry, without evidence, that increasing educational opportunities for students of color would diminish the options and resources currently available to their White children.[30] These threads of social science research and investigative journalism illuminate the ways in which White parents resist the inclusion of more Black and Brown students in opportunities that their children benefit from, and are therefore complicit in the maintenance of White privilege in schools.

Similarly, in 2018 and 2019, an organized group of Asian parents vigorously protested a plan by New York City Mayor Bill de Blasio and Schools Chancellor Richard Carranza to increase racial diversity in the city's handful of elite, specialized public high schools. Asian students represent roughly 80% of the student body at these schools, while Black and Latinx students represent less than 5%

despite constituting well over 50% of public school students in the city.[31] The plan called for the abolition of the entrance exam, which was the sole criteria for admission. The Asian parents who protested argued that scrapping the exam would discriminate against Asian students, and they were ultimately successful in their attempts to disrupt the plan. This is another example of educational opportunity hoarding.

A few months before I started writing this book, I attended an academic conference to present some of the data that appears in this chapter. My goal was to try out some new arguments—like a comedian rehearsing jokes at an open-mic night before taking their show on the road. During the question-and-answer period after my talk, someone in the audience commented that Pinnacle KPTA members were "opportunity hoarders." I did not disagree, but neither was I sure that this was the most accurate characterization of the KPTA. I offered that members of the KPTA were more opportunity seekers and creators than hoarders; they embedded their considerable ethnic community resources within the school in an effort to circumvent language barriers, increase Korean parental involvement, and, ultimately, create better academic opportunities for their children.

The early resistance from general PTA members—particularly the complaint that, in establishing a KPTA, Korean parents were trying to make the community "more segregated"—was a misreading of the group's purpose. Rather than seeking segregation and distance, which are consequences of racial opportunity hoarding, the KPTA sought integration and closeness by working to increase Korean parental engagement with the wider school community. Somewhat paradoxically, this ethnically segregated parent association has, over time, led to a more racially integrated and cohesive parental community at the school. Korean parents were not participating much before the KPTA was formed, but the establishment of the group gave these parents a platform from which to get involved and make their voices heard on campus.

TEACHING THE TEACHERS

According to one classic, sociological definition, immigrant assimilation is a process that occurs when a new immigrant group incorporates into an existing society and group boundaries steadily diminish over time.[32] This version implies that the flow of incorporation is unidirectional, as the immigrants acculturate to a new way of life in a new country. "Highly-selected" immigrant groups—those whose pre-migration levels of educational attainment and socioeconomic status outpace the median in both their country of origin and the United States—tend to do quite well in terms of cultural and structural assimilation because they have the resources to facilitate rapid incorporation into the receiving society.[33] The KPTA was a case in point, in that one of the primary objectives of the KPTA was to facilitate a seamless integration of Pinnacle's Korean families into the wider school community. They did this by providing social and cultural capital to all Korean families, and by supporting Pinnacle financially and through community outreach in ways that would ultimately enhance the opportunities and achievements of Korean students.

The provision of context-specific social and cultural capital is often essential for immigrants as they adjust to American institutions. Korean families at Pinnacle, especially those in which the parents were first-generation immigrants, made adjustments to align more closely with elements of American public school culture. But the KPTA operated from a firm belief that American educators also had an obligation to learn about and adjust to aspects of Korean culture that were relevant at school. To that end, the Korean PTA endeavored to provide Pinnacle's teachers with lessons in Korean culture. These cultural lessons included a strong emphasis on practicality and applicability—how a better understanding of Korean culture could be used by teachers to help Korean students in class.

The Korean Cultural Education Program

Every summer since 2007, the Valley View Korean Parents Organization, of which the Pinnacle Korean PTA was a subsidiary group, and the Valley View Public School Foundation have collaborated to host a three-day workshop for Valley View teachers—the Korean Cultural Education Program (KCEP). KCEP, a comprehensive introduction to South Korean history and culture, was open to all public school teachers in Valley View at the elementary-, middle-, and high-school levels. The program combined guest lecturers, music and dance performances, and discussion sessions. Space was limited to twenty-five teachers per year, and only those who had never participated in the program before were allowed to register. Teachers were paid $300 for their attendance, and a lengthy waitlist indicated that the program was popular. The money was certainly an incentive for teachers to participate, but Hannah also told me that teachers were often interested in the program simply because they routinely had several Korean students in each of their classes.

The objective of KCEP was for teachers to gain a basic familiarity with Korean history and culture so that they could better respond to the educational needs and cultural inclinations of their Korean students, particularly those who were 1.5- and second-generation immigrants:

HANNAH: For example, in our culture, in Asian culture, you're not supposed to look at a teacher who is reprimanding you because that is a sign of disrespect. Your head should be down. But in American culture, they'll say, "Look at me when I'm talking to you!" And because of those cultural differences, there are problems. I've dealt with teachers in this situation who were mad and telling the Korean parents, "Your child is being disrespectful because he doesn't look at me when I talk to him." So we teach a lot of things about cultural differences, and teachers learn that a student who looks down like that doesn't mean to be disrespectful in the classroom.

Hannah also stressed the importance of names in Korean culture, and the ways in which a lack of cultural sensitivity in the United States around Korean names caused problems for Korean students in American schools:

HANNAH: At KCEP we always distribute a book to teachers on names and how names are very important in our culture. A lot of Korean kids have names that maybe their grandparents went to a special place paid a lot of money to get that name, and the name predicts the child's future, so it's just really a good name. But then a lot of kids come here and they'll either be made fun of because other kids can't pronounce it, or the teachers screw it up all the time because they can't pronounce it. Then these kids get embarrassed and so the family will change the kid's name to an American name. So we talk to the teachers about that, telling teaches to be respectful of the names and to try their best to pronounce them.

SEAN: So the overall purpose is to help teachers bridge cultural divides?

HANNAH: Right. The purpose of the program is for teachers to learn it, take it to the classroom, apply it, and spread it to their colleagues at their school.

Hannah invited me to attend and take part in the program, and I accepted her offer.

KCEP was held at a middle school near the Valley View Civic Center, in a C-shaped multi-purpose room with wood paneling, a vaulted ceiling, and a carpeted stage. The space was decorated with posters and elaborate table displays that depicted various aspects of South Korean culture, such as food, clothing, musical instruments, literature, systems of government, education, and wildlife. A large South Korean flag hung above the stage at the front of the room. Five tables were spaced across the floor, and a packet of information had been placed on each table in front of each chair. The packet contained a daily schedule, a printout of the PowerPoint slides for each presenter's presentation, a list of famous people from South Korea,

Figure 9. Korean Cultural Education Program (KCEP)

Figure 10. Korean Cultural Education Program (KCEP)

Figure 11. Korean Cultural Education Program (KCEP) buffet lunch

and a compilation of South Korean historical facts. Beside each packet was a stack of several books, touching on topics of Korean history, politics, schools, culture, and folklore. There were twenty-five teachers in attendance—twenty White, two Latinx, and three Asian (Chinese American).

On the first day of KCEP, the program began with a buffet lunch at 11:30 a.m., followed by a visit from the mayor of Valley View. The mayor, who was White, was married to a Korean American woman, and their children were bi-racial. He delivered brief remarks welcoming teachers to the conference and encouraging them to share all that they learned with faculty and staff at their respective schools. This warm welcome was followed by a series of presentations and small group discussions from 12:00 p.m. to 5:00 p.m. A professor from a local university gave the first presentation, lecturing on the values of Confucianism, which he described as "such an integral part of Korean culture." He contrasted "Confucian values" with "American values," and challenged teachers to be mindful of these differences when dealing with Korean students in their classrooms. He also urged teachers to encourage their Korean students to take risks and get involved in extracurricular activities at school since, as he put it, "Confucianism teaches deliberation and caution."

After this presentation, which lasted about forty-five minutes and included a question-and-answer session, teachers broke into groups of four or five to read a famous Korean fable meant to instill the values of Confucianism in Korean children. Teachers were tasked with drawing a picture corresponding to the story that highlighting one or more of the Confucian themes, and then presenting that picture to the entire group. After the presentations, teachers watched a twenty-minute video on Korean history. The video focused on the South Korean economy, industry, and innovation.

The second day of KCEP featured Korean arts. The first presentation was by another local professor who specialized in the history of Korean music and dance. As part of his presentation, he played several traditional Korean instruments and sang two songs that are significant in Korean history. He then invited two young Korean women from backstage to join him, and he played a rhythm on a hand drum while the women performed a traditional and popular Korean dance. Each woman wore a Hanbok—a semi-formal style of dress often worn during important celebrations. The day ended with a thirty-minute video on the most striking differences between South Korea and North Korea, and a brief history of South Korea's relationships with the other larger, more powerful countries in the Asia-Pacific region. The documentary-style video portrayed South Korea as an impressive nation that boasted numerous global accomplishments. According to the video, South Korea's successes had been driven by a need to stand up to Japan, China, and North Korea.

Figure 12. Korean dancers and musicians performing for Valley View teachers during the Korean Cultural Education Program (KCEP)

Figure 13. Teachers learning and practicing ancient Korean drum techniques

The third and final day of KCEP began with a presentation from an ethnic studies professor at a local liberal arts college. His talk, titled "Korean Americans: Historical Experiences and Contemporary Realities for Educators," focused on best practices for teachers to connect and build rapport with Korean students and parents. His lecture was followed by a visit from five mothers of Korean students in the district, each of whom sat at a separate table with teachers. After brief introductions at each table, the teachers and parents discussed the experiences of parenting and teaching Korean children in Valley View. After these group discussions, the five mothers took seats in a row of chairs on the stage to form a panel of discussants. A member of the Pinnacle KPTA served as moderator for the panel, and she asked each panelist to describe the experience of raising Korean children in Valley View. The parents were soon joined on stage by a group of ten Korean students, who ranged in age from six- to seventeen-years-old. The students introduced themselves and joined a discussion that concluded the session. Three of the students were high school students at Pinnacle whose parents were active members of the KPTA.

The conference closed at the end of day three with a dinner in a private room at a local Korean restaurant owned by a member of the Pinnacle KPTA. KPTA parents mingled with teachers, district officials, and Valley View Public School Foundation staff. A constant wave of restaurant staff brought a boundless assortment of appetizers, main course dishes, and colorful, elaborate desserts.

Near the end of the dinner, Hannah asked the teachers to share with the entire dinner party their favorite part of the KCEP conference, as well as something that they learned that would be worth sharing with other teachers at their school. Of the twenty-one teachers in attendance for the meal, nineteen mentioned a newfound respect and admiration for Korean people, particularly those who emigrate to America for increased opportunities. One teacher named Sherry, a middle-aged blonde woman who taught math at Valley View High School, spoke last, and her comments were representative of the prevailing sentiment that evening:

SHERRY: I am just so impressed with South Korea and its incredible people! This program really makes me want to visit South Korea someday. Actually, it kind of makes me wish I *were* Korean!

Other teachers laughed and nodded in agreement. Sherry had captured the mood among those in attendance.

KCEP was a cornerstone event for the KPTA. It demonstrated that the KPTA was able to marshal sufficient resources to compel Valley View public school teachers to expand their cultural horizons and adapt their teaching practices in ways that benefitted Korean students. Through KCEP, Korean parents introduced local teachers to what they considered to be the most favorable aspects of Korean culture, the most flattering elements of their national history, and their experiences in American society and schools that teachers could draw on to support Korean students. Teachers were encouraged to hold high expectations of Korean students, and to afford Korean students the benefit of the doubt in class and on campus generally. Moreover, KCEP invited Korean American professors, parents, and students to discuss "best practices" for educating Korean children in America. These professionals—these Korean cultural fact witnesses—were compelling and persuasive.

• • • • • • • •

Classic assimilation theories conceptualize immigrant residents as disadvantaged due to cultural differences such as language barriers.[34] Indeed, the relationship between immigrant families and schools is often difficult; the expectations that most schools have for parental involvement can place an outsized burden on immigrant parents, who are often unfamiliar with educational practices in the receiving society, do not know how to become involved, or do not have the time to participate as they adapt to the work-life balance in a new country.[35] The Korean community at Pinnacle High School provides insights into how some immigrant groups are able to lever-age their co-ethnic social and economic capital to overcome these challenges.

To make sense of its impact, it is useful to conceptualize the KPTA as a racialized organization, given that one of the criteria for mem-bership was to identify as Korean. One of the principal characteris-tics of racialized organizations is that they either enhance or diminish the agency of racial groups.[36] The KPTA enhanced the agency of the Korean community at Pinnacle in three primary ways. First, it sup-ported Korean immigrants by translating and relaying critical infor-mation from general PTA meetings and announcements. Softening the language barrier kept Korean parents informed and encouraged them to participate in various school processes, such as the search for a new school principal. Second, the KPTA supported Korean stu-dents who needed extra assistance, such as providing a translator and "mediator" for the parents of a boy who was caught cheating. In another case, KPTA leadership helped a mother and her son draft a letter to school administrators after the boy was repeatedly caught smoking marijuana on campus. In both of those cases the offending student faced a harsh penalty, but each situation was resolved with little punishment and no lasting blemish on the student's academic record.

Third, the mere existence of the KPTA at Pinnacle, along with the school events it hosted, reified model minority stereotypes about the relationship between Asian cultural values and educational attain-ment. Model minority stereotypes about Asian academic success compare Asians favorable to Black and Latinx students, which, in turn, perpetuates negative stereotypes about Black and Latinx stu-dents. As we saw in chapter 1, for Asian students, the Pinnacle cam-pus was a place of "stereotype promise," which refers to the benefits of being viewed through the lens of a positive stereotype.[37] Stereotype promise can enhance opportunities and lead students to perform in ways that confirm the positive stereotype. Asian students at Pinnacle had a reputation for being the kids who "know their stuff" in class, and for contributing most to the school's academic notoriety. The KPTA unquestionably promoted this racialization of achievement.

The KPTA reminds us that assimilation is not solely a unidirectional process of immigrant incorporation and boundary dissolution in which immigrants conform to prevailing cultures in a new land.[38] Rather than strictly assimilating to the native school culture and customs, Valley View's Korean immigrant families and their school-based organizations invested in a refashioning of the institutional mainstream to align more closely with their Korean culture. The result is that, within Valley View schools, Korean families had easy access to strong co-ethnic networks and the social and cultural capital that those networks provided. Furthermore, through events like the KCEP, Korean parents encouraged and guided Valley View teachers at all grade levels to be more supportive and responsive to the needs of Korean students. Thus, this is not a case of immigrant newcomers gradually becoming more like members of a host society as their native, immigrant culture fades away. Instead, this is a unique case of a non-White group of recent immigrant origin facilitating the acculturation of important, gatekeeping members of the host society—public school teachers—to the cultural history and current needs of that immigrant group. Korean families and local teachers both worked to bridge the cultural divide between them, and both groups benefitted from those efforts.

Throughout my fieldwork at Pinnacle, parents from a variety ethnoracial backgrounds expressed unwavering commitment to the academic engagement and achievement of their children, but not all had the resources of the local Korean community. For Korean parents at Pinnacle, the institutionalization of their ethnic capital enabled them to express a resolute commitment to education in ways that were immediately accessible and legible to teachers and administrators. Korean parents, through the KPTA, worked directly with institutional actors on behalf of their children, throwing into vivid relief the commitment that these parents had to the educational attainment of their students.[39]

The absence of any Black or Latinx parent groups at Pinnacle did not signal a lesser commitment to education on the part of those groups; rather, that absence speaks to the structural disadvantages that Black and Latinx students and families often face in racially diverse suburban schools.[40] I must stress that, as I argued in chapter 1, Korean culture is not the most important factor in the general academic success of Korean students in the United States.[41] Korean immigrants' low educational attainment in Japan, where they have for decades faced consistent discrimination in many domains of economic and social life, provides strong evidence that socioeconomic status and positive stereotypes that frame Asians as inherently intelligent and studious are critical factors contributing to the general academic success of Korean Americans in the United States.

Although the Korean parents who established the KPTA faced uneasiness and resistance from White parents at first—similar to what Jiménez and Horowitz documented in a study of a similar suburban school setting in the San Francisco Bay Area—the pushback did not last long. In Valley View, the institutionalization of Korean ethnic capital ultimately streamlined Korean immigrants' incorporation into the community. They used their organization to establish a strong relationship with the general PTA and to fundraise aggressively for the school. When I was on campus, all indications were that the relationship between the KPTA and the regular PTA, whose membership was predominantly White, was amiable and cooperative.

The case of the KPTA demonstrates that immigrant groups can marshal and embed group resources within a public school district in ways that positively influence how school faculty and staff interact with them. Moreover, it provides further evidence of the ways in which immigrant incorporation involves what sociologist and immigration scholar Tomás Jiménez describes as a back-and-forth, give-and-take adjustment between immigrant "newcomers" on one hand, and more "established" individuals and institutions on the other.[42] Privileged immigrant groups can activate co-ethnic resources to cultivate social status, challenge their otherness, and create meaningful opportunities to thrive in school and society for generations to come. These social processes, which happened at Pinnacle, were an important part of what made Pinnacle and Crossroads so different.

5 "We've Failed These Kids"

MISSED OPPORTUNITIES AND SIGNS OF HOPE

Ms. Owens, the assistant principal at Crossroads, had previously held the same title at a large public high school in a neighboring district. She and I spoke briefly from time to time during her first days and weeks at Crossroads, but my first in-depth conversation with her took place when she had been with the school for about six months. I was interested in her initial impressions of Crossroads:

SEAN: What's your transition to this district been like and what are your impressions of Crossroads now that you've been here for a few months?

MS. OWENS: Well, I can say that the academic environment in Valley View has been a real adjustment. The high school where I was before, we had a lot of high achieving kids but we also had many students who were maybe not as capable academically as even the average student here at Crossroads. But those students tended to remain with us if they fell behind on credits. We had a continuation school in that district, but we tried really hard not to send kids there.

SEAN: So students who were credit deficient weren't transferred to the continuation school?

MS. OWENS: Most of the time we kept the credit deficient kids with us. We had a credit recovery program on our campus, and we enrolled kids in it, and they graduated on time without ever going to the continuation school. We just felt like those were our students, and we felt responsible for them. We wanted them to graduate with us.

SEAN: How would you contrast that with what you've experienced so far here in Valley View?

MS. OWENS: The high schools here in Valley View take a different approach and really don't hesitate to send kids to Crossroads and to put them through the continuation school system. And if you think about what the Valley View mold is, not one of these kids really fits it, so they get sent over here.

SEAN: How would you define the "Valley View mold"?

MS. OWENS: The Valley View mold is that everyone goes to a four-year college, and the schools have the best teachers and the best education. And this district does have all of those things! But not every kid fits into that; not every student is a four-year-college-bound student straight out of high school.

SEAN: That's not the path that all students are necessarily going to take.

MS. OWENS: Exactly. And I also have to say that it's been a big cultural awareness for me moving here, because I knew that Valley View was affluent, but I didn't realize that the city has a population where there's housing subsidies and everything. And the sad thing is that many of these Crossroads kids live in subsidized housing because their families are low-income. So why is it that we have a school that's disproportionately lower socioeconomic level and disproportionately students of color? It's sad that that's what makes up this school.

SEAN: Why does that make you sad?

MS. OWENS: Because it means that we failed them somewhere along the way. I think it means that we've failed these kids. We have failed to meet their learning needs and their social and emotional needs, whatever they may be. And we've failed to

make sure that our comprehensive high schools are inclusive
of all people. We do know that students, especially at the
high school level, are more likely to be successful if they feel
included and engaged—we know that that's a huge portion
of it. So, in some way, we've failed to engage them, and they
feel so disengaged from the school or the community that
their academics suffer and they end up here. So I think it's
sad because it just means that the school system has failed
these kids and let them down.

In this unvarnished assessment of Crossroads's place in the school
district, rather than lament the academic preparation or abilities of
Crossroads students, Ms. Owens asserted that the fit between students and the academic culture in Valley View was often poor. Furthermore, her comments alluded to the racial and socioeconomic
inequities in the district's approach to supporting students who fell
behind. Ms. Owens was convinced that the district could do more
to incorporate credit-deficient students at comprehensive high
schools; instead of shepherding them to a separate, unequal, and
punitive learning environment, school like Pinnacle could come up
with ways to keep them on campus and in class. Her opinion was
born of experience, as she had worked within a different model in
a nearby district. Her prior exposure to a more inclusive, equitable
approach to credit recovery provided the foundation for her belief
that comprehensive high schools could do much more to engage the
students who ended up at Crossroads.

SETTING STUDENTS UP TO FAIL

Though she had only worked in the district for a few months at
the time of our conversation, Ms. Owens was correct in her assessment that the comprehensive high schools in Valley View espoused
a college-or-bust approach to course schedules and preparing for
life after high school. Teachers and counselors constantly reminded

students of the standards necessary to be admitted to a four-year college or university, and students were encouraged to pursue a trajectory of classes and activities that would be attractive to such institutions. At Pinnacle High School, nearly 100% of graduates enrolled directly into a postsecondary institution, and 70% of those graduates did so at a four-year school. As I mentioned in chapter 1, within Pinnacle's academic culture, the "successful" students were the ones who took multiple honors or advanced placement courses, attained a 4.0+ GPA, and achieved an SAT score in the ninetieth percentile or better nationwide. These were the standards because they were considered necessary for admission to a prestigious college.

The institutional success frame at Pinnacle certainly did not align with the academic goals of all students there. Some planned to go to college but were not concerned with or interested in attending the most highly ranked college possible. Others were not sure if a "major college" was right for them, and they wanted to "try community college" first to test the postsecondary waters. Others planned to enter the workforce or attend a technical school or trade school in pursuit of a specific job or career that did not require a bachelor's degree. The institutional success frame at Pinnacle left little room for these students to feel welcome and supported. The frame pushed all students, regardless of academic performance and interests, to pursue four-year college enrollment. Those who would desire or benefit from a different trajectory often felt like fringe members of the school community, and those who struggled academically were at risk of experiencing a punishing and demoralizing transfer to Crossroads.

Paradoxically, there were signs of the district's college-or-bust paradigm at Crossroads despite the fact that the limited curriculum disqualified graduates from enrolling at a four-year college or university regardless of how well they performed academically there. For example, one of the classrooms at Crossroads was also used as a college counseling office and a space to host orientation sessions for new transfers. This room was a space in which students new to the school or nearing graduation were often thinking about and planning their futures. Three of the room's four walls were covered in colorful pennants representing various four-year colleges and universities, many of them highly ranked and with very low acceptance rates for undergraduates. The irony of this display was that Crossroads graduates were ineligible to enroll at any of those schools immediately after high school regardless of how well they performed in their classes. One day as I was leaving the room, I overhead a student seated at the desk closest to the door say to the girl beside her, "What's up with these walls? Like, why are they reminding us about all the great schools we can't get into?!" The pennants were unintentional symbols of deprivation—a glaring reminder to students of what they could not achieve.

By operating under the premise that college enrollment was the only acceptable option for students after high school, and that the true measure of success was whether one gained admission to an *elite* college, the district created unrealistic expectations for students that set them up for failure. Miguel's situation at Crossroads is a case in point. Despite a strong interest in his culinary arts class and a career goal of becoming a restaurant chef, Miguel was pulled from culinary arts by Mr. Johnson as punishment for his being repeatedly late to first-period history class. Principal Johnson justified this action by stating that, "Participation in culinary arts is a privilege that is earned, so it can be taken away." In framing all vocational classes offered by the district as extracurricular privileges that were tangential to a high school students' education, Crossroads missed opportunities to help set struggling students like Miguel on a steady path toward a fulfilling career.

Crossroads teachers often questioned the logic behind framing high school as a step on the way to immediate college enrollment for all students. Mr. Gregory, the Crossroads math and science teacher, expressed views that were representative:

MR. GREGORY: I think it's great that we want them all to go to college, but I don't think that many of them are ready for that, and I'm not sure that we're adequately preparing the ones who think they're ready.

SEAN: What incentives do these students have for coming to school every day and making an effort to do well? I'm particularly thinking of students like Miguel, the ones who aren't interested in going to college.

MR. GREGORY: That's a good question. Finishing high school is certainly an incentive by itself. But beyond that? I don't think many of them could tell you.

In contrast, Pinnacle students tended to have clear goals for their future after high school, and a belief that academic achievement in primary school was essential to the attainment of their long-term goals. Moreover, Pinnacle constantly prepared students to succeed in college. Consequently, Pinnacle students could work hard with the comfort of knowing that their hard work would be rewarded with desirable college choices and the tools to succeed at that level. Crossroads students, however, were frequently unsure of their plans and goals after high school. According to Mr. Gregory, this insecurity about their futures was amplified by the lack of preparation that Crossroads provided for them:

MR GREGORY: We're giving a high school diploma that's not opening any doors for our students. The system is set up so that they can get just what they need to get through and graduate, but we need to focus on what's after that. We are not adequately preparing them for anything after high school. A lot of these kids just want to do something where they can see a finished product. They don't respond to abstract concepts because they just aren't interested, and that's okay!

SEAN: What's something you would do to address that, if you could?

MR. GREGORY: There's a construction site down the street, and I would love to take some of these boys I have over there and hand them a shovel so they could see a result right away and feel a sense of ability and accomplishment.

Some Crossroads students stated that they were unsure if college was right for them, and that they planned to seek full-time employment immediately after graduation. Zahra, a seventeen-year-old senior whose parents emigrated to American from Iran when she was a toddler, had wanted to attend Cal State Northridge or Cal State San Bernardino for college, but, after she arrived at Crossroads, she gave up on that goal: "I really wanted to go to college when I was at Pinnacle, but I lost that confidence and that drive once I came to Crossroads," Zahra told me one day during lunch as we sat at a concrete picnic table. "The students here aren't focused on college because we don't have that many options. I wish I'd had more support at Pinnacle before and after my credits got bad." Many students, like Zahra, arrived at Crossroads clinging to their college aspirations, but soon lost the motivation to continue pursuing them. These students suffered from the segregated and punitive environment at Crossroads. A lack of college preparation in the curriculum only made matters worse.

A HOPEFUL EVENT AT CROSSROADS

During my time spent at Crossroads, I rarely witnessed students expressing intellectual curiosity or excitement in their classes. To the contrary, listlessness, disinterest, and disengagement ruled the typical day. But one particular Crossroads event stood out as a clear exception—the only time during my hundreds of hours of observation that the vast majority of Crossroads students were enthusiastic about something at school other than the end of the school day.

Crossroads faculty and staff organized a career fair for current students every year midway through spring semester. The event was held outdoors in the courtyard at the center of campus. Representatives and recruiters from several branches of the United States Armed Forces, as well as those from local professional schools, academies, and other degree-granting institutions, were on hand to participate in the event. Crossroads teachers arranged several large folding tables to accommodate dozens of recruiters. Recruiters brought pamphlets, brochures, and other informational materials that they spread or stacked neatly on each table for students to peruse and collect.

On the morning of the event, each student received a thin packet from their first-period teacher that contained a page of short-answer questions about their career goals, a list of sample questions to ask recruiters, and ample blank space for taking notes. Students could earn course credit for completing the questionnaire portion and turning it in to Mr. Johnson or Ms. Owens at the end of the day. The packet assignment was meant to incentivize students' engagement and participation in the event, in light of the fact that so many Crossroads students struggled to sustain an efficacious level of engagement in their classes. The incentive was hardly necessary, however, because the event was extremely popular with students. Students roamed around the tables in small groups, asking questions of recruiters and representatives, filling out their packets, and gathering print materials from multiple tables. Armed Forces (Army, Navy, and Air Force), cosmetology school, culinary school, and a local art institute were the most popular tables at the fair, as there was a constant crowd of a dozen or so students exploring each of those career options.

As I made my way through the bustling swarm of activity around the Armed Forces booths, I noticed Coleman speaking with an Army recruiter. We met Coleman in chapter 2, when he spoke insightfully about the ways in which, paradoxically, the academic and social context at Crossroads were distracting and made it difficult to recover credits. At the end of their conversation, Coleman and the recruiter—who was dressed in military fatigues—exchanged smiles and a handshake. The recruiter handed him a business card and brochure. Coleman, carrying a small stack of brochures from various booths, made his way to a picnic table with two of his friends—Tobias and another boy whom I recognized but did not know by name. I joined the three of them at the table.

Coleman was flipping through his collection of pamphlets as I sat down next to him, and he was unequivocal in his praise for the event:

COLEMAN: This is so good! Look at all these options! This is really good. And you see how much participation there is today for the fair? This is what gets us going because we can see a path to a job or a career.

SEAN: Can you see the same sort of path in your classes?

COLEMAN: Hell no! Classes are just about survival, man. I think folks would try a lot harder at this school if they knew it was gonna lead directly to a job.

Tobias agreed:

TOBIAS: Yeah, bro. Classes are straight up survival, but this is legit because we can see a future. Like, I think I might seriously go for the Air Force.

COLEMAN: The Air Force looks dope, right?! It's either that or the Army for me. I think my path to college is definitely gonna be through the military.

As I sat there at that table with Coleman and Tobias—listening to them talk excitedly about the fair, watching them thumb through the materials that they had collected, hearing them weigh the merits of different options—I was filled with hope for their futures. They desperately needed a practical, realistic path after high school. The career fair was showing them several possibilities and the necessary steps to move forward toward a tangible goal.

The fair was notable because it captured Crossroads students' interest like no other class, event, or activity that I witnessed at the school. For students like Coleman and Tobias, the fair lent meaning to education in a way that classes in the general curriculum simply could not. Whereas Pinnacle students were generally focused during their classes because they understand that achieving good grades and test scores in high school would enable them to attend a desirable college on their way to a lucrative career, many Crossroads students either had other plans all along, or they lost interest in college once they started at Crossroads. When we also consider that Crossroads's curriculum precluded graduates from enrolling directly in a four-year college or university, the prospect of continuing their education in a trade school, technical school, or with the Armed Forces was all the more enticing for those students.

One of Crossroads's primary goals, as stated on the school's website, was for each student to, "Leave Crossroads High School with the capacity to pursue a field of expertise that encourages each student to be a contributing member of society." The career fair was a positive step in service of that goal. The event was instructive in that it demonstrated that many Crossroads students were passionate about certain job skills and fields that did not necessarily require a four-year college degree. Nevertheless, attending trade school or finding full-time employment directly after high school were not mainstream, respectable options in this affluent, suburban school district.

FOR SOME STUDENTS, CROSSROADS WAS AN IMPERFECT ALTERNATIVE TO DROPPING OUT

Most students' experiences transferring to and attending Crossroads were demoralizing and downright embarrassing. They resented being separated from their friends. They were critical of the campus layout and punitive climate. They felt abandoned by their former high school.

I would be remiss, however, if I did not mention the handful of students for whom Crossroads was an academic safety net. This was particularly the case for students like Ernesto, an eighteen-year-old Latino senior who was on the verge of dropping out before enrolling at Crossroads. Ernesto battled anxiety and depression, and he had failed multiple courses in his second and third years of high school in Compton, a working-class city in Los Angeles County where many adolescents feel the pull of street gangs. "I definitely would have dropped out if I had stayed in Compton," he told me. "But then my mom got a new job out here in Valley View. We lived in kind of a rough neighborhood, and she'd been trying to get us up out of there for a long time." He hoped to enroll at Pinnacle to start his senior year, but he soon learned that he was woefully behind on credits and that his only chance at graduation would be to enroll at Crossroads. Ernesto was convinced that the option to attend Crossroads saved him from dropping out: "I know Crossroads has a bad reputation or whatever, but I'm actually thankful for Crossroads because being here has given me a chance to graduate."

For Ernesto and other students like him, Crossroads provided a lifeline to continue the pursuit of a high school degree. However, though he was appreciative of the opportunity that Crossroads provided for him, Ernesto was critical of the system that sent students to Crossroads, and he questioned the school's austere facilities:

SEAN: Let's pretend that you're in charge of the school district here. What would you change?

ERNESTO: First of all, I don't think schools like Pinnacle should be able to turn students like me away. Sometimes I wish I went to Pinnacle because Crossroads doesn't feel like a real high school. We don't have clubs or sports or a field. We don't even have a library! I don't see why I have to be at a separate school like this.

Ernesto's case is suggestive of the potential for continuation schools such as Crossroads to prevent or reduce high school dropout, but this function of Crossroads for some students did not negate diminish its reality as a "dumping ground" for neighboring comprehensive high schools. Ernesto's candid comments added to the chorus of students, parents, and faculty who decried the segregation and inequality between Crossroads and the district's comprehensive high schools. They expected more from their public education system.

"NOW I UNDERSTAND WHY PEOPLE GET SO UPSET ABOUT SEGREGATION!"

The notion that Crossroads students would be better served by increasing the support that they received at comprehensive high schools was widely shared among the Crossroads faculty. Ms. Turner, who taught English, frequently questioned the role of Crossroads within the district, and her views were representative:

MS. TURNER: Shifting students off of their comprehensive school site, psychologically, is very bad, because we are labeling them as failures. We're sending them to a separate campus where kids feel bad about themselves. I just don't understand why these students can't be integrated at the regular schools. The comprehensive high schools have more resources to support these students. They could get them involved in clubs and service in the community, and provide the academic support. But the comprehensive schools don't want to deal with them, so they send them here. It's segregation, it really is. And there's a racial component to it when you compare the percentage of Black and Latino students here to the percentages and the comprehensive schools . . . Now I understand why people get so upset about segregation! The longer I work here, the more I think the system is screwy.

Parents of Crossroads students shared these sentiments. Greg, a parent whom I met at Crossroads's back-to-school-night and whose daughter was a sophomore, passionately questioned the policies and practices that sent students to Crossroads, the many glaring disparities between Crossroads and the four comprehensive high schools in district, and Crossroads's overall viability as a high school in Valley View:

GREG: I just think the model of how they deal with kids that are struggling is so weird. What they're doing is taking a group of kids that are academically challenged, financially maybe

> disadvantaged, whatever the condition is, and putting them
> in an environment that's pretty bizarre for a school.
> Crossroads just doesn't seem like a friendly place. And the
> more I think about it, kids deserve better than this! I mean,
> they're in high school in Valley View. There's so much
> money here and resources to support these kids better.
> Bottom line, the kids at Crossroads deserve the support of a
> full-fledged high school instead of being relegated to an
> environment that looks and feels like a correctional facility.

My conversation with Greg took place over the phone, but the exasperation and frustration in his voice was palpable. This grievance, this feeling that the district owed more to struggling students, was typical of most Crossroads teachers and parents whom I met. Their participation in the continuation school system was far from an endorsement of that system.

THE UNIQUE HARM OF RACIALIZED, BETWEEN-SCHOOL TRACKING

Segregation and inequality between schools is potentially more harmful than segregation and inequality within schools. Eminent sociologist William Julius Wilson once wrote that, for working-class and poor communities of color, residential segregation relegates them to the margins, resulting in "a lack of contact or of sustained interaction with individuals and institutions that represent mainstream society."[1] Similarly, between-school segregation results in the social and academic isolation of disadvantaged students, consigning them to inferior institutions such as Crossroads.

Within-school segregation (i.e., tracking), though unequivocally problematic,[2] still enables students in less rigorous remedial classes to take advantage of some of the same academic supports that are available to students in honors and AP class, and provides opportunities for enriching interactions with peers in non-tracked subjects and extracurricular activities.[3] Students who ended up at Crossroads experienced between-school tracking, which meant that they were completely removed and detached from a comprehensive high school education and experience. They were unable to access and benefit from the college-going culture, academic resources, and extracurricular opportunities that were available to students at Pinnacle and other comprehensive high schools in the district. This is an example of what social psychologist Michelle Fine and colleagues have referred to as "schooling for alienation."[4]

Punitive school policies and surveillance tactics treat students as problems and potential troublemakers,[5] and this treatment can lead students to disengage from their schoolwork.[6] Indeed, the "prison" environment at Crossroads suggested to students that they were deviant and delinquent. Structuring continuation schools according to a "prison model"—as was the case at Crossroads—can have the unintended consequence of punishing students for falling behind. In Valley View, the most salient threat that students posed was not one of violence or other illicit behavior; students who struggled academically threatened the academic ethos of exceptional achievement at comprehensive high schools like Pinnacle. Valley View's comprehensive high schools dealt with this threat by "dumping" those students to Crossroads.

In his commencement address to graduating Crossroads seniors and their families, Mr. Reyes, who taught history, firmly asserted that all Crossroads students were uniformly and unfairly homogenized and labeled as "failures." Practices and policies that encourage such negative labels frame and treat students themselves as problems instead of focusing on the social, emotional, and environmental factors that might contribute to a lack of academic engagement or achievement.[7] Negative labels also perpetuate harmful stereotypes about who is likely to succeed and fail,[8] and they have an adverse impact on students' self-image and sense of school community membership.[9]

During my time spent at Pinnacle, I encountered a group of students of color who did not feel entirely welcome on campus, so they took it upon themselves to create a space at school where they felt that they belonged, and where they could counter at least some of the marginalization that they experienced. This student club was called "Blackout," and one of its objectives was to keep its members out of Crossroads.

"BLACKOUT"

Victoria, the outspoken sixteen-year-old whom we met in chapter 1, began her freshman year at Pinnacle anticipating challenges that her older sister had faced there. As one of the few Black students on campus, Victoria was keenly aware of her minoritized status, and the social and academic isolation that consistently came with it. She grew particularly disillusioned with how Black, Latinx, and Native American history were framed in her social sciences and humanities classes:

SEAN: What's it like to be the only Black student in so many of your classes?

VICTORIA: I find it funny sometimes because whenever I say something in class, I'm never just Victoria; I'm always speaking as a Black person. I'm always the Black girl no matter what. Like, in Ms. Miller's class or any other class, when we were talking about slavery, whenever they would show clips of slaves getting whipped or whatever, the teachers would go really fast through it, and I felt like, no—the whole class needs to see it. I already know about this. I already know that Black History Month is the shortest month.

SEAN: Let's pretend that you are in charge of the history curriculum here at Pinnacle. Would you change anything?

VICTORIA: Oh, that would be amazing! I would definitely change things. I really think that they should repeal Black history here. They just don't really teach us a lot about Black people. We see that slaves were whipped and all of that stuff. But we just learn about the *bad* Black history. We don't really learn about the good. Like, what did we invent? Because we invented a lot. We did a lot, we've done a lot, and we're still doing a lot. But we don't learn about that; we learn about other stuff. We're not learning about everything in US history; we're learning about White and European history. And they totally sugarcoat the Trail of Tears and Native American genocide. So I actually I started a Black club here, because we need to learn some stuff that they aren't teaching us.

SEAN: You started a club here?

VICTORIA: Yeah, it's called Blackout. It's a Black club, but we have White people and Mexicans and a couple of Asians in it, and that's actually great because I want everyone to know about good Black history.

SEAN: Why did you start the club?

VICTORIA: Because I didn't like what they were teaching us, and because I know that Black students kind of feel isolated here at Pinnacle and like they're not welcome here. They might want to make friends and not know how. So I started this social club so that Black kids here can be comfortable for who they are at this school for at least the thirty minutes that we meet every week. We can express what we want to and how we feel about the school at Pinnacle and all of that stuff. And we talk about historical things and stuff going on in the world that affects people of color. So that's what we do and it's really fun. You should come to one of our meetings!

Blackout meetings were held on Mondays in a vacant classroom during the lunch period, and there were usually around twenty students in attendance. Students talked about how they wanted to learn more about Black history than what was being taught in their classes, and they shared some of that omitted history with each other. They talked about wanting more Black students in their classes. They talked about the complete lack of Black teachers on the faculty, and how exciting it had been to recently have a Black substitute teacher for two straight days. They talked about how they had witnessed Black and Latinx students at Pinnacle face harsher discipline than White or Asian students who had engaged in the same behavior. They talked about their fear of being sent to Crossroads, and how the students who were transferred there were disproportionately Black and Latinx. Several Blackout participants had close friends who were at Crossroads, and they spoke about missing those friends at school. Victoria reminded everyone to always stay on top of their assignments to avoid the prospect of being forced out to Crossroads.

They also shared their accomplishments and congratulated each other enthusiastically. They set new goals together and wrote them down for accountability. They made a poster for Black History Month and posted it on an outdoor wall near the center of campus. They celebrated birthdays and had a dance competition. They had fun together, and those thirty minutes always passed much too fast for all of them.

Victoria and her friends supported each other and spread awareness of the brilliance of Black, Latinx, and Indigenous people to the wider school community. They created a space for themselves, and they made sure that their voices were heard. They knew that they did not fit within what Ms. Owens at Crossroads had referred to as the "Valley View mold," and they also knew that no one was going to make them feel welcome; they had to welcome each other, again and again, week after week.

·   ·   ·   ·   ·

Renowned institutions like Pinnacle have a lot to be proud of, but that pride should not preclude a careful consideration of the ways in which policies and practices, no matter how well-intentioned, can marginalize students of color and perpetuate racial inequality. Addressing racial and socioeconomic disparity means first listening to the concerns of the marginalized and disadvantaged among us and prioritizing their voices and self-expressed needs. Just because a particular group of students are a small percentage of a larger student body should not be an excuse to ignore or dismiss their concerns, or neglect to recognize their accomplishments. And no student deserves to be written off because they have fallen behind academically. The boundless opportunities of public education are meant for every student, and public schools and districts have the awesome responsibility of fulfilling that promise.

Conclusion

Examining culture at the institutional level can be useful in revealing institutionalized, cultural mechanisms by which organizations, such as schools, reproduce inequality. An *institutional success frame* is one such mechanism. At Pinnacle, the success frame was exacting, and the school's highest achievers set the standard of academic expectation. The frame was divisive, as it split the school, generally, into two types of students: high achievers taking a slate of honors and AP classes on one hand, and everyone else who was not on the other. But the success frame didn't just fracture the student body in terms of curriculum tracking and course placement; narrow interpretations of success determined which students truly belonged in the Pinnacle community, and which students were treated as though they were out of place and out of their league.

The academic and social experience at Pinnacle was especially alienating for students who were not planning to attend a highly ranked college. For example, Diana did not belong on "college sweatshirt day," an episode emblematic of her lack of belonging overall. Despite her impressive academic accomplishment as the first in her working-class family of Mexican immigrants to attend college, Diana felt like a misfit at Pinnacle since she was set to enroll at a local community college instead of a more prestigious four-year institution. For Diana, the otherness that she felt during the college application and decision process was representative of her entire experience at Pinnacle.

Jamal (the Black, standout athlete whose transfer to Crossroads expanded the focus of this study) was prohibited from taking classes at Pinnacle even as he was allowed to practice and compete in games as a member of the varsity football and basketball teams. The message was clear: he was welcomed—he belonged—on Pinnacle's fields and courts, but not in its classrooms.

In another case, Victoria recounted incidents on campus and on social media in which Pinnacle students who were enrolled in advanced courses and making top grades would openly and publicly question the values and work ethic of students who had unassuming course schedules and lower GPAs. These incidents, and warnings about Crossroads from her older sister, motivated her and a small group of friends to organize and start a student club, where they spoke candidly about the stress and struggles that came with being a Black or Brown student at Pinnacle.

The institutional success frame affected how institutional actors responded to students' needs. When Mariah (a Black, sixteen-year-old junior whom we met in chapter 2) struggled in her classes, she felt more pressure to transfer to Crossroads than she did support from Pinnacle faculty to improve her grades.[1] Hassan, Jeremiah, Coleman, and many other Black and Brown students had a similar experience and came to the same conclusion: Pinnacle was deeply invested in managing a stellar academic reputation, and could jettison lower-performing students to Crossroads instead of investing additional resources to assist those who were struggling. They felt that Pinnacle did not embrace the responsibility of educating all students regardless of past or current performance level. Ms. Owens, the assistant principal at Crossroads, shared these views.

A rigid success frame made it easier for Pinnacle to justify and rationalize their decisions to push lower-achieving students out. Pinnacle administrators stridently argued—both to families and to me—struggling students simply did not fit in, that Pinnacle was too academic for them, and that those students would be better served over at Crossroads despite the dearth of resources there. Pinnacle used Crossroads as a "dumping ground"—a place to send students whose low academic performance might damage the school's lofty reputation as a "national exemplary" and "California distinguished" school. Thus, for Pinnacle, the presence of Crossroads in the district supported the school's rigid institutional success frame by absolving the school of the responsibility of educating struggling students. Rather than seeking to modify the Pinnacle environment to be more inclusive of all students, or implementing and sustaining additional academic support for students who had fallen behind, institutional actors at Pinnacle conveniently shepherded those students to Crossroads.

. . . . .

The institutional success frame at Pinnacle was heavily racialized, and this racialization of achievement was central to its divisiveness. At Pinnacle, high academic achievement was construed and stereotyped as the province of Asian students, who were lauded as responsible for the school's sterling academic reputation. The so-called "model minority" stereotype of Asian Americans fit neatly into Pinnacle's binary frame of achievement and failure because it implies that Black and Latinx students are not "model" citizens. When Ms. Quinn instructed a group of students not to "be all Asian" about their approach to some new information, that message worked as both a joke and a directive. There was both an implicit and explicit understanding that to "be Asian" meant to be intensely studious. Overall, Asian students, and their parents—especially those in the KPTA—were regarded as institutional assets, while Black and Latinx students were frequently treated as academic liabilities and potential behavior problems to be dealt with. Shepherding those students to Crossroads was a way of dealing with them.

At Pinnacle High School, ethnoracial stereotypes were also reified by parents. The KPTA provided language support to its members who were recent immigrants, academic support for Korean students, and seminars on Korean culture for Valley View teachers. These resources, and the fact that they were available at Pinnacle, streamlined Korean families' incorporation into the school community. This *institutionalization of ethnic capital*—the establishment of co-ethnic support services and advocacy within a school—undoubtedly reinforced stereotypes and implicit racial biases about which students were likely to succeed and fail.[2] During my fieldwork, several teachers made comments to me about how they were always confident that Asian students in their classes would be better prepared and more well-behaved than their non-Asian peers, and that they could count on Asian students' parents to provide ample support and structure at home. The Korean PTA group was the only explicitly ethnic parent group at the school until a Chinese PTA was established near the end of my time spent hanging out on campus.

· · · · ·

Over the course of my fieldwork I identified distinct, concrete institutional mechanisms of segregation that disproportionately placed Black and Latinx students at risk of being pushed out to Crossroads. Pinnacle's policy for attending to struggling students included a "threshold of credit deficiency" that a given student needed to reach before they were deemed a candidate for transfer to Crossroads. Students typically reached this threshold after failing two classes in the same semester, failing the same class twice, or if their cumulative GPA dipped below 2.0. Others approached or met the threshold because they had transferred to Pinnacle from another district or state, and not all of their course credits were accepted.

This credit deficiency policy, and the low bar for reaching the threshold, disproportionately affected Pinnacle's Black and Latinx students. Black and Latinx students' grades were, on average, considerably lower than those of their White and Asian peers. Black and Latinx students at Pinnacle were roughly twice as likely as White students, and four times as likely as Asian students, to maintain a cumulative GPA in the bottom quartile. Since the threshold was so closely linked to grades, students who identified as Black or Latino were more likely to reach the threshold.

But the credit deficiency policy was arbitrary in its implementation. I found that it was common for counselors and assistant principals at Pinnacle to recommend the transfer of a student who had not yet reached the threshold. Transfer to Crossroads was voluntary, but it was customary for Pinnacle administrators to apply considerable pressure on a student and their parents when the family resisted a transfer. Administrators, like Mr. Holt, leveraged the institutional success frame during the transfer decision process, referencing the academically rigorous environment at Pinnacle to legitimize and make the case to students and parents that a transfer to Crossroads was the only viable option available to them. Students and parents often needed convincing as they routinely questioned the merits, legitimacy, and overall consequences of making the switch.

In addition to arguing that Pinnacle was simply too academically stringent for some students, Pinnacle counselors and principals would often attempt to reassure skeptical students and parents by telling them that a diploma from Crossroads was the same level of diploma that students received from Pinnacle. But Crossroads curriculum was limited such that graduates were unable to directly enroll in a four-year university. Delivering this accurate but conveniently incomplete information about the diplomas helped Pinnacle administrators legitimize the transfer process and persuade students and families to acquiesce. Credit deficient students who were able to avoid Crossroads were often those whose families possessed the resources to acquire extra academic support, such as through private tutoring (which could easily cost several hundred dollars a month in Valley View), or a switch from Pinnacle to an expensive private high school. Affluent families had access to these alternatives. Pinnacle administrators were more likely to prevail over students and families who lacked the capital to successfully resist the pressure to transfer, a result that suggests that social class played a pivotal role in who ultimately ended up at Crossroads.

The continuation school model in Valley View provides clear examples of how, in racialized organizations, what people actually do (practice) often deviates from what they are supposed to do according to the rules (policy) in ways that exacerbate racial inequality, as well as how racialized organizations "legitimate the unequal distribution of resources."[3] Education scholar and ethnographer Eve Ewing reminds us that, regardless of the intentions of the people behind them, school policies and practices can be considered racist and discriminatory if those policies and practices disadvantage students of color, and thus reproduce racial and socioeconomic inequality.[4] At Pinnacle, the "threshold of credit deficiency" policy, and the coordinated, institutional practice of pressuring students and families to transfer to Crossroads, met that criteria; they resulted in the disproportionate pushout of Black, Latinx, and lower-income students to Crossroads.

At Crossroads, students' opportunities were curtailed, which further contributed to the social reproduction of racial and socioeconomic inequality. There were no clubs or sports teams offered by the school. There was no library and barely any homework. The curriculum was so sparse that no Crossroads graduate was eligible to matriculate at any four-year college or university, even if they earned straight A's. And Crossroads students were symbolically criminalized for their academic struggles. This criminalization was readily apparent in the physical structure of the school: an iron perimeter fence; classroom buildings that closely resembled trailers; constant, conspicuous police presence and floodlights for surveillance of students; no off-campus privileges during the school day; the threat of detention for setting foot on the campus of any comprehensive high school in the district. I refer to this constellation of conditions as *the criminalization of failure.*

All of these features of Crossroads were unique among Valley View's high schools, which added to the criminalizing character of the school and the sense of relative depravation that Crossroads students felt being there. Enrollment at Crossroads often became a stigmatizing "master status" of deviance, shame, and failure that students constantly managed among their family and friends.[5] I found it routine for students to arrive at Crossroads determined to recover credits and transfer back to the school from which they were sent, but instead gradually yield to a culture of academic apathy that sapped their focus and derailed their progress. The culture of academic apathy was a byproduct of segregating struggling students in a separate and punitive school. The concentration of "credit deficient" students at Crossroads undercut the district's stated goals of facilitating credit recovery and the return of students to the comprehensive, neighborhood high school from which they were transferred.

ACTIONABLE STEPS TOWARD EQUITY AND INCLUSION FOR STUDENTS WHO STRUGGLE

Ethnography can provide a solid foundation for effective social policy. Ethnographic methods enable researchers to discover, describe, and render the cultural characteristics and lived experiences of individuals and groups within dynamic social settings. In this section, I suggest modifications to policy and practice aimed at creating a more equitable high school experience for a wide range of students in places like Valley View and beyond. In presenting these potential solutions, I draw heavily from conversations with my informants. The institutional actors whom I came to know during my time spent in the field—students, parents, teachers, and administrators at both schools—identified problems with the status quo and were often eager to offer suggestions based on their experiences in the district. My recommendations reflect a combination of those suggestions and my own ethnographic observations.

Supporting Youth in a Context of Increasing Diversity

As the ethnoracial diversity of America's youth continues to increase with steady flows of immigration, the ethnoracial makeup of America's schools will follow suit. It is critical, therefore, that teachers and administrators seek a comprehensive understanding of the ethnic and racial diversity in their student populations, and the ways in which those populations are changing, so that they can practice culturally relevant pedagogy and provide appropriate support services.[6] Educators should also promote activities and events at school that reflect and celebrate the diversity on their campuses, particularly as levels of diversity are likely to increase in the coming years. The KPTA continues to serve these functions in Valley View, helping to make sure that the needs of Korean students are consistently met. But a disproportionately high percentage of students of color— including many Cambodian-, Hmong-, Laotian-, Vietnamese-, and other Southeast-Asian American students—do not have consistent access to such resources.[7]

Lastly, educators would do well to gain an understanding of the tremendous cultural and socioeconomic diversity among contemporary Asian immigrants to the United States. Viewing all Asian Americans as members of a homogenous group promotes racial and cultural stereotypes that may place an undue burden on Asian students, pushing some to sacrifice their health for academic achievements and making others feel like ethnoracial outliers.[8] Moreover, the racialization of academic aptitude and achievement pits students of color against each other, and too often casts Black and Latinx students as culturally deficient.[9]

Creating Credit Recovery Programs
at Comprehensive High Schools

Crossroads High School, and all other continuation high schools throughout California and across the country that take a similarly punitive approach to credit recovery, should be closed. Credit deficient students should, instead, be enrolled in credit recovery courses at their comprehensive high school. This systemic reform would accomplish three important objectives: 1) alleviate the embarrassing and alienating stigma that students experience when they are transferred to a school like Crossroads; 2) allow struggling students to remain on a campus free from the culture of academic apathy and distraction that pervades schools like Crossroads; and 3) keep credit deficient students connected to the enriching academic and extracurricular resources available at comprehensive high schools. Overall, a system of credit recovery programs at comprehensive high schools would end the practices of segregating credit deficient students into continuation school systems that often fail to engage them effectively and prepare them for life after high school.

In terms of staffing, the appropriate number of teachers could be hired from Crossroads to lead credit recovery classes at each comprehensive high school in Valley View. In terms of scheduling, students could take these classes in lieu of a free period during the school day, in the afternoon or evening after school, on Saturdays, or during a summer session. If credit deficient students remained at their neighborhood high school for credit recovery, the Crossroads space could be repurposed as a vocational and technical education center, where students from each of Valley View's comprehensive high schools would be able to take Career Technical Education Program (CTEP) classes. Offering a wide variety of those classes, and making them available to all Valley View high school students at a central location, would expand the curricular options for students throughout the district, regardless of their academic standing, interests, or career goals. This plan has the potential to create a credit recovery system considerably less marginalizing and stratifying than one that promotes flagrant between-school segregation along lines of race and class.

One of the reasons that Pinnacle students succeeded in such large numbers is that they associated high school achievement with college acceptance and enrollment. This collective student culture motivated them to compete with their peers by studying hard to earn A's, even in classes that they did not enjoy. Meanwhile, Crossroads students often thought of their classes in terms of "survival" rather than as crucial steps along a path to a four-year college. Repurposing Crossroads as a vocational education hub would add value to high school for students like Coleman, Tobias, and Miguel, who were behind on traditional course credits and considering postsecondary options other than college enrollment.

Every student deserves support and an option to graduate from high school with dignity and a workable plan for their future. Shifting credit recovery responsibilities to comprehensive high schools, and refashioning continuation schools as vocation training centers for public school districts, are concrete steps toward achieving that goal. Such reform would result in a more balanced and inclusive system of credit recovery in which the schools with the most resources would be truly accountable to every student.

. . . . .

The prevailing wisdom about reducing segregation and inequality in education is to reduce residential segregation since most American children attend school in the neighborhood in which they live.[10] In this book, however, I have presented a case of between-school segregation that operates independently from forces of neighborhood segregation. The segregation of students to Crossroads was ironic because those students, who arguably needed *more* resources and support, were pushed out of a resource-rich comprehensive high school and into a scholastic setting with far fewer resources and where one's peers were far more likely to be disengaged academically. Running a tall iron fence around the small, austere campus just added insult to injury. Sending students to Crossroads was an extreme form of tracking—tracking between schools rather than within them. Tracking between schools is worse, as it results in the complete academic and social marginalization of students. Tracking between schools is *academic apartheid*. The good news—the hopeful news—is that we can do so much better if we take the time to get to know our students, and if we summon the ambition and courage to act in their best interest.

Methodological Postscript

Ethnographic research necessitates a sustained engagement with one or more field sites, such that the ethnographer is able to apprehend and render the cultural parameters, contingencies, and lived experiences of individuals and groups within dynamic social settings. As such, the issue of entrée and repeated access to field sites is a perennial one for ethnographers, and successful methods of entrée vary according to the type of setting under study. For instance, a field researcher who wishes to examine the social intricacies of a public, city park may simply travel to the park, take a seat on a park bench, and quietly observe social behavior.[1] Quasi-public spaces, such as coffee shops, bars, and clubs, while not as open to access as most public parks, are still quite accepting of strangers who wish to enter, which streamlines the ethnographer's entrée and access negotiations.[2] In these cases, entrée is relatively straightforward, as is repeated access. But a field researcher's starting point is not always so accessible, particularly when the site or sites in question are quasi-private, such drug corners,[3] schools,[4] and commercial airliners[5]; private, such as homes[6] and masonic lodges[7]; or when potential informants are vulnerable or legally protected in some fashion.[8]

In the following pages, I present, in detail, my quest for access to Pinnacle High School and Crossroads High School as field sites. In the case of each school, negotiating the gatekeepers and bureaucratic relationships among institutional actors—a process that I refer to as *phased access*—was critical. Furthermore, I extend extant considerations of entrée into different types of field sites by taking a comparative approach and highlighting the ways in which the disparate characteristics and reputations of my two field sites influence entrée. I hope that this appendix is useful to others who may be planning ethnographic research projects in schools or other spaces where access is not guaranteed.

FINESSE

Gaining entrée to Pinnacle as a research site required quite a bit of finesse at all stages. I easily found the school's phone number online, and I began by calling the main office at 9 a.m. I called early in the day because I felt as though that would give me the best chance of reaching a senior administrator before the day's affairs took them out of the office.

My call was met with a recorded message that listed several options, most of which were tailored to a parent or guardian's needs. By pressing various buttons on a phone keypad, one could report a child's impending absence from school, request transcript information, access a counseling service and new student enrollment information, contact the athletics department, or speak to an operator. I pressed zero to speak to an operator, and then silently rehearsed the tone and objective that I would convey to whomever answered the phone: I would introduce myself, say something nice about Pinnacle, and then explain my objective in terms that I felt were broad, unbiased, and truthful. I would attempt to bolster my credibility by highlighting my affiliation with a large, local research university. Sociologists David Snow, Robert Benford, and Leon Anderson refer to this access strategy as assuming the fieldworker role of a "credentialed expert."[9]

Seconds later, a woman answered the phone and said, cheerfully, "Pinnacle High School, how may I help you?" I introduced myself by name and told her that I was a PhD student in sociology at UC Irvine studying race, ethnicity, culture, and education. I said that I had heard and read great things about Pinnacle and was interested in observing classroom interactions. The receptionist responded that she would transfer me to one of the school's assistant principals, Mr. Holt, who handled such requests. Schools and other bureaucratic, hierarchical institutions and organizations tend to have a staff member whose portfolio includes managing visitors to campus, and Mr. Holt was that staff member at Pinnacle.

She transferred me, and Mr. Holt's office phone eventually went to voicemail. I left him a brief message, introducing myself and explaining my objective in as cordial a manner as possible. I made a concerted effort to sound harmless in my motives because I knew schools to be very protective of their students, especially when most of those students are minors. (In fact, I had direct experience with this protective school culture because, after college, I spent three years as a preschool teacher teaching at a school that served the campus of an elite university. I also conducted research there, as it was a child development laboratory school for the adjacent university's renowned psychology department. As such, I was familiar with the difficulties in gaining access to schools for research purposes.) Before hanging up, I also made sure to leave my phone number and email address.

On his voicemail message, Mr. Holt stated that he would get back to callers "as soon as possible," so I expected to receive a return phone call or email within forty-eight hours or so. But the next couple of days passed without a word from Mr. Holt, and I began to grow restless and nervous. My restlessness and nervousness had twin sources: my eagerness to begin field research after over two years of graduate school coursework, and my anxiety over gaining research access to a highly protected space. As the days passed without a response, I grew more and more worried about my ability to use Pinnacle as a field site. I began bracing myself mentally for a struggle to gain access, a struggle that seemed imminent. I also identified another high school to try in case Pinnacle fell through.

Four days passed and I still hadn't heard from Mr. Holt, so I decided to call again, hoping to catch him in his office. The receptionist transferred me to Mr. Holt's office phone and, to my surprise, he answered the call. My heart rate immediately increased; I had a feeling that this conversation could make or break my project since, given my research interests, Pinnacle High seemed like the ideal school for me to include in the study.

I introduced myself to Mr. Holt, explained the purpose of my research, and told him that I had called and left a message for him the previous week. He replied that he had in fact received my message, but he made no mention of an attempt to contact me. He did not thank me for taking an interest in the school or apologize for not returning my call. It seemed as though he had intentionally ignored my initial call, perhaps waiting instead to see if I would follow up on my own.

Mr. Holt asked me a series of questions about my research agenda. He wanted to know why I was interested in Pinnacle and what I hoped to see. These were not difficult questions by themselves, but the context of the conversation—the pressure I felt to say the right things—made them somewhat uncomfortable. I wanted to be honest about my objectives, and I wanted him to like my answers so that I could move forward with my research agenda. I answered truthfully and was careful not to paint my project as too complex or judgmental. I told him that I did not have a specific story that I was looking to write; rather, I was interested in social interactions on campus and the general campus culture. I figured I would say what I thought I needed to say to make him feel comfortable, without being disingenuous, and then gradually unveil my full research agenda once I had built some rapport with administrators, teachers, students, and parents on campus. Furthermore, as is the case with many ethnographic projects, the full scope of the work was unclear to me in those early days when I was attempting to gain access. I expected new avenues of inquiry to emerge as the project developed.

After hearing my nascent plan, Mr. Holt told me to send him an email introducing myself and explaining my research objectives. Later that afternoon I drafted a deferential email in which I introduced myself as a PhD student at UCI, praised Pinnacle for the academic achievements of its students, and explained my desire to observe classroom interactions at the high school. I wrote that I was currently enrolled in a graduate seminar that trained doctoral students in the art of field research, that the class required students to make several observations "in the field," and that I wished to conduct my observations at Pinnacle. I also expressed a desire to observe at least two hours of classroom interaction per week for the next four months. (I wanted to eventually observe much more than this, but two hours a week seemed like a good place to start.)

I received a return email from Mr. Holt the next morning. I was relieved that he had returned my message so quickly, but somewhat disheartened at his reply. He felt that the amount of time that I wished to observe was "excessive, given the number of classrooms that currently have regular visitors." He suggested that I make "observations with two or three teachers for a couple of weeks." I decided to counter his inauspicious message by reducing the number of hours that I wished to observe. I replied that I would be okay with observing for one hour per week for the next four months instead of two hours per week. The reduction in requested hours seemed to placate Mr. Holt somewhat; he responded that he'd send my original email out to several teachers and get back to me if he received any responses indicating that someone was willing to let me observe in their classroom.

Mr. Holt emailed me the following day saying that he had found a teacher who would be glad to let me observe in her classroom. Needless to say, I was excited and encouraged by this development. I emailed the teacher, Ms. Quinn, directly, hoping to set up an observation schedule. I introduced myself in the email and expressed my objectives. I also praised the schools stellar academic record and my interest in understanding more about what made Pinnacle a flagship institution. Ms. Quinn responded to my email later that day. Her response was friendly in tone, and she communicated an easygoing personality and willingness to help. She wrote that she taught two AP classes at Pinnacle, and her email included a link to the school's academic calendar and daily bell schedule. She also requested that I share my observations with her and wondered whether I might be able to lend relevant insights to one of her classes during an upcoming unit. I responded with my availability and told Ms. Quinn that I hoped to start making observations the following Monday. I also told her that I felt that the more I observed in her classes, the higher in quality my field notes would be. I also made sure to stress that I did not want to infringe upon her classroom dynamics and make her or the students feel uncomfortable with my presence.

I heard back from Ms. Quinn the following day, a Thursday. She thanked me for demonstrating respect for the classroom space and students in my previous message and said that she felt that the more I observed, the more comfortable the students would be with me being in class with them. We set a date for me to begin my observations the following Monday. I would be observing two periods of AP psychology and one period of AP world history—a total of over three hours on campus. This amount of time, even at the outset of my fieldwork, was much more time than what I had asked for from Mr. Holt. I was satisfied. Once I had the support of a willing teacher, I was off and running.

A VARIETY OF GATEKEEPERS

Gaining access to a particular social world is a crucial aspect of ethnographic research. My experience indicates that, when trying to garner entrée into a hierarchical bureaucracy, individuals who are in supervisory roles may know very little about the day-to-day demands of those performing other duties within the institution, and how the presence of an ethnographer would affect those employees. In my case, the Pinnacle assistant principal, Mr. Holt, cleared me to observe for a few hours per week over the course of two or three weeks, but several teachers ultimately stated that they would be "happy to have" me in their classroom, and invited me to observe "anytime." Thus, although everything worked out in the end, if I could go back and repeat the entrée process, I would begin by emailing several teachers to introduce myself and my project and ask them to reach out to other teachers who might be interested as well. Once I found one or more teachers who were willing to host me as an observer in their classes, I would email an assistant principal, such as Mr. Holt, to introduce myself and my project. In the event that one is interested in participant observation within classrooms, a teacher is one's best ally when trying to get approval from administrators who have to sign off on any arrangements.

FLEXIBILITY AND PERSISTENCE

One of the benefits of the ethnographic method is that it allows and invites the researcher to adapt their research agenda in the middle of a study in response to observations and conversations in the field. I embarked on this project intending to study Black and Brown students' experiences negotiating elite academic culture in an affluent high school community in which Asian and White students comprised roughly 90% of the student body. But Jamal's transfer to Crossroads High School changed my plans. After he was pushed out to Crossroads, I decided to expand my research to include Crossroads as a field site.

Gaining access to Crossroads took persistence. I had to make nine separate phone calls to the school over a period of six weeks, and leave six messages, before I received a return phone call. This process of calling and leaving messages was stressful because Crossroads represented a unique school site that would be central and vital to the comparative aspect of my work. Thus, gaining access to Crossroads was a high-stakes affair.

I began leaving phone messages with various members of the front office staff on January 7. I left a message with the school principal and vice principal, introducing myself and outlining my objectives in broad terms, but I heard nothing back from either of them. I also left messages, during subsequent attempts to phone in and reach the principal or vice principal, with a receptionist, student health coordinator, and counselor. I did not receive a return phone call from any of these school personnel until February 26, when I got a call from the school counselor—Ms. Carter. She acknowledged that I had been trying to gain access to Crossroads for several weeks and she apologized for the slow reply. She explained that the school had limited resources and that accommodating research requests was not high on their priority list because "no one ever wants to visit us here at Crossroads, so we just aren't used to dealing with visitor requests."

Ms. Carter expressed a genuine interest in my project and told me that she was glad that I wanted to conduct research at Crossroads. She said that there were a lot of misconceptions about the students who attended Crossroads, and that it would be nice for someone to observe and see what it was really like on campus. She told me about the various student programs that Crossroads offered and asked me what I was interested in observing. I told her that, at first, I would be interested in seeing as much of the school as possible to get a sense of the place and space. She offered to take me on a guided tour of the facility, and we set an appointment for the following week. "Crossroads has a reputation as a school for bad kids, so it will be great for you to come and see all the great work that we are doing," she said.

UNIQUE CHALLENGES AT UNIQUE INSTITUTIONS

My access to each field site was only secure once I had received approval from those who worked there, and each case presented unique challenges. At Pinnacle, I found it easy to connect with an administrator, but coming to an agreement with school officials about how much time I would need to spend on campus was a challenge. This may have been due to Pinnacle's reputation as the flagship public high school in Valley View. Was Mr. Holt worried about what I would observe and write about? Was he concerned that my findings might impugn the school's lofty reputation? I am still not sure, but I do know that he appreciated hearing about all the measures that I planned to take to maintain the confidentiality of all members of the Pinnacle school community, and he especially liked hearing that I was interested in producing a rigorous and accurate portrayal of Pinnacle's academic culture. Gaining the approval of teachers—the institutional actors with whom I would have the most direct interactions—was pivotal.

It was far more difficult to obtain an initial response from Crossroads, but school officials there readily welcomed me to campus. Their eagerness may have been rooted in a desire to show Crossroads in a positive light to an outsider like me. Ultimately, institutional actors at Crossroads were quite vocal with me about their discontent with the district's continuation school model. They wanted me to know how they felt, and they urged me on numerous occasions to "make sure you put *that* in the book."

PHASED ACCESS

I took a *phased access* approach to my entrée at Pinnacle and my initial visits there. I began observing one teacher in one subject, then expanded to other classes taught by the same teacher, then was referred to other teachers and eventually scheduled interviews with students, parents, and administrators. My access to various school spaces, and to various institutional actors, came in several phases rather than all at once.

This phased access approach is useful because it is gradual. A gradual start to fieldwork is advantageous for the ethnographer because it gives one space to reflect on time spent in the field, plan for subsequent visits, and build the rapport and trust with community members that is often essential to rich, fulsome data gathering. Phased access also helps ensure that one makes repeated observations in similar settings at first. For example, when I first started observing at Pinnacle, I observed in just one classroom— Ms. Quinn's—and during just three of her class periods. This allowed me to recognize some patterns that I might have missed had I moved around the school to observe in different classrooms from the outset of my fieldwork. I did eventually make observations in every corner of the school, but my process of expansion throughout the community was slow and methodical.

Doing ethnography is like running a marathon race—you cannot win it in the first mile, but you can definitely lose it by starting too fast and neglecting to pace yourself. A modest pace at the outset allows one the flexibility to make crucial adjustments later on. For the ethnographer, a phased access approach to entrée and initial participant and non-participant observation sets a good tempo for the long road of data collection ahead.

Notes

1. Anderson 2015.

2. Valley View is a pseudonym, as are the names of all institutions and people mentioned throughout the book.

3. For reference, according to the United States Census, in 2018 the US median household income was about $63,000, and roughly 32% of American adults held at least a Bachelor's Degree: https://www.census.gov/programs-surveys/acs/data.html.

4. During the 2013–2014, 2014–2015, and 2015–2016 school years (when I conducted fieldwork), approximately 11.2% of Pinnacle students were designated by Valley View Unified School District as "socioeconomically disadvantaged," which the district stipulated as an income of $46,000-or-less for a family of four.

5. According to the principal of Pinnacle High School, the "vast majority" of Asian students enrolled were from Korean and Chinese immigrant families.

6. Ewing 2018; Lewis and Diamond 2015; Lewis-McCoy 2014; and Shedd 2015.

7. United States Census Bureau 1960.

8. National Center for Education Statistics 2013.

9. Pew Research Center 2012.

10. Portes and Rumbaut 2014.

11. Crossroads High School opened in 1974.

12. Warren 2007; Warren 2016.

13. California Department of Education 2020.

14. Ruiz de Velasco and McLaughlin 2010.

15. Ruiz de Velasco et al. 2008.

16. Kelly 1993; Munoz 2005; and Perez and Johnson 2008.

17. Vogell 2017.

18. Vogell and Fresques 2017.

19. Pinnacle and Crossroads also differ in terms of the percentage of their students whom the district designates as "students with disabilities." During the 2014–2015 school year, 5.0% of Pinnacle students were deemed "students with disabilities," which was close to the district average of 6.1%. At Crossroads, however, 19.8% of students were "students with disabilities" during the same year. These students were not a focus of the study, but the marginalization of "students with disabilities," and the ethnoracial inequality in the assessment of learning disabilities, remain critical issues that should be examined in greater depth (see Blanchett 2006 and Harry and Klingner 2014).

20. Katz 1997; Ocejo 2013. Ethnography is the systematic study of culture, typically the culture of a place or community, that focuses on the daily lives of people there.

21. Fiel 2013; Johnson, Jr. 2014; Reardon and Owens 2014; Rothstein 2014.

22. Clotfelter, Vigdor, and Ladd 2006.

23. Clotfelter 2004.

24. Orfield 2001.

25. Coleman 1975; Johnson 2019.

26. Logan and Oakley 2004.

27. Lutz 2011.

28. Orfield 1983.

29. Reardon and Owens 2014.

30. Reber 2005.

31. Clotfelter 2004; Reardon and Yun 2003; Saporito and Sohoni 2007.

32. Wilson 1985.

33. Reber 2005.

34. Iceland and Sharp 2013; Stroub and Richards 2013.

35. Reardon et al. 2012.

36. Lutz 2011.

37. Bourdieu and Passeron 1977; Bowles and Gintis 2011; Coleman et al 1966; Domina, Penner, and Penner 2017; Fischeret al. 1995; MacLeod 1995.

38. Bowles and Gintis 1976:126

39. McDonough 1997; Willis 1981

40. Sociologist Dalton Conley has found that, among families living in poverty (measured in terms of household income), the average Black family holds $0 in assets while the average White family holds nearly $10,000. And the Black-White wealth gap is not limited to the poor; the harsh reality is that, as Conley writes, "At all income, occupational, and education levels, Black families on average have drastically lower levels of wealth than similar white families" (Conley 1999:5). See also Flynn et al. 2017.

41. Frankenberg, Lee, and Orfield 2003; Orfield 2001; Orfield and Lee 2005.

42. Carter 2005; Howard 2010; Lewis 2003; Noguera 2003a, 2003b; Rios 2011; Shedd 2015.

43. Saporito and Sohoni 2007; Logan, Minca, and Adar 2012.

44. Goldsmith 2009; Logan, Minca, and Adar 2012.

45. Hanushek, Kain, and Rivkin 2009; Johnson, Jr. 2014.

46. Guryan 2004; Johnson 2011; Reber 2010.

47. Johnson 2011; Johnson 2019.

48. Bankston and Caldas 1996; Bifulco and Ladd 2007; Bischoff 2008; Charles 2003; Denton 1995; Goldsmith 2009; Johnson 2012; Reardon and Owens 2014; Rothstein 2014.

49. Carter 2005; Ewing 2018; Lopez 2003; Shedd 2015; Valenzuela 1999.

50. Lucas 1999; Oakes 2005; Tyson 2011.

51. Lewis and Diamond 2015.

52. Lewis and Diamond 2015; Lewis-McCoy 2014; Lewis-McCoy 2016.

53. Lewis 2003; Shedd 2015.

54. In the years immediately before I began my fieldwork, levels of residential segregation in Valley View were some of the lowest in the country among cities with 200,000 or more residents (Logan and Zhang 2011).

55. Khan 2011.

56. Jack 2019.

57. Shedd 2015.

58. Kupchik 2010.

59. Rios 2006.

60. Kupchik 2016; Lopez 2003.

61. Gregory, Skiba, and Noguera 2010; Howard 2014.

62. Zussman 2004.

63. Massey and Denton 1993.

64. Malagón 2010.

65. Duneier 2011.

66. Lofland et al. 2006.

67. Snow, Zurcher, and Sjorberg 1982.

68. Biernacki and Waldorf 1981.

69. I interviewed over twice as many students at Crossroads as I did at Pinnacle both by choice and by chance. I chose to focus more on Crossroads because I was principally interested in students' experiences attending a "continuation school." I also found it much easier to schedule interviews with students at Crossroads because Crossroads teachers were far more likely to excuse students from class so that they could sit for an interview with me.

CHAPTER 1. "IF YOU'RE NOT IN AP CLASSES"

1. A neighborhood public school is a school in which students are eligible to enroll based on their neighborhood of residence, which must be within the school's residential catchment zone. Pinnacle drew its students strictly from those living in neighborhoods adjacent to the school.

2. Goffman 1974.

3. Rios 2017.

4. Lee and Zhou 2014, 2015.

5. There were no leaflets from tutoring agencies placed on cars in the Crossroads High School parking lot during back-to-school night at Crossroads.

6. Feliciano 2005a, 2005b

7. Lee and Zhou 2015.

8. Lee and Zhou 2015; Zhou and Lee 2017.

9. Zhou and Lee 2014.

10. Zhou and Lee 2017.

11. Chua and Rubenfeld 2015; Kristoff 2015.

12. Kao 1995; Lee 1994; Ngo and Lee 2007; Ocampo 2016.

13. Lee 2014.

14. Chua and Rubenfeld 2015; Kristoff 2015.

15. Yiu 2013; Zhou and Lee 2017.

16. Jiménez and Horowitz 2013.
17. Waldinger and Lichter 2003.
18. See Fischer et al. 1995. See also Flynn et al. 2017.
19. Sociologist Jennifer Lee (2014) wonders which immigrant group would be considered most successful if we measured the success of immigrant groups based on intergenerational progress and social mobility.

CHAPTER 2. THE SYMBOLIC CRIMINALIZATION OF FAILURE

1. See Darling-Hammond 2004; Lucas 1999; Noguera 2003a; Noguera 2003b; Oakes 1982; Oakes 1990; O'Connor et al. 2011; and Tyson 2011.
2. Lee and Zhou 2015.
3. See Darling-Hammond 2004; Lewis and Diamond 2015; Noguera 2008; Noguera and Wing (eds.) 2008; and Oakes 2005.
4. Rosenbaum 1978.
5. Lewis and Diamond 2015.
6. Khan 2011.
7. Roughly 63% of students enrolled in four-year colleges and universities graduate within six years (DeAngelo et al. 2011), which is nearly four times more than the percentage of those who do at community colleges. See also Moore and Shulock 2010.
8. Rios 2011.
9. Shedd 2015.
10. Lee and Zhou 2015.
11. Lee, Drake, and Zhou 2019.
12. Ray 2019.
13. Ray 2019.
14. Bourdieu and Passeron 1977; Heath 1983; Jack 2019; Lareau 1987; Lareau 2002.
15. Coleman 1988.
16. Conchas 2006; Jack 2019; Stanton-Salazar and Dornbusch 1995.
17. Carter 2005
18. Coleman 1988.
19. Ball and Vincent 1998; Lareau, Evans, and Yee 2016; Neild 2005.
20. Bodovski 2010; Lareau 2000; Smrekar and Goldring 1999.
21. Coleman's knowledge that many students at Crossroads got high on Xanax before and/or after school, and his judgement that this behavior precluded their academic progress, highlights the need for continued research on prescription drug abuse among high school students. See Sussman et al. 1995, 1998.

22. Lopez 2003.

23. See Fine 1991; Kupchik and Ward 2014; and Rios 2006, 2011, 2017.

24. Lopez 2003; Noguera 2003b; Valenzuela 1999.

CHAPTER 3. THE SEGREGATION OF TEACHING AND LEARNING

1. Kendziora and Osher 2009.

2. Lewis et al. 2005; Romi, Lewis, and Katz 2009.

3. Freiberg and Lamb 2009.

4. Freiberg and Lamb 2009.

5. Evertson and Weinstein 2006; Pigge and Marso 1997.

6. See Jacob 2007.

7. See Darling-Hammond and Sykes 2003; and Ingersoll 2001.

8. Ingersoll and May 2011.

9. See Ronfeldt, Loeb, and Wyckoff 2013.

CHAPTER 4. THE INSTITUTIONALIZATION OF ETHNIC CAPITAL

1. United States Census Bureau 2010.

2. See Gordon 1964; Warner and Srole 1945.

3. See Portes and Stepick 1993.

4. Geschwender 1978; Greeley 1971; Portes and Zhou 1993; Rumbaut 2005.

5. Caplan, Choy, and Whitmore 1992; Gibson 1988; Matute-Bianchi 1986.

6. Portes and Rumbaut 2014.

7. Alba 2009; Alba and Nee 1997.

8. Jiménez and Horowitz 2013.

9. Pew Research Center 2012.

10. Kristof 2015.

11. Chua and Rubenfeld 2015.

12. Kao 1995.

13. Feliciano 2005a, 2005b 2006; Steinberg 2001.

14. See Lee and Zhou 2015.

15. See Hsin 2016; Jiménez 2016; Wong 2015.

16. Borjas 1992.

17. See Zhou 2009; Zhou and Bankston 1994; Zhou and Lin 2005; and Zhou and Kim 2006.

18. Bankston and Zhou 1995.

19. There is now a Chinese PTA at Pinnacle that operates in much the same manner as the Korean PTA. The Chinese PTA had not yet been fully established by the time I finished conducting field work at the school, hence my focus on the Korean PTA.

20. See Tsang et al 2003; Tsong and Liu 2009.

21. Lee and Zhou 2015; Tsong and Liu 2009.

22. See Chang and Darlington 2008; and Nora Chiang 2008.

23. See Finch and Kim 2012; and Jung and Wang 2018.

24. Tsang et al. 2003.

25. Zhou 1998.

26. See Coleman 1988; DiMaggio 1982.

27. In fact, through much of American history, immigrant groups of a variety of ethnic and racial backgrounds have built social and cultural capital by forming co-ethnic organizations (Portes and Rumbaut 2014). As such, I would argue that there is nothing un-American about a Korean Parent Organization in a high school in Southern California.

28. Blumer 1958.

29. Lewis and Diamond 2015.

30. Shapiro 2019.

31. Shapiro and Wang 2019.

32. Gordon 1964.

33. Feliciano 2005a, 2006; Lee and Zhou 2015.

34. Kao and Tienda 1995.

35. Alba, Sloan, and Sperling 2011.

36. Ray 2019.

37. Lee 2012.

38. Alba and Nee 2003; Jiménez and Horowitz 2013.

39. A group of Chinese parents followed suit during my final weeks of fieldwork at Pinnacle, when they organized to establish a Chinese PTA.

40. Lewis-McCoy 2014.

41. Yiu 2013.

42. Alba and Nee 2003; Jiménez 2017; Jiménez and Horowitz 2013.

CHAPTER 5. "WE'VE FAILED THESE KIDS"

1. Wilson 1987.

2. Lewis and Diamond 2015.

3. Conchas 2006.

4. Fine et al. 2004.

5. Fine 1991; Rios 2006, 2011.

6. Lopez 2003; Noguera 2003b; Rios 2017; Valenzuela 1999.

7. Osterman 2000.

8. Flores-Gonzales 2002.

9. Deschenes, Cuban, and Tyack 2001; Rios 2011.

CONCLUSION

1. For a vivid account of how the public education system marginalizes and criminalizes Black girls, see Morris (2016).

2. Eberhardt et al. 2004.

3. Ray 2019.

4. Ewing 2018.

5. See Becker 1963; Goffman 1963.

6. Howard 2010.

7. Ngo and Lee 2007; Yang 2004.

8. Gupta, Szymanski, and Leong 2011; Wong and Halgin 2006.

9. Chua and Rubenfeld 2015.

10. Flynn et al. 2017.

METHODOLOGICAL POSTSCRIPT

1. Anderson 2011.

2. Snow, Robinson, and McCall 1991.

3. Bourgois 1993.

4. Shedd 2015.

5. Hochschild 2012.

6. Goffman 2009.

7. Mahmud 2012.

8. Goffman 2014.

9. Snow, Benford, and Anderson 1986.

Bibliography

Alba, Richard. 2009. *Blurring the Color Line: The New Chance for a More Integrated America*. Cambridge, MA: Harvard University Press.

Alba, Richard, and Victor Nee. 1997. "Rethinking Assimilation Theory for a New Era of Immigration." *International Migration Review* 31(4):826–874.

———. 2003. *Remaking the American Mainstream: Assimilation and Contemporary Immigration*. Cambridge, MA: Harvard University Press.

Alba, Richard, Jennifer Sloan, and Jessica Sperling. 2011. "The Integration Imperative: The Children of Low-Status Immigrants in the Schools of Wealthy Societies." *Annual Review of Sociology* 37:395–415.

Anderson, Elijah. 2011. *The Cosmopolitan Canopy: Race and Civility in Everyday Life*. New York: W. W. Norton.

———. 2015. "The White Space." *Sociology of Race and Ethnicity* 1(1):10–21.

Ball, Stephen J., and Carol Vincent. 1998. "'I Heard It on the Grapevine': 'Hot' Knowledge and School Choice." *British Journal of Sociology of Education* 19(3):377–400.

Bankston, Carl L., and Stephen J. Caldas. 1996. "Majority African American Schools and Social Injustice." *Social Forces* 75(2):535–555.

Bankston, Carl L., and Min Zhou. 1995. "Religious Participation, Ethnic Identification, and Adaptation of Vietnamese Adolescents in an Immigrant Community." *Sociological Quarterly* 36(3):523–534.

Becker, Howard. 1963. *Outsiders: Studies in the Sociology of Deviance.* New York: Simon & Schuster.

Biernacki, Patrick, and Dan Waldorf. 1981. "Snowball Sampling: Problems and Techniques of Chain Referral Sampling." *Sociological Methods & Research* 10(2):141–163.

Bifulco, Robert, and Helen F. Ladd. 2007. "School Choice, Racial Segregation, and Test-Score Gaps." *Journal of Policy Analysis and Management* 26(1):31–56.

Bischoff, Kendra. 2008. "School District Boundaries and Racial Residential Segregation: How Do Boundaries Matter?" *Urban Affairs Review* 44(2):182–217.

Blanchett, Wanda J. 2006. "Disproportionate Representation of African American Students in Special Education: Acknowledging the Role of White Privilege and Racism." *Educational Researcher* 35(6):24–28.

Blumer, Herbert. 1958. "Race Prejudice as a Sense of Group Position." *Pacific Sociological Review* 1(1):3–7.

Bodovski, Katerina. 2010. "Parental Practices and Educational Achievement: Social Class, Race, and Habitus." *British Journal of Sociology of Education* 31(2):139–156.

Borjas, George J. 1992. "Ethnic Capital and Intergenerational Mobility." *Quarterly Journal of Economics* 107(1):123–150.

Bourdieu, Pierre, and Jean-Claude Passeron. 1977. *Reproduction in Education, Society and Culture.* London: Sage Publications.

Bourgois, Philippe. 1993. *In Search of Respect: Selling Crack in El Barrio.* New York: Cambridge University Press.

Bowles, Samuel, and Herbert Gintis. 1976. *Schooling in Capitalist America: Educational Reform and the Contradictions of Economic Life.* New York: Basic Books.

———. 2011. *Schooling in Capitalist America: Educational Reform and the Contradictions of Economic Life (2011 Edition).* Chicago: Haymarket Books.

California Department of Education. 2020. *Continuation Education.* https://www.cde.ca.gov/sp/eo/ce.

Caplan, Nathan, Marcella H. Choy, and John K. Whitmore. 1992. "Indochinese Refugee Families and Academic Achievement." *Scientific American* 266(2):36–45.

Carter, Prudence L. 2005. *Keepin' It Real: School Success beyond Black and White*. New York: Oxford University Press.

Chang, Man Wai, and Yvonne Darlington. 2008. "'Astronaut' Wives: Perceptions of Changes in Family Roles." *Asian and Pacific Migration Journal* 17(1):61–77.

Charles, Camille Z. 2003. "The Dynamics of Racial Residential Segregation." *Annual Review of Sociology* 29:167–207.

Chua, Amy, and Jed Rubenfeld. 2015. *The Triple Package: How Three Unlikely Traits Explain the Rise and Fall of Cultural Groups in America*. New York: Penguin Books.

Clotfelter, C. T. 2004. *After Brown: The Rise and Retreat of School Desegregation*. Princeton, NJ: Princeton University Press.

Clotfelter, C. T., Jacob L. Vigdor, and Helen F. Ladd. 2006. "Federal Oversight, Local Control, and the Specter of 'Resegregation' in Southern Schools." *American Law and Economics Review* 8(2):347–389.

Coleman, James S. 1975. *Trends in School Segregation, 1968–73*. Washington, DC: Urban Institute.

——. 1988. "Social Capital in the Creation of Human Capital." *American Journal of Sociology* 94:95–120.

Coleman, James S., Ernest Q. Campbell, Carol J. Hobson, James McPartland, Alexander M. Mood, Frederic D. Weinfeld, and Robert L. York. 1966. *Equality of Educational Opportunity*. Washington, DC: US Government Printing Office.

Conchas, Gilberto Q. 2006. *The Color of Success: Race and High-Achieving Urban Youth*. New York: Teachers College Press.

Conley, Dalton. 1999. *Being Black, Living in the Red*. Berkeley: University of California Press.

Darling-Hammond, Linda. 2004. "The Color Line in American Education." *Du Bois Review* 1(2):213–246.

Darling-Hammond, Linda, and Gary Sykes. 2003. "Wanted: A National Teacher Supply Policy for Education: The Right Way to Meet the 'Highly Qualified Teacher' Challenge." *Education Policy Analysis Archives* 11(33):1–55.

DeAngelo, Linda, Ray Franke, Sylvia Hurtado, John H. Pryor, and Serge Tran. 2011. *Completing College: Assessing Graduation Rates at Four-Year Institutions*. Higher Education Research Institute at UCLA (HERI). Available online: http://heri.ucla.edu/DARCU/Completing College2011.pdf.

Denton, Nancy. 1995. "The Persistence of Segregation: Links Between Residential Segregation and School Segregation." *Minnesota Law Review* 80:795–824.

Deschenes, Sarah, Larry Cuban, and David Tyack. 2001. "Mismatch: Historical Perspectives on Schools and Students Who Don't Fit Them." *Teachers College Record* 103(4):525–547.

DiMaggio, Paul. 1982. "Cultural Capital and School Success: The Impact of Status Culture Participation on the Grades of US High School Students." *American Sociological Review* 47(2):189–201.

Domina, Thurston, Andrew Penner, and Emily Penner. 2017. "Categorical Inequality: Schools as Sorting Machines." *Annual Review of Sociology* 43:311–330.

Duneier, Mitchell. 2011. "How Not to Lie With Ethnography." *Sociological Methodology* 41(1):1–11.

Eberhardt, Jennifer L., Phillip Atiba Goff, Valerie J. Purdie, and Paul G. Davies. 2004 "Seeing Black: Race, Crime, and Visual Processing." *Journal of Personality and Social Psychology* 87(6):876–893.

Evertson, Carolyn M., and Carol S. Weinstein. 2006. "Classroom Management as a Field of Inquiry." Pp. 3–16 in *Handbook of Classroom Management: Research, Practice, and Contemporary Issues*, edited by C. M. Evertson and C. S. Weinstein. Mahwah, NJ: Lawrence Erlbaum Associates.

Ewing, Eve L. 2018. *Ghosts in the Schoolyard: Racism and School Closings on Chicago's South Side.* Chicago: University of Chicago Press.

Feliciano, Cynthia. 2005a. "Educational Selectivity in U.S. Immigration: How Do Immigrants Compare to Those Left Behind?" *Demography* 42:131–152.

———. 2005b. *Unequal Origins: Immigrant Selection and the Education of the Second Generation.* New York: LFB Scholarly Publishing.

———. 2006. "Beyond the Family: The Influence of Premigration Group Status on the Educational Expectations of Immigrants' Children." *Sociology of Education* 79(4):281–303.

Fiel, Jeremy E. 2013. "Decomposing School Resegregation: Social Closure, Racial Imbalance, and Racial Isolation." *American Sociological Review* 78(5):828–848.

Finch, John, and Seung-Kyung Kim. 2012. "Kirogi Families in the U.S.: Transnational Migration and Education." *Journal of Ethnic and Migration Studies* 38(3):485–506.

Fine, Michelle. 1991. *Framing Dropouts: Notes on the Politics of an Urban High School*. Albany: State University of New York Press.

Fine, Michelle, April Burns, Yasser Payne, and Maria Elena Torre. 2004. "Civics Lessons: The Color and Class of Betrayal." *Teachers College Record* 106(11):2193–2223.

Fischer, Claude S., Michael Hout, Martín Sánchez Jankowski, Samuel R. Lucas, Ann Swidler, and Kim Voss. 1995. *Inequality by Design: Cracking the Bell Curve Myth*. Princeton, NJ: Princeton University Press.

Flores-Gonzales, Nilda. 2002. *School Kids/Street Kids: Identity Development in Latino Students*. New York: Teachers College Press.

Flynn, Andrea, Susan R. Holmberg, Dorian T. Warren, and Felicia J. Wong. 2017. *The Hidden Rules of Race: Barriers to an Inclusive Economy*. New York: Cambridge University Press.

Frankenberg, Erica; Chungmei Lee, and Gary Orfield. 2003. *A Multiracial Society with Segregated Schools: Are We Losing the Dream?* The Civil Rights Project, Harvard University. Available online: https://www.civilrightsproject.ucla.edu/research/k-12-education/integration-and-diversity/a-multiracial-society-with-segregated-schools-are-we-losing-the-dream/frankenberg-multiracial-society-losing-the-dream.pdf.

Freiberg, Jerome H., and Stacey M. Lamb. 2009. "Dimension of Person-Centered Classroom Management." *Theory into Practice* 48(2):99–105.

Geschwender, James A. 1978. *Racial Stratification in America*. Dubuque, IA: William C. Brown.

Gibson, Margaret A. 1988. *Accommodation Without Assimilation: Sikh Immigrants in an American High School*. Ithaca, NY: Cornell University Press.

Goffman, Alice. 2009. "On the Run: Wanted Men in a Philadelphia Ghetto." *American Sociological Review* 74(3):339–357.

———. 2014. *On the Run: Fugitive Life in an American City*. Chicago: University of Chicago Press.

Goffman, Erving. 1963. *Stigma: Notes on the Management of Spoiled Identity*. New York: Simon & Schuster.

———. 1974. *Frame Analysis: An Essay on the Organization of Experience*. Cambridge, MA: Harvard University Press.

Goldsmith, Pat R. 2009. "Schools or Neighborhoods or Both? Race and Ethnic Segregation and Educational Attainment." *Social Forces* 87(4):1913–1941.

Gordon, Milton. 1964. *Assimilation in American Life: The Role of Race, Religion, and National Origins.* New York: Oxford University Press.

Greeley, Andrew M. 1971. *Why Can't They Be More Like Us? America's White Ethnic Groups.* New York: Dutton.

Gregory, Anne, Russell J. Skiba, and Pedro Noguera. 2010. "The Achievement Gap and the Discipline Gap: Two Sides of the Same Coin?" *Educational Researcher* 39(1):59–68.

Gupta, Arpana, Dawn M. Szymanski, and Frederick T. L. Leong. 2011. "The 'Model Minority Myth': Internalized Racialism of Positive Stereotypes as Correlates of Psychological Distress, and Attitudes toward Help-Seeking." *Asian American Journal of Psychology* 2(2):101.

Guryan, Jonathan. 2004. "Desegregation and Black Dropout Rates." *American Economic Review* 94(4):919–943.

Hanushek, Eric A., John F. Kain, and Steven G. Rivkin. 2009. "New Evidence about Brown v. Board of Education: The Complex Effects of School Racial Composition on Achievement." *Journal of Labor Economics* 27(3):349–383.

Harry, Beth, and Janette Klingner, J. 2014. *Why Are So Many Minority Students in Special Education?* New York: Teachers College Press.

Heath, Shirley B. 1983. *Ways with Words: Language, Life and Work in Communities and Classrooms.* Cambridge, UK: Cambridge University Press.

Hochschild, Arlie Russell. 2012. *The Managed Heart: Commercialization of Human Feeling.* Berkeley: University of California Press.

Howard, Tyrone C. 2010. *Why Race and Culture Matter in Schools: Closing the Achievement Gap in America's Classrooms.* New York: Teachers College Press.

———. 2014. *Black Male(d):Peril and Promise in the Education of African American Males.* New York: Teachers College Press.

Hsin, Amy. 2016. "How Selective Migration Enables Socioeconomic Mobility." *Ethnic and Racial Studies* 39(13):2379–2384

Iceland, John, and Gregory Sharp. 2013. "White Residential Segregation in U.S. Metropolitan Areas: Conceptual Issues, Patterns, and Trends from the U.S. Census, 1980 to 2010." *Population Research and Policy Review* 32(5):663–686.

Ingersoll, Richard M. 2001. "Teacher Turnover and Teacher Shortages: An Organizational Analysis." *American Educational Research Journal* 38(3):499–434.

Ingersoll, Richard, and Henry May. 2011. *Recruitment, Retention, and the Minority Teacher Shortage*. A CPRE Research Report Co-sponsored by the Consortium for Policy Research in Education. University of Pennsylvania and the Center for Educational Research in the Interest of Underserved Students, University of California, Santa Cruz. Available online: https://www.cpre.org/sites/default/files/research report/1221_minorityteachershortagereportrr69septfinal.pdf.

Jack, Anthony A. 2019. *The Privileged Poor: How Elite Colleges Are Failing Disadvantaged Students*. Cambridge, MA: Harvard University Press.

Jacob, Brian A. 2007. "The Challenges of Staffing Urban Schools with Effective Teachers." *Future of Children* 17(1):129–153.

Jiménez, Tomás R. 2016. "Bringing Culture Back In: The Class Origins and Ethnoracial Destinations of Culture and Achievement." *Ethnic and Racial Studies* 39(13):2385–2390

——. 2017. *The Other Side of Assimilation: How Immigrants Are Changing American Life*. Berkeley: University of California Press.

Jiménez, Tomás R., and Adam L. Horowitz. 2013. "When White Is Just Alright: How Immigrants Redefine Achievement and Reconfigure the Ethnoracial Hierarchy." *American Sociological Review* 78(5):849–871.

Johnson, Odis, Jr. 2014. "Still Separate, Still Unequal: The Relation of Segregation in Neighborhoods and Schools to Educational Inequality." *Journal of Negro Education* 83(3):199–215.

Johnson, Rucker C. 2011. "Long-Run Impacts of School Desegregation and School Quality on Adult Attainments." Working Paper No. 16664. National Bureau of Economic Research.

——. 2012. "The Effects of Residential Segregation During Childhood on Life Chances: Causal Evidence Using Historical Railroad Track Configurations." Working Paper. Goldman School of Public Policy, University of California, Berkeley.

——. 2019. *Children of the Dream: Why School Integration Works*. New York: Basic Books and Russell Sage Foundation Press.

Jung, Gowoon, and Hye Suk Wang. 2018. "The Identity Strategy of 'Wild-Geese' Fathers: The Craft of Confucian Fathers." *Religions* 9(7):1–14.

Kao, Grace. 1995. "Asian Americans as Model Minorities? A Look at Their Academic Performance." *American Journal of Education* 103(2):121–159.

Kao, Grace, and Marta Tienda. 1995. "Optimism and Achievement: The Educational Performance of Immigrant Youth." *Social Science Quarterly* 76(1):331–343.

Katz, Jack. 1997. "Ethnography's Warrants." *Sociological Methods and Research* 25(4):391–423.

Kelly, Deirdre M. 1993. *Last Chance High: How Girls and Boys Drop In and Out of Alternative Schools.* New Haven, CT: Yale University Press.

Kendziora, Kimberly T., and David M. Osher. 2009. "Starting to Turn Schools Around: The Academic Outcomes of the Safe Schools, Successful Students Initiative." Washington, DC: American Institutes for Research.

Khan, Shamus R. 2011. *Privilege: The Making of an Adolescent Elite at St. Paul's School.* Princeton, NJ: Princeton University Press.

Kristoff, Nicholas. 2015. "The Asian Advantage." *New York Times,* October 10. Available online: https://www.nytimes.com/2015/10/11 /opinion/sunday/the-asian-advantage.html.

Kupchik, Aaron. 2010. *Homeroom Security: School Discipline in an Age of Fear.* New York: NYU Press.

———. 2016. *The Real School Safety Problem: The Long-Term Consequences of Harsh School Punishment.* Berkeley: University of California Press.

Kupchik, Aaron, and Geoff Ward. 2014. "Race, Poverty, and Exclusionary School Security: An Empirical Analysis of US Elementary, Middle, and High Schools." *Youth Violence and Juvenile Justice* 12(4):332–354.

Lareau, Annette. 1987. "Social Class Differences in Family-School Relationships: The Importance of Cultural Capital. *Sociology of Education* 60(2):73–85.

———. 2000. *Home Advantage: Social Class and Parental Intervention in Elementary Education.* Lanham, MD: Rowman & Littlefield.

———. 2002. "Invisible Inequality: Social Class and Childrearing in Black Families and White Families." *American Sociological Review* 67(5):747–776.

Lareau, Annette, Shani Adia Evans, and April Yee. 2016. "The Rules of the Game and the Uncertain Transmission of Advantage: Middle-Class Parents' Search for an Urban Kindergarten." *Sociology of Education* 89(4):279–299.

Lee, Jennifer. 2012. "Asian American Exceptionalism and 'Stereotype Promise.'" The Society Pages, May 4. Available online: http:// thesocietypages.org/papers/asian-american-exceptionalism-and -stereotype-promise.

———. 2014a. "Are Mexicans the Most Successful Immigrant Group in the U.S.?" Zocalo Public Square, February 24. Available online: https://

www.zocalopublicsquare.org/2014/02/24/are-mexicans-the-most
-successful-immigrant-group-in-the-u-s/ideas/nexus.

———. 2014b. "Asian American Exceptionalism and the 'Stereotype
Promise.'" In *Color Lines and Racial Angles*, edited by Douglas
Hartmann and Christopher Uggen. New York: W. W. Norton.

Lee, Jennifer, Sean J. Drake, and Min Zhou. 2019. "The 'Asian F' and the
Racialization of Achievement." Pp. 141–154 in *Education and Society:
An Introduction to Key Issues in the Sociology of Education*, edited by
T. Domina, B. G. Gibbs, L. Nunn, and A. Penner. Berkeley: University
of California Press.

Lee, Jennifer, and Min Zhou. 2014. "The Success Frame and Achievement
Paradox: The Costs and Consequences for Asian Americans." *Race and
Social Problems* 6(1):38–55.

———. 2015. *The Asian American Achievement Paradox*. New York:
Russell Sage Foundation.

Lee, Stacey J. 1994. "Behind the Model-Minority Stereotype: Voices of
High- and Low-Achieving Asian American Students." *Anthropology &
Education Quarterly* 25(4):413–429.

Lewis, Amanda E. 2003. *Race in the Schoolyard: Negotiating the Color
Line in Classrooms and Communities*. New Brunswick, NJ: Rutgers
University Press.

Lewis, Amanda E., and John B. Diamond. 2015. *Despite the Best Intentions: How Racial Inequality Thrives in Good Schools*. New York:
Oxford University Press.

Lewis, Ramon, Shlomo Romi, Xing Qui, and Yaacov J. Katz. 2005.
"Teachers' Classroom Discipline and Student Misbehavior in Australia,
China and Israel." *Teaching and Teacher Education* 21(6):729–741.

Lewis-McCoy, R. L'Heureux. 2014. *Inequality in the Promised Land:
Race, Resources, and Suburban Schooling*. Palo Alto, CA: Stanford
University Press.

———. 2016. "Boyz in the 'Burbs: Parental Negotiation of Race and Class
in Raising Black Males in Suburbia." *Peabody Journal of Education*
91(3):309–325.

Lofland, John, David A. Snow, Leon Anderson, and Lyn H. Lofland.
2006. *Analyzing Social Settings: A Guide to Qualitative Observation
and Analysis*. Belmont, CA: Wadsworth Publishing Company.

Logan, John R., Elisabeta Minca, and Sinem Adar. 2012. "The Geography
of Inequality: Why Separate Means Unequal in American Public
Schools." *Sociology of Education* 85(3):287–301.

Logan, John R., and Deirdre Oakley. 2004. "The Continuing Legacy of the Brown Decision: Court Action and School Segregation, 1960–2000." Albany, NY: Lewis Mumford Center for Comparative Urban and Regional Research.

Logan, John R., and Charles Zhang. 2011. *Global Neighborhoods: New Evidence from Census 2010*. US2010 Project Report. Available online: http://www.s4.brown.edu/us2010/Data/Report/global final2.pdf.

Lopez, Nancy. 2003. *Hopeful Girls, Troubled Boys: Race and Gender Disparity in Urban Education*. New York: Routledge.

Lucas, Samuel R. 1999. *Tracking Inequality: Stratification and Mobility in American High Schools*. New York: Teachers College Press.

Lutz, Byron. 2011. "The End of Court-Ordered Desegregation." *American Economic Journal: Economic Policy* 3(2):130-68.

MacLeod, Jay. 1995. *Ain't No Makin' It: Aspirations and Attainment in a Low-Income Neighborhood*. 2nd ed. Boulder, CO: Westview Press.

Mahmud, Lilith. 2012. "'The World Is a Forest of Symbols': Italian Freemasonry and the Practice of Discretion." *American Ethnologist* 39(2):425–438.

Malagón, Maria C. 2010. "All the Losers Go There: Challenging the Deficit Educational Discourse of Chicano Racialized Masculinity in a Continuation High School." *Educational Foundations* 24:59–76.

Massey, Douglas S., and Nancy Denton. 1993. *American Apartheid: Segregation and the Making of the Underclass*. Cambridge, MA: Harvard University Press.

Matute-Bianchi, Maria E. 1986. "Ethnic Identities and Patterns of School Success and Failure Among Mexican-Descent and Japanese-American Students in a California High School: An Ethnographic Analysis." *American Journal of Education* 95(1):233–255.

McDonough, Patricia. 1997. *Choosing Colleges: How Social Class and Schools Structure Opportunity*. Albany: State University of New York Press.

Moore, Colleen, and Nancy Shulock. 2010. *Divided We Fail: Improving Completion and Closing Racial Gaps in California's Community Colleges*. Institute for Higher Education Leadership & Policy. Available online: https://files.eric.ed.gov/fulltext/ED513824.pdf.

Morris, Monique. 2016. *Pushout: The Criminalization of Black Girls in Schools*. New York: The New Press.

Munoz, Juan Sanchez. 2005. "The Social Construction of Alternative Education: Re-examining the Margins of Public Education for At-Risk Chicano/a Students." *High School Journal* 88(2):3–22.

National Center for Education Statistics. 2013. "Enrollment and Percentage Distribution of Enrollment in Public Elementary and Secondary Schools, by Race/Ethnicity and Region." National Center for Education Statistics, Washington, DC. Available online: http://nces.ed.gov/programs/digest/d13/tables/dt13_203.50.asp.

Neild, Ruth Curran. 2005. "Parent Management of School Choice in a Large Urban District." *Urban Education* 40(3):270–297.

Ngo, Bic, and Stacey J. Lee. 2007. "Complicating the Image of Model Minority Success: A Review of Southeast Asian American Education." *Review of Educational Research* 77(4):415–453.

Noguera, Pedro A. 2003a. "The Trouble with Black Boys: The Role and Influence of Environmental and Cultural Factors on the Academic Performance of African American Males." *Urban Education* 38(4):431–459.

———. 2003b. *City Schools and the American Dream: Reclaiming the Promise of Public Education*. New York: Teachers College Press.

———. 2008. *The Trouble with Black Boys . . . and Other Reflections on Race, Equity, and the Future of Public Education*. San Francisco: John Wiley & Sons.

Noguera, Pedro A., and Jean Yonemura Wing, eds. 2008. *Unfinished Business: Closing the Racial Achievement Gap in Our Schools*. San Francisco: John Wiley & Sons.

Nora Chiang, Lan-Hung. 2008 "'Astronaut Families': Transnational Lives of Middle-Class Taiwanese Married Women in Canada." *Social & Cultural Geography* 9(5):505–518.

Oakes, Jeannie. 1982. "The Reproduction of Inequity: The Content of Secondary School Tracking." *Urban Review* 14(2):107–120.

———. 1990. *Multiplying Inequalities: The Effects of Race, Social Class, and Tracking on Opportunities to Learn Math and Sciences*. Santa Monica, CA: The RAND Corporation.

———. 2005. *Keeping Track: How Schools Structure Inequality*. 2nd ed. New Haven, CT: Yale University Press.

Ocampo, Anthony C. 2016. *The Latinos of Asia: How Filipino Americans Break the Rules of Race*. Palo Alto, CA: Stanford University Press.

Ocejo, Richard E., ed. 2013. *Ethnography and the City: Readings on Doing Urban Fieldwork*. New York: Routledge.

O'Connor, Carla, Jennifer Mueller, R. L'Heureux Lewis-McCoy, Deborah Rivas-Drake, and Seneca Rosenberg. 2011. "Being Black and Strategizing for Excellence in a Racially Stratified Academic Hierarchy." *American Educational Research Journal* 48(6):2011: 1232–1257.

Orfield, Gary. 1983. *Public School Desegregation in the United States.* Washington, DC: Joint Center for Political Studies.

———. 2001. *Schools More Separate: Consequence of a Decade of Resegregation.* Cambridge, MA: The Civil Rights Project at Harvard University.

Orfield, Gary, and Chungmei Lee. 2005. *Why Segregation Matters: Poverty and Educational Inequality.* Cambridge, MA: The Civil Rights Project at Harvard University.

Osterman, Karen F. 2000. "Students Need for Belonging in the School Community." *Review of Educational Research* 70(3):323–367.

Perez, Lynne G., and Joseph F. Johnson. 2008. "California Continuation High Schools: A Descriptive Study." The National Center for Urban School Transformation, San Diego State University.

Pew Research Center. 2012. *The Rise of Asian Americans.* Washington, DC: Pew Research Center.

Pigge, Fred L., and Ronald N. Marso. 1997. "A Seven Year Longitudinal Multi-factor Assessment of Teaching Concerns Development Through Preparation and Early Years of Teaching." *Teaching and Teacher Education* 13(2):225–235.

Portes, Alejandro, and Rubén Rumbaut. 2014. *Immigrant America: A Portrait.* Berkeley: University of California Press.

Portes Alejandro, and Alex Stepick. 1993. *City on the Edge: The Transformation of Miami.* Berkeley: University of California Press.

Portes, Alejandro, and Min Zhou. 1993. "The New Second Generation: Segmented Assimilation and Its Variants." *Annals of the American Academy of Political and Social Science* 530(1):74–96.

Ray, Victor. 2019. "A Theory of Racialized Organizations." *American Sociological Review* 84(1):26–53.

Reardon, Sean F., Elena Tej Grewal, Demetra Kalogrides, and Erica Greenberg. 2012. "Brown Fades: The End of Court-Ordered School Desegregation and the Resegregation of American Public Schools." *Journal of Policy Analysis and Management* 31(4):876–904.

Reardon, Sean F., and Ann Owens. 2014. "60 Years after Brown: Trends and Consequences of School Segregation." *Annual Review of Sociology* 40:199–218.

Reardon, Sean F., and John T. Yun. 2003. "Integrating Neighborhoods, Segregating Schools: The Retreat from School Desegregation in the South, 1990–2000." *North Carolina Law Review Review* 81(4):1563–1596.

Reber, Sarah J. 2005. "Court-Ordered Desegregation Successes and Failures Integrating American Schools since Brown versus Board of Education." *Journal of Human Resources* 40(3):559–590.

———. 2010. "School Desegregation and Educational Attainment for Blacks." *Journal of Human Resources* 45(4):893–914.

Rios, Victor M. 2006. "The Hyper-criminalization of Black and Latino Male Youth in the Era of Mass Incarceration." *Souls* 8(2):40–54.

———. 2011. *Punished: Policing the Lives of Black and Latino Boys.* New York: NYU Press.

———. 2017. *Human Targets: Schools, Police, and the Criminalization of Latino Youth.* Chicago: University of Chicago Press.

Romi, Shlomo, Ramon Lewis, and Yaacov J. Katz. 2009. "Student Responsibility and Classroom Discipline in Australia, China and Israel." *Compare, a Journal of Comparative and International Education* 39:439–453.

Ronfeldt, Matthew, Susanna Loeb, and James Wyckoff. 2013. "How Teacher Turnover Harms Student Achievement." *American Educational Research Journal* 50(1), 4–36.

Rosenbaum, James E. 1978. "The Structure of Opportunity in School." *Social Forces* 57(1):236–256.

Rothstein, Richard. 2014. "The Racial Achievement Gap, Segregated Schools, and Segregated Neighborhoods." *Race and Social Problems* 7(1):21–30.

Ruiz de Velasco, Jorge, Greg Austin, Don Dixon, Joseph Johnson, Milbrey McLaughlin, and Lynne Perez. 2008. "Alternative Education Options: A Descriptive Study of California Continuation High Schools." John W. Gardener Center for Youth and Their Communities and National Center for Urban School Transformation, Stanford University, and San Diego State University.

Ruiz de Velasco, Jorge, and Milbrey McLaughlin. 2010. "Alternative Schools in California: Academic On-ramps or Exit Ramps for Black, Latino, and Southeast Asian Boys." Pp. 140–155 in *Changing Places: How Communities Will Improve the Health of Boys of Color,* edited by C. Edley and J. Ruiz de Velasco. Berkeley: University of California Berkeley Law.

Rumbaut, Ruben G. 2005. "Turning Points in the Transition to Adulthood: Determinants of Educational Attainment, Incarceration, and Early Childbearing among Children of Immigrants." *Ethnic and Racial Studies* 28(6):1041–1086.

Saporito, Salvatore, and Deenesh Sohoni. 2007. "Mapping Educational Inequality: Concentrations of Poverty among Poor and Minority Students in Public Schools." *Social Forces* 85(3):1227–1253.

Shapiro, Eliza. 2019. "Segregation Has Been the Story of New York City's Schools for 50 Years." *New York Times*, March 26, 2019. Available online: https://www.nytimes.com/2019/03/26/nyregion/school-segregation-new-york.html.

Shapiro, Eliza, and Vivian Wong. 2019. "Amid Racial Divisions, Mayor's Plan to Scrap Elite School Exam Fails." *New York Times,* June 24. Available online: https://www.nytimes.com/2019/06/24/nyregion/specialized-schools-nyc-deblasio.html.

Shedd, Carla. 2015. *Unequal City: Race, Schools, and Perceptions of Injustice.* New York: Russell Sage Foundation.

Smrekar, Claire, and Ellen Goldring. 1999. *School Choice in Urban America: Magnet Schools and the Pursuit of Equity. Critical Issues in Educational Leadership Series.* New York: Teachers College Press.

Snow, David A., Robert D. Benford, and Leon Anderson. 1986. "Fieldwork Roles and Informational Yield: A Comparison of Alternative Settings and Roles." *Urban Life* 14(4):377–408.

Snow, David A., Cherylon Robinson, and Patricia L. McCall. 1991. "'Cooling Out' Men in Singles Bars and Nightclubs: Observations on the Interpersonal Survival Strategies of Women in Public Places." *Journal of Contemporary Ethnography* 19(4):423–449.

Snow, David A., Louis A. Zurcher, and Gideon Sjoberg. 1982. "Interviewing by Comment: An Adjunct to the Direct Question." *Qualitative Sociology* 5(4):285–311.

Stanton-Salazar, Ricardo D., and Sanford M. Dornbusch. 1995. "Social Capital and the Reproduction of Inequality: Information Networks among Mexican-Origin High School Students." *Sociology of Education* 68(2):116–135.

Steinberg, Stephen. 2001. *The Ethnic Myth: Race, Ethnicity, and Class in America.* Boston: Beacon Press.

Stroub, Kori J., and Meredith P. Richards. 2013 "From Resegregation to Reintegration: Trends in the Racial/Ethnic Segregation of

Metropolitan Public Schools, 1993–2009." *American Educational Research Journal* 50(3):497–531.

Sussman, Steve, Clyde W. Dent, Alan W. Stacy, and Sande Craig. 1998. "One-Year Outcomes of Project towards No Drug Abuse." *Preventive Medicine* 27(4):632–642.

Sussman, Steve, Alan W. Stacy, Clyde W. Dent, Thomas R. Simon, Elisha R. Galaif, Mary Ann Moss, Sande Craig, and C. Anderson Johnson. 1995. "Continuation High Schools: Youth at Risk for Drug Abuse." *Journal of Drug Education* 25(3):191–209.

Tsang, A. Ka Tat, Howard Irving, Ramona Alaggia, Shirley B. Y. Chau, and Michael Benjamin. 2003. "Negotiating Ethnic Identity in Canada: The Case of the 'Satellite Children.'" *Youth & Society* 34(3):359–384.

Tsong, Yuying, and Yuli Liu. 2009. "Parachute Kids and Astronaut Families." Pp. 365–380 in *Asian American Psychology: Current Perspectives*, edited by N. Tewari and A. N. Alvarez. New York: Taylor & Francis Group.

Tyson, Karolyn. 2011. *Integration Interrupted: Tracking, Black Students, and Acting White after Brown*. New York: Oxford University Press.

United States Census Bureau. 1960. "Estimated Population by Sex, Color, and Age: 1950 to 1959." Available online: http://www2.census.gov /prod2/statcomp/documents/1960-02.pdf.

———. 2010. "The Asian Population: 2010." Available online: http://www .census.gov/prod/cen2010/briefs/c2010br-11.pdf.

Valenzuela, Angela. 1999. *Subtractive Schooling: U.S.-Mexican Youth and the Politics of Caring*. Albany: State University of New York Press.

Vogell, Heather. 2017. "How Students Get Banished to Alternative Schools." *ProPublica*, December 6. Available online: https://www.propublica.org /article/how-students-get-banished-to-alternative-schools.

Vogell, Heather, and Hannah Fresques. 2017. "'Alternative' Education: Using Charter Schools to Hide Dropouts and Game the System." *ProPublica*, February 21. Available online: https://www.propublica.org /article/alternative-education-using-charter-schools-hide-dropouts -and-game-system.

Waldinger, Roger, and Michael I. Lichter. 2003. *How the Other Half Works: Immigration and the Social Organization of Labor*. Berkeley: University of California Press.

Warner, William L., and Leo Srole. 1945. *The Social Systems of American Ethnic Groups*. New Haven, CT: Yale University Press.

Warren, Paul. 2007. *Improving Alternative Education in California.* Sacramento: Legislative Analyst's Office.

———. 2016. *Accountability for California's Alternative Schools.* San Francisco: Public Policy Institute of California.

Willis, Paul E. 1981. *Learning to Labor: How Working Class Kids Get Working Class Jobs.* New York: Columbia University Press.

Wilson, Franklin D. 1985. "The Impact of School Desegregation Programs on White Public-School Enrollment, 1968–1976." *Sociology of Education* 58(3):137–153.

Wilson, William Julius. 1987. *The Truly Disadvantaged: The Inner City, the Underclass, and Public Policy.* Chicago: University of Chicago Press.

Wong, Frieda, and Richard Halgin. 2006. "The 'Model Minority': Bane or Blessing for Asian Americans?" *Journal of Multicultural Counseling and Development* 34(1):38–49.

Wong, Janelle S. 2015. "The Source of the 'Asian Advantage' Isn't Asian Values." *NBC News*, October 13. Available online: http://www.nbcnews.com/news/asian-america/editorial-source-asian-advantage-isnt-asian-values-n443526.

Yang, KaYing. 2004. "Southeast Asian American Children: Not the 'Model Minority.'" *Future of Children* 14(2):127–133.

Yiu, Jessica. 2013. "Calibrated Ambitions: Low Educational Ambition as a Form of Strategic Adaptation among Chinese Youth in Spain." *International Migration Review* 47(3):573–611.

Zhou, Min. 1998. "'Parachute Kids' in Southern California: The Educational Experience of Chinese Children in Transnational Families." *Education Policy* 12(6):682–704.

———. 2009. "How Neighborhoods Matter for Immigration Children: The Formation of Educational Resources in Chinatown, Koreatown and Pico Union, Los Angeles." *Journal of Ethnic and Migration Studies* 35(7):1153–1179.

Zhou, Min, and Carl L. Bankston III. 1994. "Social Capital and the Adaptation of the Second Generation: The Case of Vietnamese Youth in New Orleans." *International Migration Review* 28(4):821–845.

Zhou, Min, and Susan Kim. 2006. "Community Forces, Social Capital, and Educational Achievement: The Case of Supplementary Education in the Korean and Chinese Immigrant Communities." *Harvard Educational Review* 76(2):1–29.

Zhou, Min, and Jennifer Lee. 2014. "Assessing What Is Cultural about Asian Americans' Academic Advantage." *Proceedings of the National Academy of Sciences* 111(23):8321–8322.

———. 2017. "Hyper-selectivity and the Remaking of Culture: Understanding the Asian American Achievement Paradox." *Asian American Journal of Psychology* 8(1):1–32.

Zhou, Min, and Mingang Lin. 2005. "Community Transformation and the Formation of Ethnic Capital: Immigrant Chinese Communities in the United States." *Journal of Chinese Overseas* 1(2):260–284.

Zussman, Robert. 2004. "People in Places." *Qualitative Sociology* 27(4):351–363.

Index

academic achievement and values, racialization of, 46–50, 200

academic apartheid, 17–18, 21, 208. *See also* academic apartheid, process of

academic apartheid, process of, 82–83; and the coordinated pressure to transfer, 85–89; and the "threshold of credit deficiency," 83–85, 94

academic apathy, 204; and the effect of the school schedule on, 99–100; and the ramifications of clustering "credit deficient" students in one school, 97–100

academic aptitude, racialization of, 205

Alejandro, 127

alternative schools: number of students enrolled in nationwide, 8; operation of as private charter schools in Florida and Michigan, 8; in Pennsylvania, 8

Anderson, Elijah, 2

Anderson, Leon, 210

Andy, sloppy classroom habits of, 118–19

Angulo, Jonathan, 139; interview with concerning the stigma of being a continuation-school teacher at Crossroads, 140

Anthony, 60

Asian Americans, 205; and the Confucian emphasis on education, 147; population of in Valley View, 145; proposed explanations for their high level of academic achievement, 147–48; role of hyper-selectivity in Asian American academic achievement, 49–50; shame of on being transferred to Crossroads, 81–82; stereotyping of as a "model minority," 45–46, 147, 200

Benford, Robert, 210

Blackout meetings, 194–96

Blacks, 200–201; criminalization of, 16–17; economic inequality of, 219n40; as overrepresented among the nation's poorest individuals, 14; stereotyped as culturally deficient, 205

Brown v. Board of Education (1954), 10–11

Bush, George W., administration emphasis of on improving public school test scores, 7

California High School Exit Exam (CAHSEE), 9
Candace, 56; interview with concerning the difficulty of academics at Pinnacle, 56
"career technical education program" (CTEP), 101–2, 206; interest of students in, 102
Carlos, 123–24
Carranza, Richard, 165
Celia, 78–79, 81; interview with concerning her view of Crossroads, 79
cell phones, use of by students during class time, 129
Chicago, public schools in the South Side of, 16
Cindy, 58–59
Civil Rights Act (1964), 11, 14
Coleman, 187, 199; excitement of concerning the Crossroads' career fair, 188; interview with concerning the changes in students once transferred from Pinnacle to Crossroads, 97–98; on student drug use before and after school, 221n21
Confucianism, 147, 172
continuation high schools (continuation school model/system), 7–10, 63–64, 65, 105–6, 138–39, 203, 206; number of in California, 7; purpose of, 8
credit deficiency, 202–3; clustering of "credit deficient" students in one school, 97–100 "threshold of credit deficiency" at, 83–85, 203
criminalization, 106–7, 203–4; of Blacks and Latinx persons, 16–17
Crossroads High School, 10, 17, 71*fig.*; arrangement with Valley View's four comprehensive high schools regarding the transfer of students to Crossroads, 70, 72; Asian Americans' profound sense of shame on being transferred to Crossroads, 81–82; between-school tracking at, 193; career fair of featuring Armed Forces recruiters, 186–89;

classroom culture of, 110; confinement and surveillance of students at, 73–75, 76–77; as a continuation high school, 138–39; demographic disparities between Crossroads and Pinnacle, 68; disabled students at, 218n19; as a "dumping ground" for underachieving Pinnacle students, 18, 94–97; ethnoracial composition of, 9, 10*tab.*; fear and shame manifested by parents and students when sent to Crossroads, 79–81; frustration of some students with their fellow students' behavior, 121; as an imperfect alternative to dropping out of high school, 189–90; lack of facilities and opportunities at, 69; lack of material resources at, 69–70; lack of a PTA at, 69; main quad of, 72*fig.*; and the mismatch between students' goals and the Crossroads curriculum, 132–37; as not a disciplinary school, 75–77; as an outlier compared to other high schools in Valley View, 68–69; percentage of students designated as "socioeconomically disadvantaged" at, 9, 66–67, 89; perimeter fence surrounding, 71*fig.*, 72, 76; presence of the Valley View Police Department at, 73–74, 74*fig.*, 75, 76; prevailing perception in Valley View of Crossroads as a school for failed students and delinquents, 66; proposed solutions to the problems at, 22–23; relationship with Pinnacle High School, 16; role of in the Valley View Unified School District, 96–97; as serving the interests of academically elite high schools like Pinnacle, 106; small class sizes of, 130; structuring of to a "prison model," 106–7; students feeling as if they were "delinquents" at, 75–76; successful students at, 142; symbolic criminalization of students at, 203–4; transfer process between Pinnacle and Crossroads, 21; truncated/limited curriculum at, 70, 87–88, 202
"cultural success frames," 31–33, 148

David, 127–28
de Blasio, Bill, 165
Deborah, 26–27, 34, 35
desegregation, societal benefits of, 14
Diamond, John, 165
Diana: feeling of as a "misfit" at Pinnacle, 198–99; interview with concerning "College Sweatshirt Day," 60–61
Dominique: interview with concerning the limitations of a Crossroads diploma, 88; perfect attendance record of, 88

Edson, 93; interview with concerning his transfer to Crossroads, 93–94
Eisenhower, Dwight, 11
Eric, 124, 125–26
Ernesto, 189–90; interview with concerning his disappointment with Crossroads, 190
Esther, 54; full slate of AP courses taken by, 43; interview with concerning the pressure for grades and the pressure of parents to succeed, 43–44; interview with concerning race, culture, and education, 48
ethnic capital: institutionalization of, 149; sources of external to schools, 148; utility of, 148–49
ethnography, 204, 216, 218n20; ethnographic research and observations, 9, 16, 17, 19, 23, 114, 205, 210, 212, 213, 214
Eugene, 39–40, 54, 56; interview with concerning his view of Crossroads, 78; interviews with Eugene and Ryan, 40–43, 47
Ewing, Eve, 203

Feliciano, Cynthia, 38
Frame Analysis (Goffman), 31
Francine, 103–5; arduous road of from the Democratic Republic of the Congo to the United States, 103–4; effect of the continuation school model on, 105; enrollment of at Valley View Community College, 105; as an exemplary student at Crossroads, 104; interview with concerning her frustration with fellow

students, 121; interview with concerning her struggles at Crossroads, 105; problems with her mother, 104

Goffman, Erving, 31
grade point averages (GPAs), 25; GPAs of Pinnacle minority students, 83–84, 84*tab.*
Greg, interview with concerning his questioning of Crossroads' policies and practices, 191–92

Hassan, 95–96, 106, 199; interview with concerning the pressure by Pinnacle for huis transfer to Crossroads, 96
Horowitz, Adam, 147
"hyper-selectivity, 38, 39; role of in Asian American academic achievement, 49–50

immigrant groups, 22, 38, 47, 148, 176, 221n19; Asian, 147; "highly-selected" immigrant groups, 167, 223n27; privileged immigrant groups, 178–79
immigrants (to the United States), 146–47, 205; education levels of Chinese and South Korean immigrants, 38; and "hyper-selectivity, 38–39; and the immigrant assimilation process, 167, 175, 177; influence of, 147; and "positive selectivity," 38; relationship between immigrant families and schools, 175–76; and the reshuffling of racial hierarchy in schools, 147; "success frame of," 38, 148. *See also* immigrant groups; immigrants, ethnic resources of and their effect on academic achievement
immigrants, ethnic resources of and their effect on academic achievement, 146–48, 177; and the utility of ethnic capital, 148–49
immigration law, changes in (since 1965), 38
inequality, in the US educational system as reproducing the inequality in society itself, 13, 207–8
institutional success frame. *See* Pinnacle High School, institutional success frame of

Jack, Anthony, 16

Jamal, 199; as an athlete, 5, 63; diagnosis of OHI (Other Health Impairment), 63; disinterest of in class when the subject matter was presented visually, 5–6; engagement of in class when worksheets were involved, 6; poor vision of, 63; transfer of to Crossroads from Pinnacle, 6–7, 62–64, 66

Janet, 75; interview with concerning the police presence at Crossroads, 75

Jeremiah, 99, 199; interview with concerning the behavioral changes in once he transferred from Pinnacle to Crossroads, 98

Jessica, heavy academic load and extracurricular activities of, 50–51

Jessie, interview with concerning his experience at Crossroads as an Asian American, 81–82

Joey, 126–27

Johnson, Rucker, 14

Jolene, 48, 54; interview with concerning race, culture, and education, 49

Juan, 79, 81

Khan, Shamus, 16

Kim, Hannah, 151, 158–59; interview with concerning the image of Korean students and families promoted by the KPTA, 161–62; interview with concerning the KPTA, 151–52; interview with concerning the objective of the KCEP program, 168–69; interview with concerning the relationship between the general PTA and the KPTA, 163–64; interview with concerning the role of the KPTA in keeping Korean students out of trouble, 154–56; interview with concerning the "tremendous opportunity" for KPTA members to be heard, 153

Korean Cultural Education Program (KCEP), 168–69, 170fig., 171–72, 171fig., 174–75; lecture given at concerning Confucianism and "Confucian values," 172; objective of, 168; opening day of, 171–72; second day presentation featuring Korean arts, 172,

173fig.; setting of, 169, 171; third day presentation of on the best practices for teachers to connect and build with Korean students, 174

Korean Parent Teacher Association (Pinnacle High School [KPTA]), 22, 90–91, 200–201, 205; and achieving solidarity with the general Pinnacle PTA, 162–64; and the framing of Korean culture as exceptional and thus responsible for the academic achievement of Korean students, 150; impact of, 176; key objective of, 152–53; as "opportunity hoarders," 166; as a racialized organization, 176; as a reliable source of ethnic capital, 149–50; view of the "general PTA" by, 152. See also Korean Parent Teacher Association (Pinnacle High School [KPTA]), academic and social support of for Pinnacle's Korean students; "Teacher Appreciation Luncheon"

Korean Parent Teacher Association (Pinnacle High School [KPTA]), academic and social support of for Pinnacle's Korean students, 153–54, 167; role of in keeping Korean students out of trouble, 154–56

Kristof, Nicholas, 147

Latinx persons, 200–201; criminalization of, 16–17; as overrepresented among the nation's poorest individuals, 14; stereotyped as culturally deficient, 205

Lee, Jennifer, 31, 148, 221n19

Lewis, Amanda, 165

Little Rock Central High School, 11

Little Rock Nine, 11; racial slurs and death threats experienced by, 11

Mariah, 83–84, 85, 106; interview with concerning her experiences at Pinnacle, 84

Matthew, 124–25

Max, 163

Megan, 58–59

Michael, interview with concerning his experience at Crossroads as an Asian American, 82

Miguel, 100–101, 184; as chronically late to the first period of school (and the reasons why), 101–2; enrollment of in the "career technical education program" (CTEP) for culinary arts, 101, 102; as not comporting with the institutional success frame of Pinnacle, 103; preference of for vocational training, 103; transfer to Crossroads, 10

Min Zhou, 31, 148

Miranda, 79–80; interview with concerning her embarrassment and shame on being sent to Crossroads, 80–81

Mr. Bradley, 36; interview with concerning the acceptance of transfer students from Pinnacle to crossroads, 85

Mr. Davis, interview with concerning the behavioral changes in students that transferred from Pinnacle to Crossroads, 99

Mr. Gregory, 139; belief that the Valley View Unified School District is "setting up Crossroads kids for failure," 133–35; interview with concerning the inadequate preparation of students for life after high school, 185; interview with concerning Miguel and the CTEP culinary arts program, 102; interview with concerning the mission of Crossroads, 132–33; interview with concerning the incentives for students coming to school, 184–85; interview with concerning the role of Crossroads in the Valley View Unified School District, 96–97; on the mismatch between curriculum demands and student aspirations, 135–36

Mr. Holt, 34, 85–86, 210–13; interview with concerning Asian American students, 45; interview with concerning the decision to transfer students to Crossroads, 86; interview with concerning persuading students to transfer to Crossroads, 87

Mr. Jefferson, interview with concerning teaching at Pinnacle, 110–11

Mr. Johnson, 75, 101, 184, 187; interview with concerning the perimeter fence surrounding Crossroads, 76

Mr. Reyes: excerpt from his commencement address, 65–66; experiences as a history teacher at Crossroads, 122

Mr. Thompson, interview with concerning the difficulty of getting students to transfer to Crossroads, 91–92

Ms. Bright, 90

Ms. Carter, 214–15

Ms. Kitayama, 46; presentation of at back-to-school night, 36, 37

Ms. Miller, 5–7

Ms. Owens, 121–22, 187, 199; interview with concerning the academic environment in Valley View and the effect of students, 180–82; interview with concerning student discipline, 120

Ms. Quinn, 26, 27–29, 46, 110; at back-to-school night, 34–36; disdain of for the "Teacher Appreciation Luncheon," 157–58; interview with concerning her opinion of teaching at Crossroads even though she had never been there, 108–9; interview with concerning her students and AP courses, 29–31; interviews with concerning the "Teacher Appreciation Luncheon," 157, 162–63; personality of, 29

Ms. Reynolds, 109, 110; refusal of to teach at Crossroads, 78

Ms. Turner, 138; as a classroom manager of disruptive students more than a teacher (fourth-period English class), 126–28; as a classroom manager of disruptive students more than a teacher (second-period English class), 128–30; as a classroom manager of disruptive students more than a teacher (third-period English class), 123–26; ethnoracial composition of her English class, 123; experiences of with Tobias, 122, 128, 130–31; interview with concerning the role of Crossroads within the larger school district, 191

neighborhood public schools, 14–15, 67, 95, 204, 206, 207, 220n1

New York City, plan of to increase racial diversity in elite, specialized public schools, 165–66 "opportunity hoarding," 165, 166

Parent Teacher Association (Pinnacle High School), 34, 162–64
pedagogy, research concerning, 141
Pinnacle High School, 9–10, 17, 69, 77, 196–97; absence of Black or Latinx parent organizations at, 178; academic culture of, 26, 110, 111, 207; as an academically elite school, 4; administration building and auditorium of, 27*fig.*; back-to-school night activities at, 33–38; baseball field and equipment of, 27*fig.*; college pennants displayed in, 32; "College Sweatshirt Day" at, 58–61, 198; commitment of students to academics at, 111; demographic disparities between Pinnacle and Crossroads, 68; disabled students at, 218n19; discomfort of Black students at, 193–94; ethnoracial composition of, 4–5, 10*tab.*, 25–26, 26*tab.*; hallmarks of popular students at, 25; as the leading public school in Valley View, 25; negative opinion of Crossroads by students and teachers at Pinnacle, 77–78; number of honors and advanced placement (AP) courses offered at, 25; number of students identifying as either Korean American or Chinese American at, 39, 217n5; as an "open campus," 24–25; percentage of graduates enrolled in postsecondary education, 25, 183; percentage of students designated as "socioeconomically disadvantaged" at, 9, 66–67, 89, 217n4; physical facilities of, 4, 24; as a place of "stereotype promise" for Asian students, 176–77; racialized nature of institutional success frames at, 45; recent formation of a Chinese PTA at, 223n19; relationship with Crossroads High School, 16; "threshold of credit deficiency" at, 83–85; transfer process of students from Pinnacle to Crossroads, 21, 67–68, 92–94, 95. *See also* Pinnacle High School, institutional success frame of

Pinnacle High School, institutional success frame of, 31–33, 33*fig.*, 54, 61–62, 103, 183, 198, 199–200; racialized nature of, 200–201
Pinnacle High School/Crossroads High school, fieldwork concerning, 18–20; data collection methods (observations and interviews), 19–20, 220n69; self-identified race of student interviewees, 20*tab. See also* Pinnacle High School/ Crossroads High School, fieldwork concerning, and the quest for access to Pinnacle and Crossroads high schools
Pinnacle High School/Crossroads High school, fieldwork concerning, and the quest for access to Pinnacle and Crossroads high schools, 209–10; unique challenges of, 215; use of finesse in order to gain access, 210–13; use of flexibility and persistence, 214–15; use of a phased access approach, 216; and the variety of gatekeepers of the schools, 213–14
"positive selectivity," 38
Potter, Emily, on teaching AP chemistry classes at Pinnacle, 111–16; demeanor of while teaching, 114; ethnoracial composition of her classes, 112, 113; her class as representative of the everyday classroom culture at Pinnacle, 115; "person-centered" approach of as opposed to a "teacher oriented" approach, 115; students helping other students in her class, 114–15
Privilege (Khan), 16
Privileged Poor, The (Jack), 16
public schools. *See* neighborhood public schools

racial groups, maintenance of their privileges by the monopolization of resources, 164–66
racialization, of organizations, 82–83, 88–89, 203. *See also* academic achievement and values, racialization of
racial stratification, in the United States, 47–48
Roberta (lead security resource officer [SRO]), 128

Ryan, 39–40, 54, 56; interviews with Ryan and Eugene, 40–43, 47

San Francisco, 1; and the dearth of colored students and faculty at schools in, 2–4
Sarah, interview with concerning the role of the KPTA in keeping Korean students out of trouble, 154–55
Savannah, 92; interview concerning her transfer to Crossroads, 92; interview with her mother (Tanya) concerning Savannah's transfer to crossroads, 93
school segregation: between-school segregation, 192, 207; institutional mechanisms of, 9–10, 201; reducing segregation and inequality, 207–8; research on in ethnoracially diverse school districts, 67; within-school segregation, 192–93. *See also* school segregation, summation of in the United States since 1954
school segregation, summation of in the United States since 1954, 10–13; and the effect of "White flight," 12–13; hampering of integration efforts at the turn of the century (1990s through 2010), 13; lawsuits concerning, 10–12; progress made in desegregation, 12; and the ramifications of a racially and economically segregated school system, 13–14; segregated classrooms in integrated schools, 14–15; segregation in the aftermath of legal victories for desegregation, 11–12; and stratified schooling conditions, 13
segregation, residential, 1, 12, 13, 14–15, 17, 192, 207, 219n54
Shedd, Carla, 16
Snow, David, 210
social, cultural, and economic capital, use of to resist student transfers to Crossroads, 89–92, 167; and the lack of social capital, 89–90; and "middle-class cultural capital," 89; and the use of private tutors to avoid transfer, 91; and the use of social processes at Pinnacle to resist transfer, 90
Stacy, interview with concerning her frustration with fellow students, 121

students: clear goal of Pinnacle students for their future after high school, 185; and the college or bust culture of Valley View, 182–83; Crossroads students' insecurity about their future after high school, 185; disproportionate amount of disadvantaged students pushed to transfer to Crossroads, 92–94; poor fit between students and the academic culture of Valley View, 182–84; setting students up to fail, 182–86. *See also* students who struggle, actionable steps toward equity and inclusion for
students who struggle, actionable steps toward equity and inclusion for, 204–5; creating credit recovery programs at comprehensive high schools, 206–7; supporting youth in a context of decreasing diversity, 205
success frames: of immigrants, 38, 148; institutional success frames, 20, 31–33, 61–62; racialized nature of institutional success frames at Pinnacle High School, 45;
surveillance, 16–17, 21, 73, 107, 193, 203; panoptic surveillance, 72, 77; surveillance cameras, 17
Swann v. Charlotte-Mecklenburg Board of Education (1971), 12

"Teacher Appreciation Luncheon," 160*fig.*; details of, 158–61; Ms. Quinn's view of, 156–58
teachers, 107; on the behavioral changes in students that transferred from Pinnacle to Crossroads, 98–99; day-to-day classroom experiences of, 21–22. *See also* Korean cultural education program; teachers, at Crossroads; teachers, at Pinnacle
teachers, at Crossroads, 109–10, 137–38; as classroom managers, 119–22, 141; effect on teachers of the chaotic nature of class time at Crossroads, 130; and the mismatch between students' goals and the Crossroads curriculum, 132–37; and the stigma of teaching at Crossroads, 138–40; struggle of to keep students on task, 112; teaching

teachers, at Crossroads (*continued*)
an English class at Crossroads, 123–26; teaching a history class at Crossroads, 122; uniqueness of teaching at Crossroads, 136–37. *See also* Mr. Reyes; Ms. Owens; Ms. Turner
teachers, at Pinnacle, 109–10, 141, 142; individual attention of teachers to students despite large class sizes, 115–16; student assistance to teachers at Pinnacle, 112; teaching of an AP chemistry class at, 111–16; teaching of marine science class at, 116–19. *See also* Potter, Emily; Ventura, Mark
Thomas, 91
Tina, 50; interview with concerning her daughter Jessica's heavy academic load and extracurricular activities, 50–51
Tobias, 187; behavior of in the classroom, 122, 128, 130–31; excitement of concerning the Crossroads' career fair, 188
tracking/tracking policies, 15; extreme/severe form of, 17–18, 67–68, 208; and the placement of Black and Brown students in lower-level and remedial courses, 15; racialized tracking, 15; the unique harm of racialized between-school tracking, 192–94
Tremont, 86–87; interview with concerning his transfer to crossroads and being "credit deficient," 87
tutoring agencies, 37–38, 220n5

Unequal City (Shedd), 16
US Department of Justice, 11

Valley View, California, 217n2; Asian American population of, 145; ethnoracial change in and its effect on school districts, 145–46; ethnoracial composition of, 4, 10*tab*.; hidden mechanisms of school segregation and inequality in, 15–17; median household income in, 4; patterns of migration to, 145
Valley View Korean Parents Organization, 168
Valley View Public School Foundation, 168
Valley View Unified School District, 7, 9, 83, 123–26
Ventura, Mark, 116–19; demeanor of while teaching, 119; ethnoracial composition of his marine science class, 117; interview concerning the collective sloppy work of his students, 118; interview with concerning laughter in his class, 117–18; interview with concerning an overview of his students and subject matter, 116
Victoria, 55, 196; interviews with concerning difficulty of being one of the few Black students at Pinnacle, 55–56, 194–95; interview with concerning her overall experiences at Pinnacle after being there three years, 56–58; interview with concerning warnings about the difficulty of academic at Pinnacle, 55; motivation of to start a Black student club at Pinnacle, 199
Vivian, 160–61

Wendy (Korean mother of two teenage daughters): decision of to move from South Korea to Valley View including interview concerning, 144–45; as a member of the KPTA, 150
"wild-geese families," 151
Wilson, Julius, 192

Yuki, 52; interview with concerning the academic struggles of, 52–54; interview with concerning "College Sweatshirt Day," 59–60

Zahra, 186

Founded in 1893,
UNIVERSITY OF CALIFORNIA PRESS
publishes bold, progressive books and journals
on topics in the arts, humanities, social sciences,
and natural sciences—with a focus on social
justice issues—that inspire thought and action
among readers worldwide.

The UC PRESS FOUNDATION
raises funds to uphold the press's vital role
as an independent, nonprofit publisher, and
receives philanthropic support from a wide
range of individuals and institutions—and from
committed readers like you. To learn more, visit
ucpress.edu/supportus.